THE DAILY STUDY BIBLE

(OLD TESTAMENT)

General Editor: John C. L. Gibson

TWELVE PROPHETS

Volume 1

TWELVE PROPHETS

Volume 1

HOSEA, JOEL, AMOS, OBADIAH, AND JONAH

PETER C. CRAIGIE

THE WESTMINSTER PRESS
PHILADELPHIA

Published by
The Saint Andrew Press
Edinburgh, Scotland
and
The Westminster Press®
Philadelphia, Pennsylvania

Printed in the United States of America

Library of Congress Cataloging in Publication Data

Craigie, Peter C.
Twelve prophets.

(Daily study Bible series)
Bibliography: p.
1. Bible. O.T. Minor Prophets—Commentaries.
I. Title. II. Title. 12 prophets. III. Series: Daily study Bible series (Westminster Press)
BS1560.C72 1984   224'.9077   84-2372
ISBN 0-664-21810-5 (v. 1)
ISBN 0-664-24577-3 (pbk. : v. 1)

GENERAL PREFACE

This series of commentaries on the Old Testament, to which Professor Craigie's first volume on the *Twelve Prophets* belongs, has been planned as a companion series to the much-acclaimed New Testament series of the late Professor William Barclay. As with that series, each volume is arranged in successive headed portions suitable for daily study. The Biblical text followed is that of the Revised Standard Version or Common Bible. Eleven contributors share the work, each being responsible for from one to three volumes. The series is issued in the hope that it will do for the Old Testament what Professor Barclay's series succeeded so splendidly in doing for the New Testament—make it come alive for the Christian believer in the twentieth century.

Its two-fold aim is the same as his. Firstly, it is intended to introduce the reader to some of the more important results and fascinating insights of modern Old Testament scholarship. Most of the contributors are already established experts in the field with many publications to their credit. Some are younger scholars who have yet to make their names but who in my judgment as General Editor are now ready to be tested. I can assure those who use these commentaries that they are in the hands of competent teachers who know what is of real consequence in their subject and are able to present it in a form that will appeal to the general public.

The primary purpose of the series, however, is *not* an academic one. Professor Barclay summed it up for his New Testament series in the words of Richard of Chichester's prayer—to enable men and women "to know Jesus Christ more clearly, to love Him more dearly, and to follow Him more nearly." In the case of the Old Testament we have to be a little more circumspect than that. The Old Testament was completed long before the time of Our Lord, and it was (as it still is) the sole Bible of the Jews, God's first people, before it became part of the Christian Bible. We must take this fact seriously.

Yet in its strangely compelling way, sometimes dimly and sometimes directly, sometimes charmingly and sometimes embarrassingly, it holds up before us the things of Christ. It should not be forgotten that Jesus Himself was raised on this Book, that He based His whole ministry on what it says, and that He approached His death with its words on His lips. Christian men and women have in this ancient collection of Jewish writings a uniquely illuminating avenue not only into the will and purposes of God the Father, but into the mind and heart of Him who is named God's Son, who was Himself born a Jew but went on through the Cross and Resurrection to become the Saviour of the world. Read reverently and imaginatively the Old Testament can become a living and relevant force in their everyday lives.

It is the prayer of myself and my colleagues that this series may be used by its readers and blessed by God to that end.

New College   JOHN C. L. GIBSON
Edinburgh   General Editor

CONTENTS

CONTENTS

CONTENTS

TWELVE PROPHETS

INTRODUCTION

Of the multitude of prophets who lived and ministered in ancient Israel, only a few survived by name in the narrative of the Old Testament. Our knowledge of these named prophets comes from two different kinds of sources. Some of them left no writings, but an account of their lives and teachings has been preserved in the historical books of the Old Testament. Others are known from the books named after them; they were not in every case the writers of the books, for prophets were primarily preachers and activists, rather than authors. But their books contain a record of their preaching, and in some instances brief fragments of biography.

The prophets after whom books have been named are sometimes divided into *major* prophets and *minor* prophets, a distinction going back to the time of St. Augustine in his treatise, *The City of God*. The division between major and minor prophets does not refer in any sense to the significance, or otherwise, of the prophets so designated, but only to the length of the books bearing their names. The major prophets are those whose names are appended to long books: Isaiah (66 chapters), Jeremiah (52 chapters), and Ezekiel (48 chapters). The books of the minor prophets vary in length, but all are relatively short: Hosea, Joel, Amos, Obadiah, Jonah, Micah, Nahum, Habakkuk, Zephaniah, Haggai, Zechariah, and Malachi, twelve in all.

Ancient Jewish books were written, not in the modern form, but on a scroll, a long rolled strip of parchment or papyrus. The books of the three major prophets would each have been written on a single scroll; those of the twelve minor prophets, which taken together are approximately the same length as one major prophet, would all have been written on a single scroll. Apparently the works of the twelve minor prophets were collected together on a single scroll at quite an early date, perhaps as early as the third century B.C. The single "book" that was formed in this manner became in effect an anthology of the shorter prophetic writings of ancient Israel. It was called, in the early Jewish canon, the "Book of the Twelve Prophets", and it is this title, rather than the "Minor Prophets", which most accurately describes the substance.

There is variety in the sequence of the books as they occur in ancient manuscripts and versions of "The Book of the Twelve". Whereas in the Hebrew manuscripts there was some attempt to arange the books in chronological sequence, the old Greek version begins its arrangement of some of the books by virtue of length, beginning with the longest (Hosea). But for the modern reader of the Twelve Prophets, each book can be read as a more or less independent unit. This commentary has followed the sequence of the books as they occur in the English Bible, but the reader should not feel compelled to read them in the same sequence. Indeed, there is some value in studying certain prophets together, even though their books do not follow in direct sequence. Hosea and Amos, for example, were contemporaries; though they addressed Israel at the same period in history, it is instructive to see the very different theological perspectives which they bring to bear in their preaching.

The twelve books that comprise this prophetic anthology differ considerably in substance and style. Some contain elements of biography that supplement the prophetic preaching with some insight concerning the preacher (Amos, Hosea). Others remain for practical purposes anonymous, despite the names attached to them (Obadiah, Malachi). They range in date from periods separated by more than three centuries (from about 750 B.C. to 400 B.C.). They reflect different geographical locations, some reflecting life in the ancient monarchical states of Israel and Judah, others pertaining to the period after the Exile. But for all the differences between them, the books share common ground. All are concerned with prophecy, namely the declaration of God's word to the people of God. And taken together, the

Twelve Prophets provide us with a panorama of Israel's religion during one of the most critical periods of its history. From the false confidence of the time of the monarchy, to the despair of those in exile, and finally to the new hopes and aspirations following exile, we are provided with an understanding of the transition from an old state-religion to the birth-pains of a newly-formed community of God's people.

A century or so after the completion of the Book of the Twelve Prophets, Joshua ben Sira wrote his famous wisdom work, in which he extolled the fame of Israel's past heroes. His words concerning the Twelve Prophets indicate not only their greatness in bygone years, but also their potential contribution to the future:

> May the bones of the twelve prophets
>   also send forth new life from the ground where they lie!
> For they put new heart into Jacob [Israel],
>   and rescued the people by their confident hope.
>
> Ecclesiasticus 49:10

INTRODUCTION TO THE BOOK OF HOSEA

There were few persons in Old Testament times of such remarkable perception and such sensitivity of character as Hosea, and
yet all too little is known of this man. A part of his life is laid bare
for us in the opening three chapters of his book, for his life was for
a time a public ministry. But as to his background, his upbringing
and circumstances in life, we can only speculate. Apart from his
short book, there are no external sources that have survived to
illuminate for us the life of this extraordinary prophet.

He lived in the eighth century B.C. and his ministry as a prophet
probably took place within the years 750–722 B.C.; the references
to kings who reigned in Israel and Judah provide the chronological framework of the book. Hosea was a resident of the northern
of the two Hebrew kingdoms, Israel, and in retrospect we perceive that he ministered to that kingdom during the last decades
of its existence; Israel was defeated and destroyed by the Assyrian armies in 722 B.C. To a nation in moral and spiritual
decline, Hosea functioned as a messenger and a warner from
God. Though his message was not widely heeded during his
lifetime, it possessed such remarkable spiritual insight and force
that it was preserved after his death. It is probable that, after
Hosea's death, friends and companions compiled his book from
fragments of sermons, prophetic pronouncements and private
writings; it is to them that we owe this extraordinary legacy from
one of the greatest of all the prophets of Israel.

The times in which Hosea lived were characterized by both
moral and spiritual decline. But whereas the prophet's contemporary, Amos, focused primarily on moral issues, it was the
decline in spiritual values which grasped Hosea's attention and
exercised his soul. The faith of Israel, as he perceived it, was

being polluted by external influences and the grave inroads of foreign religion. A certain form of the religion of Baal, popular in part because of the sexual activity which accompanied it, was undermining the faith of Israel in the one and true God. For the prophet Hosea, the loss of the true essence of the religion of the fathers was the gravest issue of the time; all other evils flowed from the corruption which he perceived to have infiltrated to the very core of Israel's religion. And it was to counter that loss of true faith among the chosen people that Hosea was called to be a prophet, a spokesman of the Living God.

THE BOOK OF HOSEA

The fourteen short chapters of Hosea provide us with only a limited insight into the man and his message. The book is neither a comprehensive biography nor a complete collection of his sayings and writings; it is in the form of an anthology of collected pieces from the prophet. And precisely because it is an anthology, there is no clear and dominant literary structure which permeates the book as a whole. The first three chapters have a certain unity, focusing as they do on the marriage and family life of Hosea. But, for the most part, the remainder of the book is a collection of different sayings from different periods of the prophet's life and ministry and as such it is not easy to understand fully at first reading. It is as if the speeches of a contemporary politician, delivered over a lifetime in public service, were compiled into a single anthology; while each speech would have made perfect sense at the time and in the place where it was first delivered, each one would be more difficult to understand later when the specific occasion for the speech was forgotten. And so it is with Hosea; the substance of some of his speeches and sermons remains, but frequently the circumstances in which they were spoken can only be surmised. But for all the difficulty in reading this little book, certain dominant themes and insights emerge which are of lasting religious value.

THE MESSAGE OF HOSEA

There are two dominant themes running through the sayings of Hosea which appear at first sight to be mutually exclusive: they are the *judgment* of God and the *love* of God. But they are not mutually exclusive; there is a sense in which they are the two faces of a single coin. Hosea preached God's coming judgment, not because God was by nature a bad-tempered deity, but because the evil of Israel was so gross and unyielding that it invited divine judgment. Judgment operated on the basis of law; it was a reaction to sin, the breaking of the law. Yet for Hosea, there was something more central in the nature of God than law and judgment; underlying and supporting everything else was the love of God. And the love of God constantly breaks through in the words of Hosea; the dark gloom evoked by the message of judgment is frequently brightened by an insight of love that is irrepressible. Although, with some justice, Hosea has been called the prophet of doom *par excellence*, it is also true to say that no Old Testament book contains such extraordinary insight into the love of God; the fundamentals of the gospel are clearly present in the words of this prophet from ancient times.

Hosea also possessed a remarkable sense of history. He was not an historian in the modern sense of the term, but he perceived world events on a large canvas and understood them in relation to God and Israel. With respect to the "history of God", he recalled Israel's marvellous beginnings, when God in love had drawn his people from slavery in Egypt; for the present and immediate future, Hosea perceived that divine love was cast in the shade of judgment, but there was hope ultimately that what God had begun in love would also culminate in love. Israel's history was seen in a different light; the past was stained with failures and lost opportunities, the present with hypocrisy and evil, and the future deserved no bright prospect, though still there remained hope in God's love. Hosea used his awareness of history as only an astute preacher can do; the past evoked memories of God's faithfulness and Israel's failures, but memory of the past may function as a powerful influence upon present thinking and future action.

Hosea must also be classed among the most radical of Israel's prophets. The radical nature of his message lay not only in its substance (the stubborn insistence of God's love), but also in the striking language with which he sought to grasp the attention of his audience. The extraordinary analogy of human love and marital faithlessness in the opening chapters would have been as surprising and disturbing to his contemporaries as it is to modern readers. And the similes with which the prophet described the nature of God were also unconventional and striking; it is hardly the language of theology to say that God is like a mother bear, a wild lion, a moth or dry rot (Hosea 5:12; 13:7-8)! But he had a message which must not only be proclaimed, but also heard; the evidence which has survived in the book of Hosea indicates that few could have failed to listen.

HOSEA'S CALL TO BE A PROPHET

Hosea 1:1-3

[1]The word of the Lord that came to Hosea the son of Beeri, in the days of Uzziah, Jotham, Ahaz, and Hezekiah, kings of Judah, and in the days of Jeroboam the son of Joash, king of Israel.

[2]When the Lord first spoke through Hosea, the Lord said to Hosea, "Go, take to yourself a wife of harlotry and have children of harlotry, for the land commits great harlotry by forsaking the Lord." [3]So he went and took Gomer the daughter of Diblaim, and she conceived and bore him a son.

Though Hosea was certainly one of the greatest of Israel's prophets, he is nowhere explicitly identified as a prophet in the book. We are simply given his name, the name of his father (who is not otherwise known), and the names of some of the kings of Israel and Judah during whose reigns he lived. For us in the modern world, there is a certain fascination in biography. It would be interesting to know about his upbringing, his education and profession, or his experience in the world of men and affairs. But very little of this is recorded; just brief snippets of biography emerge in the book, and such as remain are only those directly relevant to Hosea's ministry. It is clear that those friends or companions who compiled Hosea's book had no particular intention of preserving a comprehensive account of the prophet's life for posterity; it was his message that mattered. But because a part of the message was intimately related to the prophet's life, a certain amount of biography has survived. At the beginning of the book, Hosea is a fully grown adult and his earlier life is a blank, but some details of his marriage and family life are recounted because they played a role in his ministry.

Of all the prophetic calls, that of Hosea is surely the most peculiar and the least "religious" in form. The Lord *spoke* to Hosea, and that is the beginning of any vocation. But the nature and content of God's initial call are entirely different from those experienced by other prophets. There was for Hosea no burning bush or mountain-top experience, as there was for Moses. He saw no glorious vision in the Temple, as did Isaiah. There is no record of a great inner struggle, a spiritual battle, as there was for Jeremiah. When the Lord spoke to Hosea, he issued a most extraordinary command: "Go, take yourself a wife of harlotry"! The word *harlot* is an archaic word in English; it is not the normal speech of people in the street. Hosea was to take a wife of *prostitution*, yet still the meaning of the ancient text is not entirely clear. It could mean that God commanded Hosea to marry a prostitute, namely a common street prostitute, but the form of the Hebrew word which is used, and the times in which Hosea lived, suggest a slightly different sense. Religion in Israel had been debased by the religion of Baal. In that foreign religion, both men and women engaged in sexual relationships as a part of their worship of Baal. And a "wife of prostitution" probably designated an ordinary Hebrew woman of that time, not one who made a living as a common prostitute, but one who had offered her body to men in the debased worship of Baal.

For a man such a Hosea, whose sensitivity emerges from every page of his book, this was an extraordinary command and a most unusual form of prophetic vocation. Though the book is written with great simplicity and offers no insight concerning Hosea's reaction to the divine call, it must have involved him in terrible

spiritual turmoil. Why should he marry such a woman, of precisely the kind that represented the sorry state of life and faith in
Israel at that time? And though the godless masses would have
cared little whom he married, intimate friends would surely have
been shocked at such a marriage by a man of Hosea's character.
But this is speculation; all we are told is that Hosea was obedient.
He married a woman called Gomer; we know little of her beyond
her name and the fact that she was not a virgin at the time of her
marriage.

There are two significant facts which emerge from this all too
brief account of Hosea's vocation.

(i) The first point is obvious, but should be stressed nevertheless. It is that Hosea, when we are first introduced to him, was a
man whose walk with God was so intimate that he heard and
clearly understood the divine vocation. And having heard, he
obeyed. For us in the modern world, it is a reminder of the danger
of stereotyping God and reducing all vocations to a set pattern or
form. One can scarcely imagine the reaction of a committee in the
contemporary Church, commissioned to examine young people
who offer themselves for ordination, if they were faced with a
modern-day Hosea and such an account of vocation. There are
times when the sense of vocation is real, though its form makes no
human sense; but vocation demands a response and Hosea
offered it.

(ii) The second point emerges in relation to the nature of
prophecy. God called Hosea, and Hosea responded, but initially
there is no suggestion that God intended his prophet to speak or
preach. That came later, but it had no part in the initial ministry
to which Hosea was summoned. He was called to *do* something
and his obedience and fulfilment lay in action; his first act was to
undertake a rather strange marriage. But all this lies within the
definition of prophecy which is stated so concisely within this
passage: the Lord "spoke *through* Hosea". The prophet was by
definition a spokesman of God; God would speak *through* him.
But whereas God might normally speak through the *words* of
prophets, he could also speak through their *lives*. In the first
instance Hosea was called to a marriage, specifically a marriage

through which God would speak to his people. We always need to be reminded that God may speak through his people to the world, not only through the words they speak, but also through the lives of obedience which they live. I have heard, over the years, many preachers and many sermons, and they are almost all forgotten; but on a few occasions I have met men and women of great spiritual stature and profound Christian character, and the memory of them has remained printed indelibly on my mind.

THE BIRTH OF HOSEA'S CHILDREN

Hosea 1:4–9

> 4 And the Lord said to him, "Call his name Jezreel; for yet a little while, and I will punish the house of Jehu for the blood of Jezreel, and I will put an end to the kingdom of the house of Israel. 5 And on that day, I will break the bow of Israel in the valley of Jezreel."
>
> 6 She conceived again and bore a daughter. And the Lord said to him, "Call her name Not pitied, for I will no more have pity on the house of Israel, to forgive them at all. 7 But I will have pity on the house of Judah, and I will deliver them by the Lord their God; I will not deliver them by bow, nor by sword, nor by war, nor by horses, nor by horsemen."
>
> 8 When she had weaned Not pitied, she conceived and bore a son. 9 And the Lord said, "Call his name Not my people, for you are not my people and I am not your God."

Hosea's marriage resulted in the birth of three children, two sons and one daughter; the naming of the children constituted the second stage of Hosea's ministry (after the marriage itself), for in the name of each child a message was conveyed to the people of Israel.

(i) The first son to be born was called Jezreel, and though the name may sound normal enough to those of us who belong to a foreign culture and a different age, it was a distinctly unusual name. An analogy might be seen if some future American prophet were to call his son "Vietnam" or "Watergate", the names of places which designate events in America's history. Jezreel, too, was primarily a place name with a particular historical significance in ancient Israel. It was at Jezreel that the royal house of Omri had been exterminated by the house of Jehu in a terrible massacre (2 Kings 9–10). At the time of the massacre, a century before Hosea's ministry, the death of that royal dynasty may have seemed a good thing, for the true faith of Israel had been corrupted under the rule of the house of Omri. But the new dynasty in Israel, that of Jehu, was still in control a century later in the person of King Jeroboam II, and the state of the faith was as bad as it had ever been in the past. Thus the massacre had been in vain, but the name of the place where the massacre had been carried out still contained ominous overtones. To speak the word *Jezreel* conjured up the image of awful bloodshed; when the prophet named his first son Jezreel, he intimated a coming judgment to the royal house in Israel.

(ii) The second child, a daughter, was also given an unusual name; she was called *Lo-ruhamah*, or "Not pited". It was not a normal name; one can scarcely imagine the pain of a parent in so naming a child or the difficulty of a child in growing up with such a name. But again, the name carried a message, and through the naming of his children Hosea was performing his role as a prophet. As a little girl was called "Not pited" by her parent, so too the Lord had come to the end of his pity for Israel. The birth of the second child, at least a year after the birth of Jezreel, marks an awful progression in this prophecy of doom. The birth of the first child carried a message to the royal household; that of the second child carried a message to the entire nation of Israel. And while the first message indicated a coming judgment, the second spoke a still more solemn word: God's love or pity for Israel had reached at last its limit.

(iii) Finally, a year or so later, a third child was born and he carried the most terrible name of them all: *Lo-ammi*, or "Not my people". When God had promised the Covenant, back in the time of Moses, he had said to Israel: "I will take you for my people [*ammi*], and I will be your God" (Exod. 6:7), but now that ancient promise was negated in the birth of a boy. Israel would no longer be God's ancient people, and the Lord would no longer be their God. To a nation whose entire existence and faith were based upon the Covenant, there could be no more terrible pronouncement for those who had ears to hear it!

The life of the prophet and his family were now set before Israel as a living and permanent message of judgment. Hosea had not merely preached a sermon which could quickly be forgotten by a thoughtless audience. He had acted as he had been commanded, and the character of his wife and the names of his children set permanently before Israel a symbolic reminder of the nation's own standing before God. It was Israel who was God's unclean wife; it was her children who symbolized the judgment and separation from the husband, God.

Hosea's prophetic acts were undertaken before a particular nation state in the ancient world and thus seem somewhat distant from us in the twentieth century. Yet from those prophetic actions and from the meaning attributed to them, there emerge two points of considerable significance; one pertains to God and the other to mankind.

(a) The naming of the three children indicates a severe progression in God's announcement of judgment. First, he declares a coming act of judgment against the royal family, second a limit to his pity, and finally the end of the covenant relationship with Israel. And yet, as we reflect upon this progression of judgment, we can see that it involves a move from the active to the passive. First, God threatens action, but finally he simply announces the withdrawal from relationship with the chosen people. Judgment has always a purpose; it is not merely punitive or an angry reaction. The first stage of active judgment still contains within it the possibility that the people will be prompted to turn back to God; the last stage is nothing, for a people who have steadfastly refused a relationship eventually have the possibility of a relationship withdrawn from them. And the final terror of judgment is not that of a God active against mankind, but that of a God who has ceased to be concerned with mankind. Hidden within this judgment theme lies the nucleus of the meaning of human life. Life finds its meaning and fulfilment in relationship with God, who is the giver of all life. But Israel constantly turned away from that relationship and sought love and fulfilment elsewhere; that was the ultimate evil, and the ultimate response was that God's pity would be exhausted and his offer of relationship terminated. And in all the relationships with the Living God, love and judgment go together: love is the essence of relationship, judgment seeks to draw us back into relationship, but when there is response neither to love nor judgment, the possibility of finding meaning in human existence slips finally from our grasp.

(b) If the opening verses of Hosea contained the entire message of the prophet, then it would be a very solemn book indeed, for the birth of the third child, taken by itself, appears to mark the end. There is in fact more to the prophet's message and it begins to emerge even before the end of the first chapter, but the opening nine verses set a proper perspective on the human condition. Israel had sinned and resisted the warnings of God, and so the judgment of a terminated Covenant was announced: Israel would no longer be God's people. There was more to the message than that; there was also hope, but the prophet's audience was in no position to hear of hope until first they had realized with full clarity the terrible predicament in which they were situated. Thus the beginning of the prophet's ministry and the opening verses of his short book set forth the human predicament in all its bleakness. Only then may it be possible to look beyond the black clouds and glimpse a future hope. And in this sense, Hosea anticipates an element of the gospel. We cannot perceive the ultimate hope in God unless first we perceive the sad estate of the human race. If, in the last resort, the love of God depended upon us and upon our response to the offer of relationship with God, the ninth verse of Hosea would toll as a dreary epitaph: "Not my people". But those who recognize the human predicament, whether in Hosea's time or our own, are in a position to hear another word, a word of hope.

HOPE FOR THE FUTURE

Hosea 1:10–2:1

[10]Yet the number of the people of Israel shall be like the sand of the sea, which can be neither measured nor numbered; and in the place

where it was said to them, "You are not my people," it shall be said to them, "Sons of the living God." ¹¹And the people of Judah and the people of Israel shall be gathered together, and they shall appoint for themselves one head; and they shall go up from the land, for great shall be the day of Jezreel.

¹Say to your brother, "My people," and to your sister, "She has obtained pity."

The dismal prospects elicited by the naming of Hosea's children in verses 4–9 are here contrasted by words offering hope of a brighter future. But the reader of the book needs to be careful; although this prophetic saying directly follows the account of the naming of the children in the narrative, it was delivered originally at a much later point in the prophet's ministry. The naming of the children took place early in the ministry; when life in Israel appeared to be prospering, the ominous names of the children indicated that a future of judgment lay ahead. Later in Hosea's ministry, between 733 and 722 B.C., when the signs of the end were plainly to be seen in Israel, the prophet declared these words, offering a message of hope that lay beyond the doom that must by then inevitably fall. Yet in the compilation of the book, the placing of this saying immediately after the terrible naming of the children enables the reader to perceive the full range of the prophet's thought. He begins his work with a message of judgment; as the days of judgment begin to dawn, he has a word of hope for the more distant future.

The prophet's message begins with a promise, reminiscent of a more ancient promise given in the days of Abraham: "the number of the people of Israel shall be like the sand of the sea" (verse 10; see also Gen. 22:17). As the population of Israel in Hosea's time was not large (perhaps in the vicinity of 150,000), the words evoked hope of a more splendid future. But it was not just the anticipation of growth that provided basis for hope; much more significant was the transformation in the nation's condition that would occur. Whereas, as a consequence of judgment, they had been called "Not my people", in the future they would be known as "Sons of the Living God".

The prophet then specifies three distinctive aspects of the future restoration (verse 11). (a) The people of the two kingdoms would be reunited into a single nation, as they had been in the past. (b) They would be led by a single "head" (or chief). (c) They would "go up from the land", probably meaning that they would control once again their own territory, which in Hosea's later life was becoming little more than a colonial territory belonging to a foreign power. In anticipation of these future transformations, the prophet cries out: "Great shall be the day of Jezreel." Although there is debate as to the precise meaning of these words, they appear to refer back to the earlier mention of Jezreel (verse 4). The original day of Jezreel had been one of hope, that out of the bloodshed of slaughtered idolatry a new faith might arise; it did not, and the naming of Hosea's first child intimated the coming of further bloodshed. Yet now, further on in time, Hosea perceives that, out of the bloodshed anticipated in the naming of his son, there would yet be a new birth of living faith. And as the significance of the name Jezreel has been changed in this saying from a later period in the prophet's life, so too would the other children's names be changed. Jezreel would start calling his brother "My People", and his sister "She has obtained Pity". The future action of God would negate the negatives incorporated into the names of those children.

This short saying, located as it is in the narrative of Hosea's book, illuminates both the manner of God's dealing with people and also his desire for all people.

(i) The preceding part of the prophecy (verses 4–9), taken alone, might appear to reveal the countenance only of a holy and wrathful God. In his holiness, he could not countenance sin; his word, transmitted through the naming of the children, was one of judgment. It was not God's last word, but it was the only word the people heard when the prophet began to minister. Later in time, as we perceive from the juxtaposition of these two passages, a word of grace was to follow.

The prophet thus illuminates the full nature of God in his dealing with his people. The divine desire is that all should be his children. But we cannot always explicitly discern that from his immediate word to us. Frequently the circumstances of our lives, fully of our own making, elicit only a word of judgment; the judgmental word tells no less of the character of God than it does of the condition of ourselves. We know what God desires for us; if his word indicates less than blessing, it points further within us to the need for self-examination and a return to fellowship with God. Only then may the word of hope be heard again.

(ii) The divine word of judgment to Israel had been: "You are not my people". This awful dictum shattered the Covenant upon which Israel's faith was based. But Hosea promised a time when it would be changed and when the new divine address would be: "Sons of the Living God".

The word to Israel carries also implicit hope for gentiles. We cannot claim by any right to be God's people; we can only aspire, perhaps forlornly, to the title "Sons of the Living God". But as the New Testament writers make clear, these prophetic words were understood in the early Church to embrace both Gentiles and Jews. Paul explicitly makes such an assertion in his letter to the Church in Rome (Romans 9:24–26), as does Peter in his description of the new community of God's people (1 Peter 2:10). We no more deserve such privilege than did those to whom Hosea first addressed the words. Yet we have failed to grasp the fulness of the faith unless we perceive that it has made us "Sons of the Living God". The expression *Living God* designates above all he whose character it is to impart the power of life. To be the children of such a God is to have fulness of life and to discover that the meaning of our lives is to be found in relationship with the Father of all Life.

THE GREAT DIVORCE

Hosea 2:2–15

> 2"Plead with your mother, plead—
>   for she is not my wife,
>   and I am not her husband—

that she put away her harlotry from her face,
and her adultery from between her breasts;
³lest I strip her naked
and make her as in the day she was born,
and make her like a wilderness,
and set her like a parched land,
and slay her with thirst.
⁴Upon her children also I will have no pity,
because they are children of harlotry.
⁵For their mother has played the harlot;
she that conceived them has acted shamefully.
For she said, 'I will go after my lovers,
who give me my bread and my water,
my wool and my flax, my oil and my drink.'
⁶Therefore I will hedge up her way with thorns;
and I will build a wall against her,
so that she cannot find her paths.
⁷She shall pursue her lovers,
but not overtake them;
and she shall seek them,
but shall not find them.
Then she shall say, 'I will go
and return to my first husband,
for it was better with me then than now.'
⁸And she did not know
that it was I who gave her
the grain, the wine, and the oil,
and who lavished upon her silver
and gold which they used for Baal.
⁹Therefore I will take back
my grain in its time,
and my wine in its season;
and I will take away my wool and my flax,
which were to cover her nakedness.
¹⁰Now I will uncover her lewdness
in the sight of her lovers,
and no one shall rescue her out of my hand.
¹¹And I will put an end to all her mirth,
her feasts, her new moons, her sabbaths,
and all her appointed feasts.

> [12]And I will lay waste her vines and her fig trees,
>> of which she said,
>> 'These are my hire,
>>> which my lovers have given me.'
>> I will make them a forest,
>>> and the beasts of the field shall devour them.
> [13]And I will punish her for the feast days of the Baals
>> when she burned incense to them
> and decked herself with her ring and jewelry,
>> and went after her lovers,
>> and forgot me, says the Lord.
>
> [14]"Therefore, behold, I will allure her,
>> and bring her into the wilderness,
>> and speak tenderly to her.
> [15]And there I will give her her vineyards,
>> and make the Valley of Achor a door of hope.
> And there she shall answer as in the days of her youth,
>> as at the time when she came out of the land of Egypt."

The focus of attention now swings back to an earlier period in the prophet's life and ministry; the words of hope in the preceding verses (1:10–2:1) are followed by this bleak passage concerning divorce. For a number of reasons, it is a difficult passage to read. Unlike the preceding prosaic verses, this section is written in poetry. And it must be interpreted on two levels: the initial level concerns Hosea and his family, but this is merely the foundation for the second level, which is an allegory of God's relationship to Israel. While at first the passage may appear to be in the normal forms of biblical poetry, it is in fact characterized by technical expressions and style that indicate its true character. It is a speech, specifically a speech related to a lawsuit, which is spoken in court in complaint concerning the person against whom the suit is brought.

The two levels on which the speech must be interpreted are at times so intimately interrelated that it is difficult to distinguish between them. On the first level, one must envisage Hosea and his children in the court; they address words to the judge in the presence of Gomer. Hosea's purpose in the lawsuit is to obtain a decree of divorce from his wife, and indeed his speech begins with the formal proclamation of divorce: "She is not my wife and I am not her husband" (verse 2). The reason for bringing the suit was to be found in the actions of the wife. She had been persistently unfaithful, committing adultery with other men. (Whether the acts in question were simply adulterous liaisons, or whether Gomer had resorted once again to the sexual activities of the fertility cult, remains uncertain; the latter is most likely, given the language of the speech and the intent of the allegory.) The entire scene is a tragic one: a deserted husband and three children are compelled by the actions of the wife-mother, and by the requirements of Hebrew law, to take the case to court. But the second level of interpretation is no less tragic, for Hosea's family life is still functioning as an allegory of God's relationship to Israel.

In the divine court, Israel is arraigned; God is present in a multiple role, as at once offended party, prosecutor, and judge. And to the divine court, the nation's crimes are proclaimed; its unfaithfulness to God and its pursuit of false faith are such that the marriage of covenant can no longer continue. God must seek divorce from Israel. For all the bleakness of the scene, it is not without a slim ray of hope. Adultery, according to Hebrew law, was punishable by death (Deut. 22:22); yet at neither level of interpretation is the death penalty sought. Indeed, for all the pathos of the passage, it is not without the remnants of warmth. Hosea, despite the action he takes, still loves his wife, just as God continues to love Israel, despite the divorce which the covenant stipulations compel him to seek.

In the course of the divorce proceedings three condemnations are made, each followed by a statement of judgment introduced by the word *therefore* (verses 6, 9, 14). The condemnations and judgments refer first to Gomer, and then in allegory to Israel, but they also have a more lasting message beyond the immediate context of their initial usage.

(i) The first condemnation is based on the woman's intention to pursue other lovers; indeed, her words are quoted to the court: "I will go after my lovers" (verse 5). She had consciously set off on her unfaithful path, deluding herself into the false belief that other lovers could make rich provision for her needs. And so the judgment is stated: she would be forced to continue down the path of life she had chosen, to its bitter and frustrating end. She would chase her lovers, but never catch them, seek them, but never find them, until at last in desperation she would perceive that the only hope lay with her first love. In the allegory, it is clear that Israel's judgment was a continuation in the path the nation had consciously chosen, but in its passage the hollowness of heathen love would become dreadfully apparent.

To have known the love of God, and then quite deliberately to choose another path, is to invite the frustration of a loveless existence. For having once known true love, all the rest of love's allures tantalize, but remain always beyond our grasp. The pursuit of other loves, the searching for what we think it may provide, becomes eventually a cul-de-sac in which, if we have any wisdom at all, we may perceive that there is only one love in which full provision and full satisfaction may be found. And we perceive a further truth in the prophet's words. Even as we chase and strive in the cul-de-sac of empty human love, we are pursued and hounded by a greater love that will not cease.

(ii) The second condemnation was addressed to the wife's wilful ignorance. She did not know that her husband provided the needs of life; it was not simple ignorance, but wilful ignorance. She would seek the fulfilment of her needs elsewhere. Likewise, Israel was wilfully ignorant that God provided the "grain, the wine, and the oil" (verse 8) on which life depended; yet those three things were explicitly a part of the provision of the Covenant, a sign of God's love (see Deut. 7:13). In the judgment, ignorance was to be treated by the withdrawal of all provisions (verse 9); only in the absence of God's life-sustaining gifts would Israel return to its senses and a knowledge of God.

The wilful ignorance that is here condemned is a commoner affliction than we might think. It is induced by the conscious setting aside of the realities of existence, as revealed by faith. We know that we have needs, but we think we are the ones best equipped to seek them out. As Israel sought to fulfil its needs in the resort to alien faith, so too do we. There are times when only destitution, whether physical or spiritual, can bring us back to the clear-sighted knowledge of the great Provider. The removal of God's provision, though it may be an act of judgment, provides nevertheless an opportunity to learn again the source of that which sustains true life.

(iii) The third condemnation points to the failure that is *forgetfulness* (verse 13). In going her own way, Gomer had forgotten Hosea; in pursuing other gods, Israel had forgotten the Lord. It is not normal amnesia that is meant, nor the simple forgetting of facts; rather it is that foregetfulness of the bonds of faithful relationship that makes possible the faithless pursuit of alien liaisons. But the third judgment (verses 14–15) turns condemnation into promise. Israel would be taken into the wilderness, a place of trial, but would learn again such dependence upon the love of God that a new entry into the promised land would be possible. The Valley of Achor, which in the past had been a "Valley of Trouble" (see Josh. 7:22–26), would become a "Valley of Hope" through which access to a new land would be gained.

Persons who commit adultery do not literally forget that they are married; they forget rather the bonds of marriage and the commitments of faithful love. And the person who turns aside from the faith does not literally forget it all, but forgets only its obligations on life and love. For all such, the experience of wilderness is a time both of hardship and of hope. It is a hardship to be cut off from the comforts and self-sufficiency of normal life; it is a source of hope to learn again that the valley of trouble through which we walk may become a "door of hope" (verse 15).

THE HOPE OF A NEW COVENANT

Hosea 2:16–23

[16]"And in that day, says the Lord, you will call me, 'My husband,' and no longer will you call me, 'My Baal.' [17]For I will remove the names of the Baals from her mouth, and they shall be mentioned by name no

more. [18]And I will make for you a covenant on that day with the beasts of the field, the birds of the air, and the creeping things of the ground; and I will abolish the bow, the sword, and war from the land; and I will make you lie down in safety. [19]And I will betroth you to me for ever; I will betroth you to me in righteousness and in justice, in steadfast love, and in mercy. [20]I will betroth you to me in faithfulness; and you shall know the Lord.

[21]"And in that day, says the Lord,
> I will answer the heavens
> and they shall answer the earth;

[22]and the earth shall answer the grain, the wine, and the oil,
> and they shall answer Jezreel;

[23]　and I will sow him for myself in the land.
> And I will have pity on Not pitied,
> and I will say to Not my people, 'You are my people';
> and he shall say, 'Thou art my God.'"

The pendulum of chronological perspective has now swung forward again, as it did at the end of chapter 1. The awful address to the divorce court, with its anticipation of coming separation, now lies in the past; the prophecy in verses 16–23, though it cannot be dated precisely, comes from a later period in Hosea's ministry. His children, whose names are mentioned in this message, are by now young adults. But as before, the brighter prospect seen in these verses must be viewed against the darker background of the time of judgment in which they were delivered. From a time in which God's wrath is already being experienced, Hosea looks forward to a new and future work of God; he cannot tell how far in the future lies the era of which he now speaks, yet his words concerning the distant days of salvation are penetrated through and through by hope and conviction.

The prophecy is divided into three parts, each part introduced by a Hebrew expression translated "on [or in] that day"; see verses 16, 18 and 21. "That day" is the future period, lying beyond the present day of judgment, in which God's salvation would be known once again. In a sense, the prophecy is a prediction, not in the sense of specifying a *day* or *time* when certain things would happen, but rather in the sense of affirming that some day God *would* act again. For both ancient Israel and the modern reader of Hosea's book, the day of which the prophet writes has a futuristic ring to it. Yet for all the future focus, the prophetic words, in each of the three sections of this passage, express something which may have in part a present reality.

(i) The first part of the prophecy anticipates a *new marriage* (verses 16–17). The marriage would be between God and Israel, though the language is a haunting reminder that Hosea is divorced from Gomer. The prophet engages in effective word-play; to appreciate it, a little knowledge of Hebrew is required. The noun *baal* in Hebrew may mean "husband", with the cultural overtones of "lord and master". The noun may also function as a name, that of the Canaanite "Master" god, and as such it should be translated *Baal*. The Hebrew word *'ish* means simply *man*, but it may also be translated "husband", as such having the nuance of endearment. In the future, the prophet affirms, Israel would address its Lord as my *'ish* (beloved husband), not my *baal* (husband and master). But the transformation would be more than that, for the return to the Lord as true *husband* would concurrently be an abandonment of *Baal* as false master. The names of the various local manifestations of Baal would no longer soil Israel's lips.

The prophecy is one of the restoration of love and intimate relationship, and it is not without its glimpses of grief. The *Baals* on Israel's lips in the past caused grief to the still-loving divine husband. Gordon Lightfoot, a Canadian folksinger, sang a popular blues song a few years ago: "I heard you talking in your sleep". But the loved one, in sleep, was murmuring another name, dreaming of another lover. And as in human experience, the sleeping murmur of another's name can cause terrible grief to a husband or wife, so too the words on Israel's lips cut to the heart of God. Perhaps it is only when we perceive how deeply we have hurt God that we can also perceive how gracious is the promise of new marriage, of a love restored.

(ii) The second part of the prophecy anticipates a *new Covenant* (verses 18–20). In many ways, it is a repetition of the essential substance of the preceding section, but it has a new focus; whereas in the first part, the focus is on the internal intimacy of love, here it is on the external implications of the new covenant relationship of marriage. The new Covenant of the future would be one characterized by peace, which would be experienced on two fronts. Israel would experience peace with the world of nature, with the animals and birds and all living things. But in addition, God would destroy the weapons of war and grant the nation peace from its enemies. This peace from all external powers would be a period of new intimacy in the marriage of a renewed Covenant. And the prophecy of peace and new Covenant is rooted in the conviction that the Lord was God both of the world of nature and of the affairs of human beings and nations.

The perspectives of these prophetic words lie still in the future, as they did in the prophet's time. Although the Prince of Peace has visited this world, its nations have continued relentlessly in the practice of war. Yet there is an insight here that is perpetually and presently relevant: it is that war is rooted in mankind's separation from God's love. The words were first declared to a nation threatened on every side, destined for destruction. And the world today is little different, for the stormclouds of war have not ceased to gather. We must always strive for peace among the nations of the world, but it will remain a distant dream until the human race makes its peace with God.

(iii) In the third and final part of this prophecy, the names of Hosea's children are changed. The changes are introduced by a chain of speech, bringing the news from heaven to earth. (a) *Jezreel's* name remains the same, but its meaning is changed. Initially, the name recalled the place of bloody massacre and doom; it was an ominous name. But in the name's transformation, it is the etymology that is drawn out. *Jezreel* means "God shall sow"; in its new sense, it intimates God's new "sowing" of his people in their land. (b) On the child "Not pitied", God would exercise compassion and change the name to "Pitied". (c) The child "Not my people" would be called "My people", and in return would respond to God, as if in a wedding ceremony, "Thou art my God."

HOSEA'S REMARRIAGE

Hosea 3:1–5

[1]And the Lord said to me, "Go again, love a woman who is beloved of a paramour and is an adulteress; even as the Lord loves the people of Israel, though they turn to other gods and love cakes of raisins." [2]So I bought her for fifteen shekels of silver and a homer and a lethech of barley. [3]And I said to her, "You must dwell as mine for many days; you shall not play the harlot, or belong to another man; so will I also be to you." [4]For the children of Israel shall dwell many days without king or prince, without sacrifice or pillar, without ephod or teraphim. [5]Afterward the children of Israel shall return and seek the Lord their God, and David their king; and they shall come in fear to the Lord and to his goodness in the latter days.

This short chapter brings to both climax and conclusion the episodes from Hosea's life that began in chapter 1. Though the chapter is brief, it is not without difficulties of interpretation, in part because of the conciseness of the writing and in part because of the difficulty in translating some parts of the first three chapters from Hebrew. The form of language changes in these verses; now the prophet employs the first person ("I", "me"), and we must suppose that the compiler of the book had access to an account related by the prophet himself. The use of the first person adds to the humanity and the pathos of the passage.

The word of the Lord comes to Hosea again; indeed, there is a sense in which this event can be seen as a second vocation, a repetition of the call first described in chapter 1. And the substance of this renewed call is similar to the first, though there are some subtle and important differences. We do not know precisely when Hosea experienced this further vocation; we may suppose that the event took place some fifteen or twenty years after the first call. Hosea is now an older man, divorced, and with a family of grown-up children.

As before, the call is curious by comparison with the norms of prophetic vocation. Hosea is told: "Go again, love a woman" (verse 1). The name *Gomer* is not used, though it is implied both by the preceding story and by the interpretation that follows (verses 4–5). So the prophet is told to love again (though one suspects he had never ceased to love) his former wife, who is described here as an adulteress loved by other men. One of the subtle differences from the first vocation is to be seen in the divine command; initially, he was told to "take" a woman (1:2, "take" being a technical expression meaning "marry"), but now he must go a step further and "love" a woman—the same woman. And the force of the command is enhanced by the description of the one to be loved; to paraphrase, God says in effect: "love one who is unlovely, unlovable, and who loves others." As before, Hosea obeys. Recalling the hardship that had ensued the first time he had obeyed such a command, he must have acted with some trepidation, but he obeyed anyway.

The response to the divine command posed some difficulties for the prophet. His ex-wife was no longer "available" and had to be purchased. The implication of verse 2 is either that Gomer had become somebody's slave or concubine and thus must have her freedom purchased; alternatively, and more probably, she had become a slave or possession of the temple of Baal, where false religion prospered. There, she would have been engaged in the sexual practices of the fertility worship of Baal. From such enslavement, Hosea purchased her, the price paid (verse 2) being approximately the amount required to redeem a person from slavery. Having purchased her freedom, Hosea would live in seclusion with Gomer for many days, seeking in the shared loneliness to restore the intimacy of love that once had existed.

In the interpretation (verses 4–5), the life of Hosea is shown once again to portray and foreshadow God's dealings with Israel. Beyond the disruption of covenant relationship would lie a long period of separation between Israel and God, but beyond that a renewed relationship would be formed between the Lord and his people.

This conclusion to the story of Hosea's marital and family experiences is remarkable for the insights it offers concerning the biblical message as a whole.

(i) It demonstrates the supremacy of *love* over *law*. When

Hosea is commanded to love and marry Gomer again, he is faced with a terrible impasse. The divine call impels him to action, but the divine law appears to prohibit the action to which he is called. According to the ancient law, a man who has divorced a woman may not remarry the same woman, after she has been married to, and divorced from, another man (Deut. 24:1–4). How can God ask Hosea to do what is prohibited in divine law? The question is phrased wrongly! Love always precedes law. If law took preeminence, there would be no gospel in either Old or New Testament. And as Hosea is asked to go beyond law in the pursuit of love, so too does he demonstrate God's purpose of love that transcends law. Here, in a nutshell, is the Gospel of Love in the Old Testament. If law were the sole criterion, God could not have sent his Son to redeem the world, any more than Hosea could have gone out to redeem Gomer. But divine love is a force that knows no bounds; law may follow love to give some structure to the forms of love, but it can never have pre-eminence.

(ii) These verses also demonstrate the unflagging pursuit of God's love. When, by every standard, he should have ceased to love Israel, still God loves relentlessly, pursuing through the years those in whom the flames of love have long since died.

Francis Thompson, the English poet (1859–1907), captured splendidly this knowledge of the pursuit of God's love. As a young man, following certain disappointments in life, he had become addicted to drugs, and his addiction had reduced him to the life of a tramp on the streets of London in his twenties. At the age of 31 (in 1890), while struggling to break the chains of his addiction, he wrote the poem, "The Hound of Heaven"; like Hosea, he perceived the pursuit of a divine love that will not cease from its course.

> I fled Him, down the nights and down the days;
>   I fled Him, down the arches of the years;
> I fled Him, down the labyrinthine ways
>   Of my own mind; and in the midst of tears
> I hid from Him, and under running laughter.
>   Up vistaed hopes I sped;
>   And shot, precipitated,

Adown Titanic glooms of chasmed fears,
From those strong feet that followed, followed after.
   But with unhurrying chase,
   And unperturbed pace,
Deliberate speed, majestic instancy,
   They beat—and a Voice beat
   More instant than the Feet—
'All things betray thee, who betrayest Me.'

(iii) This third chapter in the account of Hosea's experience demonstrates further the many faces of *love*; the word *love* is used four times in verse 1. Hosea is to *love* the woman, as God *loves* Israel; but the woman is *loved* by other men, and she herself appears to *love* the dainty raisin cakes (associated with Baal worship) more than anything else in the world! In English, as in Hebrew, the word *love* can designate a wide range of emotions, from profound passion to preference in food. And yet, despite the superficial differences between the forms of love we know, there is a deeper commonality. For love designates that which is most important to us: it may be a profound relationship with another person, or a petty preference for food or trinkets. The tragedy of Gomer, as portrayed here, is not the *object* of her love, the dainty raisin cakes, but the shrivelling of her capacity to love. Having abused the capacity to love for so long, she was no longer capable of true and deep love for persons. As the muscles of the legs will shrivel if we do not walk, so too will the muscles of love shrink if they are not exercised in the true and profound forms of loving. We know what true love is, in these verses, when we reflect on God's unrelenting love for Israel; like Hosea, we are called upon to love "even as the Lord loves" (verse 1).

THE LORD'S COMPLAINT AGAINST ISRAEL

Hosea 4:1-3

[1]Hear the word of the Lord, O people of Israel;
   for the Lord has a controversy with the inhabitants of the land.

> There is no faithfulness or kindness,
>> and no knowledge of God in the land;
> ²there is swearing, lying, killing, stealing, and committing adultery;
>> they break all bounds and murder follows murder.
> ³Therefore the land mourns,
>> and all who dwell in it languish,
> and also the beasts of the field,
>> and the birds of the air;
>> and even the fish of the sea are taken away.

The short prophetic oracle contained in these verses serves as an introduction to Part II of the collected sayings of Hosea. The first three chapters constitute Part I, in which a degree of thematic unity is provided by the story of Hosea's family life. Part II is different in form; it is simply a collection of the prophetic sayings of Hosea, without the sense of unity provided by a story-line. But there is nevertheless a degree of unity and continuity in Part II (chapters 4–14); it is provided by the subject matter of the prophet's oracles, which is given its most precise and condensed expression in these opening three verses. It is best to view Part II as a complementary and companion volume to Part I. In the first part, we have seen the progression of the prophet's thought over a period of time, from the oracles of judgment that characterized Hosea's early ministry, to the oracles of salvation from the later period of his life. The same kind of general progression is evident in Part II. And just as Part I was introduced as the "word of the Lord" (1:1), so too is Part II (4:1); these are the only two verses in the Book of Hosea in which the expression is used.

The opening oracle of the second part of the book sets down concisely God's fundamental complaint against the nation as a whole; later, the prophet will address the divine word to specific groups within the nation. The saying is in a kind of legal form; the Lord "has a controversy" (verse 1) with the entire population, namely a formal complaint of the kind that would be declared in a court of law. The complaint is expressed first in negative terms (verse 1*b*), then in positive terms (verse 2), and is followed by a statement of the judgment that must come as a consequence of the nation's failure (verse 3).

The negative expression of the complaint (verse 1) has three parts to it. Israel, as a nation, is condemned for the absence of (a) faithfulness, (b) kindness, and (c) the knowledge of God. The first two parts of this complaint pertain to the question of relationships, with both God and fellow human beings. *Faithfulness* describes the continuity and steadfastness of a relationship, whereas *kindness* portrays its depth and intimacy; both are characteristic of God's relationship to Israel, and both are absent in the relationship of the Israelites with God and with one another. The third part of the complaint, namely the absence of the knowledge of God, points to something other than a thin theology or inadequate religious education; it refers rather to that knowledge which should culminate in a knowledge of God's law and purpose, and it is this that is so conspicuously absent in Israel. It is the absence of knowledge that is developed in the positive statement of complaint in verse 2.

The positive statement of complaint is an appalling indictment of Israel's behaviour. All the ethical components of the Ten Commandments have been broken. "There is swearing"; the reference is not simply to bad language, but to the formal cursing of a neighbour in the name of God, thereby breaking the third commandment (Deut. 5:11). "Lying" involved in all probability not only false statements, but also false testimony in court, thereby undermining the entire judicial system. "Killing" refers to premeditated murder. The word translated "stealing", though it can designate simple theft, implies something like kidnapping ("stealing" a person's life and liberty). And "adultery" no doubt encompasses both the secular act and also the sexual activities associated with the false faith in Baal. This massive outbreak of social disorder and decline all stemmed from the absence of "knowledge of God in the land" (verse 1).

Verse 3, in the RSV translation, sounds at first like a description simply of the consequences of Israel's sin in the world of nature. But the words are stronger than that, judgmental in tone; the introductory *therefore* clearly indicates that the substance of the verse is to be seen as a coming judgment directly consequent upon the nation's evil. The language implies a massive drought, causing the land to languish and affecting all living creatures. The dire consequences in the world of nature are seen as a direct result of the collapse of the moral structure of human society.

These opening verses of Part II of Hosea establish the underlying themes that will be developed in various ways in the chapters and verses that follow. The most fundamental flaw in Israel is the failure in all forms of relationship. At the heart of the faith, relationships gave structure to all of life; the relationship with God fulfilled life's meaning and gave shape to the various relationships with fellow human beings. Conversely, rich relationships with fellow human beings gave added depth to the relationship with God. But in all this, Israel had failed; there was no faithfulness or kindness, none of that profound knowledge of God which could form and shape all the various modes of interaction between human beings.

It is a sobering passage, despite its brevity. Israel only remained the chosen people of God so long as they maintained their intimacy with God, which in turn should flow forth in relationships of love and justice between one another. And the same is no less true of the Church. The knowledge of God and proper treatment of our fellow human beings are intimately interrelated. It is impossible to divorce theology from ethical behaviour, and remain true to the faith revealed; when it is attempted, a drought must follow and the Church must languish.

CONDEMNATION OF THE PRIESTHOOD

Hosea 4:4–19

⁴Yet let no one contend,
  and let none accuse,
  for with you is my contention, O priest.
⁵You shall stumble by day,
  the prophet also shall stumble with you by night;
  and I will destroy your mother.
⁶My people are destroyed for lack of knowledge;

because you have rejected knowledge,
  I reject you from being a priest to me.
And since you have forgotten the law of your God,
  I also will forget your children.

[7]The more they increased,
  the more they sinned against me;
  I will change their glory into shame.
[8]They feed on the sin of my people;
  they are greedy for their iniquity.
[9]And it shall be like people, like priest;
  I will punish them for their ways,
  and requite them for their deeds.
[10]They shall eat, but not be satisfied;
  they shall play the harlot, but not multiply;
because they have forsaken the Lord
  to cherish harlotry.

[11]Wine and new wine
  take away the understanding.
[12]My people inquire of a thing of wood,
  and their staff gives them oracles.
For a spirit of harlotry has led them astray,
  and they have left their God to play the harlot.
[13]They sacrifice on the tops of the mountains,
  and make offerings upon the hills,
under oak, poplar, and terebinth,
  because their shade is good.

Therefore your daughters play the harlot,
  and your brides commit adultery.
[14]I will not punish your daughters when they play the harlot,
  nor your brides when they commit adultery;
for the men themselves go aside with harlots,
  and sacrifice with cult prostitutes,
and a people without understanding shall come to ruin.

[15]Though you play the harlot, O Israel,
  let not Judah become guilty.
Enter not into Gilgal,
  nor go up to Bethaven,
  and swear not, "As the Lord lives."

¹⁶Like a stubborn heifer,
    Israel is stubborn;
  can the Lord now feed them
    like a lamb in a broad pasture?

¹⁷Ephraim is joined to idols,
    let him alone.
¹⁸A band of drunkards, they give themselves to harlotry;
    they love shame more than their glory.
¹⁹A wind has wrapped them in its wings,
    and they shall be ashamed because of their altars.

The first three chapters of the book have illuminated only one aspect of the prophet's life, namely the manner in which Hosea's family life served as an allegory of God's dealings with Israel. But through all the years of trauma and grief that characterized Hosea's life at home, he also had a life and ministry beyond the confines of his family; he was a prophet who, by words and action, addressed the contemporary issues of his time. In this long passage, we are provided a glimpse into his continuing struggle with the official priesthood of his day.

From a literary perspective, verses 4–19 have at first the appearance of a single speech or sermon addressed to the priests. But a closer examination of the form and style suggests that the narrative is a condensation; from numerous arguments and speeches against the priests this summary account has been put together, either by the prophet himself or by his faithful disciples. To grasp the power of these words, we must read them in the context of real conflict and confrontation, though it is not easy to reconstruct the setting from the words as such. The sermons and statements, here in summary form, were in all probability declared in public to the priests in Bethel, one of the principal sanctuaries in the northern state of Israel. And one must suppose that the words evoked a hostile response from those priests to whom they were addressed, though of this no details are given. But it is important to remember the setting. Hosea was not an essayist, writing polemical tracts from the safety of the ivory tower, but one who was engaged in a public and bitter conflict.

His words reflect in part his courage, and in part they portray the intense and profoundly moving struggle in which Hosea was engaged against the paganizing tendencies of his time.

The principal focus of his critique is the official priesthood of his nation, though as the polemic progresses the people as a whole come into view once again. The solemn tone at the beginning of the address sets the mood for what is to follow: "With you is my contention, O priest" (verse 4); the one who was supposed to be God's servant and intimate friend is immediately set in sharp relief as an enemy. The priests had failed in their task; though they continued to hold the title, in reality they had ceased to be the true priests of God.

The failure of the priests may be seen in several dimensions. (a) They failed in their responsibilities as teachers; consequently the people, no longer knowing God and his law, had departed far from the path of faith (verse 6). (b) Rather than condemning the national apostasy, they encouraged it and prospered from it, turning a nation's disgrace into personal profit (verse 8). (c) Though they above all should have known the true faith, they delighted in practising the false and syncretistic rites of their time, seducing their people into doing the same (verses 11–13). Such terrible behaviour invited divine judgment, but the true tragedy of such priestly actions is that their consequences were not limited to the priests; they pervaded the entire nation, making Israel "like a stubborn heifer" (verse 16). The wayward leadership of the priests had led the people to an abandonment to the practice of idolatry, a love of its new and drunken shame that had replaced the glory of the old days of true faith (verses 17–19).

It is a sombre word that the prophet speaks, having implications both for those engaged in formal ministry and for the laity as a whole.

(i) The priests had been given great responsibility; their failure was thus all the more dramatic. Those to whom the privilege of leadership is given, but who systematically mislead, are responsible not only for their own actions, but for the fate of those that follow.

The role of ministry to God's people is always both privileged and perilous. It is a privilege to share in God's work, to extend his compassion to those who know no love, to teach his way, to lead in the worship of a community. But it is also a perilous task, for leaders must know where they are going, and a hundred things conspire to change that direction. Israel's priests had lost sight of their priorities and accommodated themselves to the ethos of their age. And once one has turned aside from the straight and narrow path of leadership, one becomes accustomed to the new and more liberal path after a while. The old religion was too narrow, too inflexible, not in touch with the changing tenor of the times; it takes a Hosea sometimes to reveal to the leadership of the Church that some new forms of religion have abandoned the very heart of the ancient faith.

(ii) For all the responsibility that is carried by priests and ministers, the people as a whole cannot absolve themselves from their own responsibility for the crisis in the community of faith. The leaders must have followers, but the followers in turn must exercise discrimination in choosing to follow. In Israel, they chose the easy way, succumbing to the seductive allures of a pagan faith and convincing themselves that the easy path must be the right path, for it was the path in which the leaders were walking.

In a sense, this passage sets forth some of the dilemmas of the democratic process, whether in nation or church. The people want true and courageous leadership, thinking themselves willing to follow. But the leaders fear to go it alone, and so they constantly turn to the polls of public opinion, seeking the direction in which they must lead. The consequence is frequently confusion among the masses, and a meandering leadership from the rear.

Leadership gains its strength when its goals and objectives are stated clearly and with objectivity. In the Church, the criteria of leadership are the priorities of the gospel, which the people as a whole can clearly see and follow. We are responsible, as God's people, for knowing the directions in which we must go and following those who would take us there. But we are no less responsible for refusing to follow when the leaders choose to walk in the wrong path, away from the clear direction of the gospel. In the last resort, we are responsible for our own actions, whether leader or follower.

A MESSAGE TO PRIESTS, CHIEFS, AND THE KING'S COURT

Hosea 5:1-7

¹Hear this, O priests!
    Give heed, O house of Israel!
Hearken, O house of the king!
    For the judgment pertains to you;
for you have been a snare at Mizpah,
    and a net spread upon Tabor.
²And they have made deep the pit of Shittim;
    but I will chastise all of them.

³I know Ephraim,
    and Israel is not hid from me;
for now, O Ephraim, you have played the harlot,
    Israel is defiled.
⁴Their deeds do not permit them to
    return to their God.
For the spirit of harlotry is within them,
    and they know not the Lord.

⁵The pride of Israel testifies to his face;
    Ephraim shall stumble in his guilt;
    Judah also shall stumble with them.
⁶With their flocks and herds they shall go
    to seek the Lord,
but they will not find him;
    he has withdrawn from them.
⁷They have dealt faithlessly with the Lord;
    for they have borne alien children.
Now the new moon shall devour them with their fields.

In this short prophetic passage, we have once again a condensation of what was originally a longer discourse. The first three verses are expressed as the direct words of God, declared by

Hosea; verses 4–7 are the prophet's own words, spoken perhaps by way of response to the complaints and excuses that were evoked by the initial divine speech. The divine speech is addressed to three categories of leaders in Israel: (a) the priests (see also 4:4–19); (b) the chiefs of the clans and local regions (namely the "House of Israel", verse 1); and (c) the Royal Court ("House of the King"). These various groups of persons, by virtue of their failure to fulfil their responsibilities of leadership, are the subject of divine criticism and the object of coming chastisement. The background to these proclamations of the prophet was no doubt the city of Samaria, where the Royal Court was situated; and from the substance of the prophet's words, one may assume that his outspoken critique evoked a hostile reaction from those who had been administered such a scathing rebuke in public.

The initial complaint is expressed as a metaphor. The actions of the leaders in Israel had been like a "snare", a "net", and a "pit". The three terms of the metaphor are drawn from the vocabulary of hunting: the snare and the net were used for the entrapment of birds, whereas the pit was used for the capture of game. All three aspects of the hunting metaphor illustrate the loss of freedom for the victim; likewise, Israel's leaders, by their actions, had removed any real freedom from their people. The three places mentioned (Mizpah, Tabor, and Shittim) were probably locations which typified the actions of ensnarement by Israel's leaders; though no doubt highly significant to the first audience, the reference to places is now somewhat elusive. Mizpah (though there are several places bearing the name) may have been close to the southern border of the northern kingdom, Tabor was a mountain in the north, and Shittim lay to the east of the Jordan. In addition to alluding to specific events, no longer known, the place-names may be indicative of the widespread failure of Israel's leaders, from south to north, and from west to east.

Israel (for which *Ephraim* in this context is a synonym: verse 3) had engaged in the sexual rites of the fertility religion, lured into such false practices by the delinquent leadership of its priests, chiefs, and the royal household. In response to Hosea's public words of denunciation, many of the leaders must have claimed, by way of self-defence, that the proper forms of worship were still being conducted in Israel. But Hosea cannot countenance such a shallow excuse. There may indeed still be some surviving semblance of the true worship, but those who "seek the Lord" will not find him (verse 6); the Lord, in reaction to the dissemination of pagan practice, has withdrawn from Israel. As a result of the failure of the nation's leadership, God's judgment would inevitably come. It is expressed in the last line of verse 7, but the meaning of the words in the Hebrew text (and in the English translation) is obscure. It is possible that the early Greek translation preserves the original meaning: it refers to a coming plague of locusts, perceived as an act of divine judgment.

This concise summary of the prophet's encounter with the nation's leaders has both negative and positive messages to impart.

(i) The people had lost their liberty as a consequence of false leadership. When they should have been free as a bird in God's fresh air, they had become ensnared in the fowler's net. The freedom of the gazelle to roam the country ranges had been exchanged for the confines of the hunter's pit. A nation which had been built on the celebration of freedom from ancient slavery was once again enslaved, captured by the chains of an alien faith. Of all the losses that a person may endure, the loss of the freedom of faith is one of the most severe. And it is not always imposed by a foreign power with its repressive legislation; the loss of freedom may as easily be experienced by the abandonment of the faith which brought that freedom in the first place.

(ii) When the exclusive commitments of the faith have been abandoned, it is only a self-deception to maintain the old ways in the hope that all will be well. The leaders in Israel had both practised and promulgated the alien faith of Baal, but they sought to cover all options by maintaining the formal worship of Israel's God. And when their false ways were condemned, they pointed self-righteously to the continuity of all the forms of worship that belonged to the true faith (verse 6). But the double standard wasn't effective, indeed it was pointless. For the continuity of the true forms of worship did not preserve the faith in times of rampant paganism; it echoed only the hypocrisy of leaders who no longer perceived the exclusive requirements of the old way.

The hollow exercise of maintaining the veneer of the true faith, while indulging in the fleeting pleasures of paganism, brings a stern word from the prophet. Such people will seek the Lord, but will not find him, for he has withdrawn from them. It is the very opposite of the promise of the gospel, "seek, and ye shall find". But you only find when you are really seeking; the pantomime of Israel's worship was simply a cover for the actions of a people who no longer desired to find God. And so God withdrew, no longer able to be found.

(iii) For all the power of the prophet's critique, there remains an element of hope in the divine words he declares. He says, on behalf of God: "I will chastise all of them" (verse 2), and the chastisement is announced at the end of verse 7. But the Hebrew word translated *chastise* is a word with positive connotations; it designates disciplinary actions of the kind that are intended to instruct. A parent chastises a child, not only as a consequence of a naughty act, but also to teach the child how to behave. And so again we perceive the divine mercy penetrating the clouds of judgment. By our wayward actions, we may invite the divine judgment, but that judgment in turn may be a form of chastisement, not God's last word. And when we perceive God's discipline for what it is, we may learn from it. Though a child suffers from parental chastisement, it also learns to discern the love behind the frown and thus to discover the true path in life.

THE ALARM IS SOUNDED

Hosea 5:8–9

8Blow the horn in Gibeah,
   the trumpet in Ramah.
 Sound the alarm at Bethaven;
   tremble, O Benjamin!
9Ephraim shall become a desolation
   in the day of punishment;

among the tribes of Israel
I declare what is sure.

These two short verses introduce a collection of Hosea's sayings which extends from 5:8 to the end of chapter 7. The collection forms a homogeneous whole, with a common theme and common goal, although, as with other portions of the book, in its present form it is a condensation and summary of an episode in Hosea's ministry. The background to this portion of the prophet's ministry can be only partially reconstructed from the verses as such, supplemented by the historical account given in 2 Kings 15–17. The verses probably reflect the crisis that was reached in Israel in the year 733 B.C.; some further information on that crisis may help to illuminate the meaning of 5:8–7:16 as a whole.

When Hosea began his prophetic ministry, the state of Israel was ruled by King Jeroboam II. The state, during his reign, prospered by the external and human measures of success. Israel was a powerful military nation with considerable wealth and influence in international affairs. Nevertheless, the country was sick at heart; the decline in the nation's faith was accompanied by a breakdown in the social structure that did not bode well for the future. All that held the nation together was the firm hand of Jeroboam II, but in the year 746 B.C. he died. The following year, another significant event took place: in 745 B.C. Tiglath-Pileser III became the new ruler of Assyria and set himself the goal of rebuilding the once mighty Assyrian Empire. The death of a king in Israel, coupled with the coronation of a man determined to dominate the world from Assyria, created a new politico-historical environment in which the fate of the northern kingdom was to be worked out until its eventual demise in 722 B.C.

The years following the death of Jeroboam II were marked by chaos in Israel. Over the next ten years the nation was ruled by five kings, few of them with any legitimate claim to the throne. Violence was established as the new means by which power in Israel was sought, and periodic civil war characterized the internal life of the nation. Jeroboam's son, Zechariah, succeeded to his father's throne; after a reign of only six months, he was murdered and succeeded by his slayer, Shallum. He too was slain, after only a month in the royal seat, and was succeeded by the one who killed him, namely Menahem (745–737 B.C.). During Menahem's reign, Israel became virtually a colony of Assyria, to whom heavy tributes were paid. He was succeeded by his son Pekahiah (737–736 B.C.); this unfortunate king was assassinated by a military officer, Pekah, who ruled from 736 to 732 B.C. With the rise of Pekah to royal power, the national policy changed; the former pro-Assyrian policy of Menahem was changed to an anti-Assyrian policy by Pekah (who may have hoped for Egyptian help as a consequence of his new political alignment).

Thus, from 736 B.C., the small nation of Israel embarked on a foreign policy that was doomed from the beginning. It sought to resist the tide of Assyria's rising power and to that end engaged in an alliance with Damascus to the north; but the anti-Assyrian policy in Israel also created an enemy in the south, for the state of Judah was still supportive of Assyria, all too well aware that Egypt was a weak reed, providing no real help in crisis. And so Israel, allied to a pagan power in Damascus, invaded Judah, which in turn was compelled to ask Tiglath-Pileser for assistance in response to the invasion from the north by its sister state. Tiglath-Pileser promptly responded; his armies destroyed Israel's alliance, removed much of the nation's territory and, by 733 B.C., only Israel's heartland, the central mountainous region of Ephraim, retained a degree of relative freedom from Assyria.

Such was the international and political environment in which this portion of Hosea's book (5:8–7:16) must be interpreted. For most people living in Israel at the time, attention would have been focused on international events. What would happen next? Would the alliance with Damascus hold firm? Would the invasion of Judah be successful? Would Egypt send help against the Assyrian menace? But while dozens of questions such as these were asked, and while the political pundits sought to answer them, none sought to determine what was the divine purpose in the tumultuous events of the time—except for a few of God's prophets, of whom Hosea was one.

The beginning of his message is striking in its style: "Blow the horn ... sound the alarm!" His speech opens with the words traditionally employed to announce an imminent attack and the need for defence. The danger is seen as coming most immediately from the south, for Gibeah, Ramah and Bethaven were in the border territories between Israel and Judah; that was the direction in which the nation's anti-Assyrian thrust had been directed, and that was the direction from which a new threat would emerge. Yet the new foe, as Hosea perceives it, lies literally neither to the north nor the south. The new foe is a former ally, none other than the God of Israel. For behind the gathering clouds of international conflict, Hosea perceives an even greater threat, namely that God has turned against Israel on the basis of the nation's sin.

What we shall be reading, then, in the verses that follow is in part historico-political analysis, but it is profoundly penetrated with theological critique. We are reading the words of a remarkable man who perceived clearly not only the events of his time, but the presence and purpose of God within those events. And even more, we are reading the words of a man of remarkable courage; it is not easy to speak home truths plainly in a time when national courage has failed and calamity piles upon calamity. People did not want to hear Hosea's message, which made it all the more imperative that it be proclaimed with insistence.

THE FAILURE OF TWO NATIONS

Hosea 5:10–6:3

> [10]The princes of Judah have become
>   like those who remove the landmark;
>   upon them I will pour out
>   my wrath like water.
> [11]Ephraim is oppressed, crushed in judgment,
>   because he was determined to go after vanity.
> [12]Therefore I am like a moth to Ephraim,
>   and like dry rot to the house of Judah.

¹³When Ephraim saw his sickness,
and Judah his wound,
then Ephraim went to Assyria,
and sent to the great king.
But he is not able to cure you
or heal your wound.
¹⁴For I will be like a lion to Ephraim,
and like a young lion to the house of Judah.
I, even I, will rend and go away,
I will carry off, and none shall rescue.

¹⁵I will return again to my place,
until they acknowledge their guilt and seek my face,
and in their distress they seek me, saying,
¹"Come, let us return to the Lord;
for he has torn, that he may heal us;
he has stricken, and he will bind us up.
²After two days he will revive us;
on the third day he will raise us up,
that we may live before him.
³Let us know, let us press on to know the Lord;
his going forth is sure as the dawn;
he will come to us as the showers,
as the spring rains that water the earth."

Having sounded the alarm, the prophet now turns to the substance of his message; although it is addressed immediately to the northern state of Israel, its words also embrace the neighbouring state of Judah. The initial comment about the "princes of Judah" (verse 10) may have been prompted by an audience complaint. Hosea had begun by sounding the alarm against "the tribes of Israel" (verse 9), suggesting by reference to place-names that judgment would come from Judah. And no doubt a self-righteous member of the audience, suspecting the prophet of pro-Judean politics and even treason, complained: "What about Judah? They are no better than us!" The prophet promptly agreed and affirmed unequivocally that Judah too would experience God's wrath. (The reference to "those who remove the landmark" may be an allusion to long-standing border disputes between Israel and Judah; the three towns mentioned in verse 8 were in the disputed border territory.) But the fact that Judah too would experience judgment did not in any way blunt the prophet's affirmation concerning Israel's fate. The northern state's determination to "go after vanity" (verse 11) was such that judgment must come.

Israel, called here *Ephraim* after the small portion of territory in the nation that retained a degree of freedom, would discover that its relationship with God had gone sour. The words in verse 12 are difficult to translate: rather than "moth" and "dry rot" (as in RSV), the translations "festering sore" and "canker" (NEB) may catch better the sense of the Hebrew and indicate the link between this verse and "sickness" and "wound" referred to in verse 13. God, who should have been Ephraim's (viz. Israel's) close friend in covenant, would be an irritant to both nations, a festering sore in the lives of both that reminded them of the deep-seated sickness in their relationship to God. Indeed, the northern state knew well enough that all was not well, but not knowing the cause they had turned to the wrong remedy. They had sent a message to the Assyrian emperor for help (verse 13); the reference may be to such an action taken by King Menahem (745–737 B.C.), or to a similar action taken by King Hoshea, who succeeded Pekah in 732 B.C. But any such action was misguided; no foreign power could heal the sickness which afflicted the spiritual life of the nation of Israel. The only one who could help, ironically, had become the new enemy. God, with the ferocity of a young lion, would pounce on the apostate nations as his prey (verse 14), and there could be no rescue from the divine hunter.

And so God would withdraw from the nations of his chosen people and stay withdrawn until at last a penitent people returned to him and sought new health and life. The words of chapter 6:1–3 are typical of a penitential psalm; if used with honesty and understanding, they would pave the way for a return to the nation's true source of life and faith.

There is little that is cheering in this part of the prophet's proclamation, but its themes are important nevertheless.

(i) The prophet spoke in a time of political crisis and international catastrophe, and the contagion of fear in society was such that neither pious nor apostate could understand the true state of affairs. The "festering sore" that disfigured the nation's life was there for all to see; what few could see was the underlying cause of the sickness. And to such blindness, whether wilful or warranted, Hosea's proclamation comes as a shock—indeed, it cannot be easily accepted. God was in effect the festering sore, but the sore merely revealed on the surface the rot that lay within.

Whether as individuals or as members of a community, most of us would prefer not to know the cause of the sores in our lives. The individuals who precipitate disaster in their personal circumstances would prefer to discern the causes in a hundred external circumstances, than see that the responsibility lies within. The church that has lost the integrity of its faith would prefer to analyze its decline against the backdrop of uncontrollable external forces, rather than see the sickness within. And the same is no less true of a nation: the fault of national decline is always placed on international causes, rather than being acknowledged at home where it belongs. Hosea compels us to reflect. Is our crisis outside ourselves in its origin? Or is the ravaging lion that rends our lives none other than God, whose grace and love have been thus changed by perpetual refusal?

(ii) God may withdraw (verse 15), but it is the people who must return (6:1). The sickness is such that only God can heal the nation's wound; life is so nearly lost, that only God can restore it. The prophet's message is clear enough to the mind, but harder to grasp with the spirit, as the remainder of chapter 6 will make clear. But there is hope in these verses; perhaps after a couple of days the process of revival will begin, and after three days new life will be restored (6:2). The reference to the "third day", with its nuance to Christian ears of the Resurrection, is not messianic in its initial sense; it expresses only the hope that could be born in the heart of the penitent, if he truly turned back to God.

The brief hope of the "third day" had no reality in Hosea's time; nor, from a strictly human perspective, would it have much hope for our time. For we, like Hosea's audience, have a deeply stubborn streak, compounded by a wilful blindness to the nature of our position. Yet in the early Church, a ray of messianic light was seen in these words of the ancient prophet; Paul writes to the Church in Corinth "that he was raised on the third day in accordance with the scriptures" (1 Corinthians 15:4), alluding no doubt to Hosea's words. It is the Resurrection of Jesus Christ which imparts new meaning to the ancient message, transforming its tone of despair to one of hope for all human beings.

LOVE LIKE A MORNING CLOUD

Hosea 6:4–11a

⁴What shall I do with you, O Ephraim?
  What shall I do with you, O Judah?
 Your love is like a morning cloud,
  like the dew that goes early away.
⁵Therefore I have hewn them by the prophets,
  I have slain them by the words of my mouth,
  and my judgment goes forth as the light.
⁶For I desire steadfast love and not sacrifice,
  the knowledge of God, rather than burnt offerings.

⁷But at Adam they transgressed the covenant;
  there they dealt faithlessly with me.
⁸Gilead is a city of evildoers,
  tracked with blood.
⁹As robbers lie in wait for a man,
  so the priests are banded together;
 they murder on the way to Shechem,
  yea, they commit villainy.
¹⁰In the house of Israel I have seen a horrible thing;
  Ephraim's harlotry is there, Israel is defiled.

¹¹For you also, O Judah, a harvest is appointed.

The brief days of summer, during which these paragraphs on Hosea are being written, have permitted a temporary escape from the city. The wilderness of the Arrow Lake, in the heart of British Columbia, provides the setting in which to reflect on Hosea's words. Every morning the unruffled waters of the lake are shrouded with white clouds, hemmed in by the mountains that rise on every side. And the rough grass and pine forests

surrounding the lake glisten with dew in the early light. But by
mid-morning, the scene begins to change: the warmth of the sun
penetrates the morning mist; the new clouds drift up the moun-
tainside, soon to dissipate, and the dew disappears in the rays of
the morning sun. And such is the simile that Hosea employs for
Israel's love. It is real enough for a while, but it is quickly
dispelled in the dawning heat of the day.

Even if Ephraim and Judah should use the words of the penitential psalm that the prophet has quoted (6:1–3), it would be to
little avail. Such words, to be effective, must come from deep
within a nation's soul; they must reflect a love that is strong and
lasting. But the love of this nation, as has been demonstrated so
frequently in the history of Hosea's age, is thin and insubstantial;
it has no substance, no resistance to the changing circumstances.
Despite the persistent and faithful words of God's prophets, his
people steadfastly refused to perceive the true nature of the faith.
They thought that ritual was enough, that the offering of sacrifices was sufficient (verse 6); they could not understand that
steadfast love and knowledge of God were the fundamentals
from which ritual and sacrifice should flow as the outer
expression.

Thus the prophet declares a catalogue of crime (verses 7–10),
the substance of which shows clearly the hypocritical nature of
the continuing activities of formal worship. Three places are
mentioned, in each of which recent crimes had taken place; we
know nothing of the events in question beyond the bare summary
presented here, but the prophet's audience would have known
precisely the events to which he referred. (a) The Covenant had
been broken by a faithless act at Adam (verse 7), a town beside
the River Jordan where the River Jabbok joins the larger stream
some twenty miles north of Jericho. (b) In the town of Gilead,
also in Transjordan, blood had flowed (verse 8); whether the
allusion is to an act of murder, or perhaps to the awful practice of
child sacrifice, remains uncertain. (c) The priests had banded
together to murder some of those who travelled to Shechem
(verse 9). Shechem, one of the most ancient shrines of the
Hebrew tradition, was also one of the places set aside as a "city of

refuge" (Josh. 20:7); the prophet implies that those who sought the security it offered were set upon by violent priests on their journey towards safety.

Thus, in the prophet's summary words, Israel's sin had defiled the nation; Judah was no better, and a "harvest" of judgment was appointed for that nation too. The massive proportions of the nation's sin and its coming calamity might detract us, if we are not careful, from recognizing that great disasters may find their beginnings in what seemed to be small failings.

(i) *The people had failed in love* (verse 4). It was not that love was absent altogether, but just that there was no steadfast love, no strength and continuity in the character of their relationship to God.

Love that is not steadfast, that is fickle in the fluctuation of its affections, can be a terrible thing. And Hosea knew whereof he spoke; he had loved deeply and over a long time, but the one whom he loved knew nothing of love's depths. Love that is like a morning cloud is eventually a mockery of true love, for it promises, but never delivers, it offers hope, but no fulfilment. If we would learn the meaning of love, we would do well to reflect on St. Paul's words: "Love bears all things, believes all things, hopes all things, endures all things. Love never ends" (1 Corinthians 13:7–8).

(ii) *The people had failed in worship* (verse 6). The failure in love led inevitably to a failure in worship and the replacement of the praise of God with the clamour of hypocrisy. True worship arises from true love; it is a response of the whole life to the revealed love of God. But if love is gone, it is better not to worship, for the words and actions in God's temple become only the hollow echoes of empty lives. Hosea opposed worship no more than did the other prophets; he opposed only its perpetuation when the heart of the faith had long since died. For the continuation of empty worship, long past faith's demise, is not only an insult to God, but promulgates among its participants the false conviction that all is well. Like the pills that soothe the pain of headache, shallow worship may promote the delusion that all is well. In reality, it only makes matters worse.

NATIONAL APOSTASY

Hosea 6:11b–7:16

When I would restore the fortunes of my people,
 [1]when I would heal Israel,
the corruption of Ephraim is revealed,
  and the wicked deeds of Samaria;
for they deal falsely,
  the thief breaks in,
  and the bandits raid without.
[2]But they do not consider
  that I remember all their evil works.
 Now their deeds encompass them,
  they are before my face.
[3]By their wickedness they make the king glad,
  and the princes by their treachery.
[4]They are all adulterers;
  they are like a heated oven,
 whose baker ceases to stir the fire,
  from the kneading of the dough until it is leavened.
[5]On the day of our king the princes
  became sick with the heat of wine;
  he stretched out his hand with mockers.
[6]For like an oven their hearts burn with intrigue;
  all night their anger smoulders;
  in the morning it blazes like a flaming fire.
[7]All of them are hot as an oven,
  and they devour their rulers.
 All their kings have fallen;
  and none of them calls upon me.

[8]Ephraim mixes himself with the peoples;
  Ephraim is a cake not turned.
[9]Aliens devour his strength,
  and he knows it not;
 grey hairs are sprinkled upon him,
  and he knows it not.
[10]The pride of Israel witnesses against him;
  yet they do not return to the Lord their God,
  nor seek him, for all this.

¹¹Ephraim is like a dove,
   silly and without sense,
   calling to Egypt, going to Assyria.
¹²As they go, I will spread over them my net;
   I will bring them down like birds of the air;
   I will chastise them for their wicked deeds.
¹³Woe to them, for they have strayed from me!
   Destruction to them, for they have rebelled against me!
 I would redeem them,
   but they speak lies against me.

¹⁴They do not cry to me from the heart,
   but they wail upon their beds;
 for grain and wine they gash themselves,
   they rebel against me.
¹⁵Although I trained and strengthened their arms,
   yet they devise evil against me.
¹⁶They turn to Baal;
   they are like a treacherous bow,
 their princes shall fall by the sword
   because of the insolence of their tongue.
 This shall be their derision in the land of Egypt.

Political commentary, in a modern state, can be devastating to the authorities at the time that it is delivered. It is not without reason that many corrupt nations have sought to silence the press, for the news of their actions and the comment on their political and moral behaviour can seriously undermine corrupt authority. And yet, with the passage of time, the political comment that was so powerful and dangerous in its moment seems to lose its power; when the events that prompted such scathing comment recede into the past and are forgotten, the comment too has its teeth pulled.

Such is the difficulty we face as we continue to read Hosea's words. This part of the text is a mixture of political comment and religious critique; it was rooted originally in matters of state, crises of terrible moment that dominated people's minds at the time. The prophet's audience followed the daily news bulletin with fascination and fear—what would happen next? And when the prophet spoke to the people, common people and government leaders alike, they knew precisely whereof he spoke. They may have loved his words or hated them, but they understood them perfectly. But with the passage of time the events that prompted these prophetic declarations have receded from memory. We can guess what some of the events were from the prophet's words; others have literally been lost from the annals of history, beyond the shadow of their substance that is retained in these verses. And so it is difficult for us now to read the prophet's words and grasp the impact and urgency that they would have had on first delivery. We can discern only the outlines of the occasion and the attendant circumstances.

(i) *The prophet continues to speak as God's messenger.* When Hosea says "I", he refers to God, who is speaking through his words. And the prophet's role as divine messenger makes his critique all the more powerful. The pen is mightier that the sword, spoken words can be more powerful than weapons, but when the speech is said to be divine, it is all the more critical. For if the modern secular political commentator can evoke such wrath from a government, imagine the anger of those who are criticized in the name of God. They are not only criticized, but their ways are condemned by the standards of the official religion of the state; if people started to believe Hosea, the successive governments would be perceived not only as failures, but also as traitors. As we reflect on this, we see once again the extraordinary courage Hosea required for his task. His job was not only difficult, but dangerous.

(ii) *The prophet condemns a nation's apostasy.* The entire passage is full of condemnation, and a principal target for criticism is the royal house, in effect the government in power (see especially verses 3–7). The government has failed in every way. In international affairs, it has fluctuated back and forth, now turning to Egypt for help in crisis, now turning to Assyria (verse 11). Like a silly dove, flying furiously in one direction and then without reason flying furiously back in the other, the nation has no direction. With this and other metaphors, the prophet condems a nation that tries out every policy but the right one. They will not turn back to God, the true Head of State. The critique is political (verse 11), moral (e.g. verse 2), and religious, for the nation continues to embrace the adulterous cult of Baal (verse 16). And we shall only begin to capture the force of Hosea's words as we re-create in our minds the context and society in which they were delivered. The nation was literally on the verge of collapse: it was marred by violence and crime, morally bankrupt, spiritually apostate, and worse still it was in the hands of rulers who were both bungling and corrupt. The prophet speaks out in such a time, for he is compelled to, but one suspects that he held few illusions about the success of his mission.

(iii) *The prophet declares the mercy of God.* Hosea does not explicitly call for repentance or a return, though the message is there if any had ears to hear it. God would have liked to heal Israel, had its corruption not prevented the application of divine healing (6:11*b*–7:1). God wanted to redeem his people, but their only response to him was lies (verse 13). For all the divine provision, the people continued to rebel (14–15).

The scene is like that of a stormy day. The dark clouds have gathered and rain falls on the land, but here and there sun pokes through and illumines the droplets of the rainbow. But eventually the cloud grows so dense that the sun is blocked out and the rainbow fades. So too the clouds of Israel's sin were obliterating all the last rays of God's mercy. A few strands of light remain in these verses, a few reflections of divine mercy, but the light has almost gone. Israel has gone too far; the storm of judgment soon must break.

SOWING THE WIND, REAPING THE WHIRLWIND

Hosea 8:1–14

> [1]Set the trumpet to your lips,
>   for a vulture is over the house of the Lord,
>   because they have broken my covenant,
>   and transgressed my law.

²To me they cry,
  My God, we Israel know thee.
³Israel has spurned the good;
  the enemy shall pursue him.

⁴They made kings, but not through me.
  They set up princes, but without my knowledge.
With their silver and gold they made idols
  for their own destruction.
⁵I have spurned your calf, O Samaria.
  My anger burns against them.
How long will it be
  till they are pure ⁶in Israel?

A workman made it;
  it is not God.
The calf of Samaria
  shall be broken to pieces.

⁷For they sow the wind,
  and they shall reap the whirlwind.
The standing grain has no heads,
  it shall yield no meal;
if it were to yield,
  aliens would devour it.
⁸Israel is swallowed up;
  already they are among the nations
  as a useless vessel.
⁹For they have gone up to Assyria,
  a wild ass wandering alone;
  Ephraim has hired lovers.
¹⁰Though they hire allies among the nations,
  I will soon gather them up.
And they shall cease for a little while
  from anointing king and princes.

¹¹Because Ephraim has multiplied altars for sinning,
  they have become to him altars for sinning.
¹²Were I to write for him my laws by ten thousands,
  they would be regarded as a strange thing.
¹³They love sacrifice;
  they sacrifice flesh and eat it;
  but the Lord has no delight in them.
Now he will remember their iniquity,

and punish their sins;
they shall return to Egypt.
14For Israel has forgotten his Maker,
and built palaces;
and Judah has multiplied fortified cities;
but I will send a fire upon his cities,
and it shall devour his strongholds.

This passage begins with a further announcement of warning (see also 5:8), indicating that the chapter which follows is another summary of an incident in Hosea's ministry. The subject matter is such that this period of ministry should probably be dated very close to that described in the preceding section of the book (5:8–7:16). The newh is about 733 or 732 B.C.; the northern state of Israel is still in crisis, threatened by enemies outside and corruption within. And in this context Hosea, as if he were the captain of the guard, is instructed to "set the trumpet" to his lips, to sound the alarm concerning the danger that is approaching. But the prophet's words in this passage are even darker than in the preceding section; the judgment is closer than ever, and Hosea leaves no doubt in his listeners' minds as to the reason for its advent. In this depressing catalogue of national failure, the words focus on sin after sin and their echo has continued to carry the mournful message to subsequent generations in synagogue and church.

(i) *They were guilty of hypocrisy*. They said to God: "We know thee" (verse 2), but their actions denied their words, and thus they would be judged. Their mendacious words could not deceive God, but the tragedy of lies is that they may deceive the liar. The real horror of the nation's plight is that they really believed they knew God. They could not see that their lives contradicted the proclamation of their creed. And the prophet's message has lost none if its urgency. All who say to God, "We know thee", should ask themselves whether their lives and speech condemn them as liars in this most fundamental of statements that any human being can make.

(ii) *They deliberately sought their own leaders and rejected God's leadership* (verse 4). First this person became king, then that, all depending upon the ebb and flow of international affairs. The people had forgotten that their true king was God and they sought salvation in any human leader who offered promise of better times. It is easier to condemn them than to learn from their failure; in times of terrible crisis, when faith and courage fail all round, a great leader may offer hope. But if the leader is chosen when the truth of God has been abandoned, there will be no guidance toward the path of deliverance.

(iii) *They resorted to idolatry*. By constructing a golden calf, a supposed image of God (verses 4*b*–5), they broke the second commandment. They exchanged faith in the invisible and almighty God for empty obeisance before a visible and powerless lump of metal. Their actions are not so different from their contemporary counterparts. The calf was the product of technology, what humans hands can make. And in this age, more than most ages, we rest our hopes in technology, in the vain hope that human beings can build the salvation of the world. But to paraphrase verse 5, God says, "I have spurned your technology"; there is no salvation there.

(iv) *They sought security in foreign alliances*. They went to Assyria for help, then sought friends and allies in other nation states (verses 8–10). Forgetting they had a Covenant exclusively with God, they made covenants and treaties with other nations, wherever and whenever the terms seemed to offer security. But to a nation on the edge of divine judgment, no other nation and no treaty alliance can offer help. Throughout human history, the great nations and empires have seemed to be the ultimate expression of human power: Assyria, Babylon, Rome, the British Empire, the United States, the Soviet Union. But no imperial power, whether hostile or friendly, can offer the ultimate security and salvation for which human beings long.

In these and other words of criticism, Hosea not only lays bare his nation's sin, but also by the cut and lash of his words strips away any deceitful hope for help apart from God. "For Israel has forgotten his Maker" (verse 14), and when that knowledge is lost, no truth remains. The irony of Israel's position is that it was caught in a circle of its own making. Having forgotten its Maker, the nation sought elsewhere what the Maker had always provided, security and salvation. It pursued what it had lost down a multitude of false trails, each one taking it further from its Maker, each one leading closer to disaster. But the fault lay within. Having turned from God and looked elsewhere, Israel had sown the wind (verse 7); now, the prophet declares, it is caught up in the whirlwind of judgment and it cannot avoid the destruction. It is a frightening insight into the downward career of those who have forgotten their Maker. Just a little deed here, a little turn there, and the wind has been sown. But the wind is the harbinger of the whirlwind, which destroys all that lies in its path.

THE END OF THE COVENANT

Hosea 9:1–9

1Rejoice not, O Israel!
  Exult not like the peoples;
 for you have played the harlot, forsaking your God.
  You have loved a harlot's hire
  upon all threshing floors.
2Threshing floor and winevat shall not feed them,
  and the new wine shall fail them.
3They shall not remain in the land of the Lord;
  but Ephraim shall return to Egypt,
  and they shall eat unclean food in Assyria.

4They shall not pour libations of wine to the Lord;
  and they shall not please him with their sacrifices.
 Their bread shall be like mourners' bread;
  all who eat of it shall be defiled;
 for their bread shall be for their hunger only;
  it shall not come to the house of the Lord.

5What will you do on the day of appointed festival,
  and on the day of the feast of the Lord?
6For behold, they are going to Assyria;
  Egypt shall gather them,
  Memphis shall bury them.
 Nettles shall possess their precious things of silver;
  thorns shall be in their tents.

⁷The days of punishment have come,
 the days of recompense have come;
 Israel shall know it.
The prophet is a fool,
 the man of the spirit is mad,
 because of your great iniquity
 and great hatred.
⁸The prophet is the watchman of Ephraim,
 the people of my God,
yet a fowler's snare is on all his ways,
 and hatred in the house of his God.
⁹They have deeply corrupted themselves
 as in the days of Gibeah:
he will remember their iniquity,
 he will punish their sins.

As fate would have it, I am sitting down to write these pages of commentary on July 1; it is "Canada Day", a day on which a nation celebrates its "birthday" and its heritage of history. On July 4, a similar celebration will be observed in the United States. And in different nations around the world, special festive days are set aside to mark the observance of a nation's birth and its legacy of history. On just such a day, not long after the events described in the preceding chapters, Hosea undertook the portion of his ministry summarized in these verses. It was a festival time, a day of national rejoicing, and perhaps the celebration was even more frantic than usual, as temporarily the international crises appeared to have abated. It was above all a time to be happy.

"Rejoice not, O Israel" (verse 1); thus does Hosea open his new address to the festive crowds. He addresses the people gathered at the "threshing floors", open areas employed both for threshing wheat and for celebrations at harvest time. And his message to them is a bleak one: they are celebrating the land and its produce, but Hosea proclaims that "they shall not remain in the land of the Lord" (verse 3). Indirectly, he is announcing the end of the nation's Covenant with God. Israel had come out of Egypt in the past; from Egyptian slavery, they had been brought into a land of harvest and freedom. But now, the prophet declares, "Ephraim shall return to Egypt"; those who so joyfully ate the festival bread of harvest soon would eat the bread of captivity in Assyria (verse 3). The national Covenant, celebrated in the festivities that Hosea interrupted, soon would end, and the end of covenant would also be the end of freedom. In the coming captivity, the people would no longer be able to celebrate harvest home or a nation's birthday (verse 4); there would be no harvest and there would be no nation. In different directions, the people who celebrated freedom would be dispersed once again into captivity, some going to Assyria, others to Egypt. And their captivity would not be temporary, but it would be in the place where eventually they would die: "Memphis shall bury them" (verse 6). It is perhaps ironical that what has survived almost intact from the ancient city of Memphis in Egypt are its burial places. Memphis is a place of ancient and splendid pyramids, and its graveyards are of phenomenal proportions. In 1850 a young Frenchman, Auguste Mariette, arrived in Egypt with money from the Louvre with which to purchase Coptic manuscripts. Instead, he spent the money in Memphis, excavating the Serapeum, an extraordinary underground cemetery of the sacred Apis bulls. It was in Memphis, the city of cemeteries, that many of Israel's festival-goers would end their days. For although it was the festival days that were foremost in the people's mind, the prophet solemnly declares that "the days of punishment have come" (verse 7a).

Hosea's disruption of the festal occasion could not pass unnoticed; they would have shouted him down and called him a fool. The prophet accepts the criticism and abuse, incorporating it into his address. "The prophet is a fool, the man of the spirit is mad" (verse 7b), he says; but the criticism is turned into condemnation, for only a nation that has turned from its God would reject the words of his messenger as folly. Only those who have abandoned their faith would fail to heed the words of their watchman. As in Gibeah, centuries before, a Levite had been violently and shamefully abused (verse 9; see also Judg. 19–21), so too Israel had abused the prophets. And thus the divine word is final, carrying no suggestion of a call to repentance: "he will remember their iniquity, he will punish their sins" (verse 9). The words, like those of an epitaph, convert the festival occasion into a mockery; it becomes like a funeral in which those present unwittingly celebrate their own impending deaths.

If one were to choose a day in the Church's calendar on which to reflect upon these words of Hosea, it would be Whitsunday, or Pentecost, the festival on which the Church celebrates its birthday. It is appropriately a day of rejoicing, a commemoration of God's gift of the Holy Spirit, of the birth and history of the Church. But it is also a day on which to recall the substance of Hosea's ancient speech: "Rejoice not!" There are no grounds for rejoicing if the ancient faith has been abandoned. There are no grounds for celebration if the freedom of the gospel has been exchanged for a new slavery to sin and to self. Like all birthdays, the celebration should be accompanied by moments of reflection, by examining the present in the light of the past, by asking ourselves if the faith of the early Church continues to be our own faith and that of our Church. Only then may we convert Hosea's opening speech to a single word: "Rejoice!"

LOVE'S LAMENT

Hosea 9:10–17

10Like grapes in the wilderness,
  I found Israel.
Like the first fruit on the fig tree,
  in its first season,
  I saw your fathers.
But they came to Baal-peor,
  and consecrated themselves to Baal,
  and became detestable like the thing they loved.

11Ephraim's glory shall fly away like a bird—
  no birth, no pregnancy, no conception!
12Even if they bring up children,
  I will bereave them till none is left.
  Woe to them

when I depart from them!
[13]Ephraim's sons, as I have seen, are destined for a prey;
    Ephraim must lead forth his sons to slaughter.
[14]Give them, O Lord—
    what wilt thou give?
Give them a miscarrying womb
and dry breasts.
[15]Every evil of theirs is in Gilgal;
    there I began to hate them.
Because of the wickedness of their deeds
    I will drive them out of my house.
I will love them no more;
    all their princes are rebels.
[16]Ephraim is stricken,
    their root is dried up,
    they shall bear no fruit.
Even though they bring forth,
    I will slay their beloved children.
[17]My God will cast them off,
    because they have not hearkened to him;
    they shall be wanderers among the nations.

The tone of these verses has changed dramatically from that of the preceding passage. There is no longer the strident note of conflict, nor the proclamation of judgment against the noisy bustle of the festal activities. Indeed, it is possible that the public reaction to Hosea's speech on the festival day was so great that he was forced to retreat for a while and to refrain from public ministry. In these verses, we detect a more reflective note, a personal encounter between the prophet and his God, perhaps with only a few close friends present. But the theme of Hosea's ministry on the festival day continues; he had declared, in effect, that the end of Israel's nationhood was near. It was one thing to declare such finality in public ministry, but now Hosea begins to reflect more deeply on the significance of what he has said. Could the end really be coming? What about God's election of his chosen people and all his promises for the future? What about the love that was supposed never to die? Did not the prophetic word he had delivered in the present somehow contradict the funda-

mentals of the ancient faith? Gripped with such uncertainties and
worries, Hosea enters a dialogue. First, the Lord speaks (verses
10–13), and then Hosea responds (verse 14). The Lord speaks
again (verses 15–16), and Hosea adds his closing word (verse 17).

(i) In God's first address to his prophet in this personal encounter, the passage of love is traced from its fresh beginning to
its later transformation into hatred.

In the beginning God had loved Israel; there had been fresh-
ness and joy in the relationship at the start of the wilderness days.
But from early on, Israel had demonstrated its propensity to
wander and the shallowness of its love. Even before the Israelites
had entered the promised land, they had been seduced by the
sensuous cult of Baal at the place called Baal-peor in Transjordan
(see Num. 25:1–5). From that sad sin in the past down to Hosea's
time, the chosen people had persisted in their perverse and loveless ways. At last they had gone too far; devoted to detestable
things, the nation had become itself detestable in the eyes of God.
The nation's glory had flown away like a bird (verse 11); the
children, in whom the future might have been found, would be no
more (verses 13–14). They were indeed the chosen people, but
they had been chosen for the privilege of a relationship with God;
having perpetually rejected that relationship, the people had
themselves transformed their election, becoming thereby a
nation chosen for judgment.

The prophet responds with a prayer (verse 14). He begins as if
he is going to pray that the people be given one last chance, but he
cannot complete what he started to say. For even as he speaks, he
remembers his own experience of love. He had loved deeply, but
time and time again Gomer has spurned that love, going off on
her own adulterous way. There had been a hundred last chances,
but none had done any good; finally the line had to be drawn.
And so Hosea changes his prayer: he concurs with the divine
words and asks that they be fulfilled.

There is a terrible pathos to this passage. Hosea is able to enter
into the agony and grief of God's love precisely because he has
experienced the same agony throughout his own life of love. And
those who spek critically of the Old Testament, deploring its

emphasis on judgment, would do well to reflect on these verses. Judgment is rooted in love; it is not desired by the lover, but pursued and invited by the loveless. To play with love, to treat it lightly, to trample on the affections of another, as Gomer had done with Hosea, is to make mockery of life's meaning and values. Likewise, the persistent abuse of God's love releases eventually the landslide of self-induced judgment.

(ii) After Hosea's response, God addresses the prophet a second time (verses 15–16). Again, the words begin with an historical reflection, this time associated with Gilgal. "There," God says, "I began to hate them." It was at Gilgal that Saul had become Israel's first king (I Samuel 11:15) and it was at Gilgal that the long history of the failure of Israel's kings had begun (I Samuel 15:10–11). And so the terrible judgment is declared again, "I will love them no more" (verse 15), for nothing had really changed from Saul's time to that of Hosea.

"I will love them no more": it is a horrifying word to reflect upon in the light of all human history, of which Israel's history is in so many ways simply a paradigm. Century after century has been marred by violence; nation after nation has re-created within itself the ills that plagued ancient Israel. And it seems, from the historical vantage point of the twentieth century, that in the important matters we humans never learn. In science, medicine, technology and the like, civilization surges forward; but in matters of violence, evil and social sickness, each generation repeats only the muddy achievements of the past. If justice were the criterion by which human history were to be judged, the prophet's ancient declaration on behalf of God would still ring true: "I will love them no more". But Hosea's message is not yet complete, nor is that of the Bible as a whole. A further word of love is still to come, bringing with it hope where none is deserved.

OF KING AND CALF

Hosea 10:1–8

[1]Israel is a luxuriant vine that yields its fruit.
The more his fruit increased

the more altars he built;
as his country improved
  he improved his pillars.
[2]Their heart is false;
  now they must bear their guilt.
The Lord will break down their altars,
  and destroy their pillars.

[3]For now they will say:
  "We have no king,
for we fear not the Lord,
  and a king, what could he do for us?"
[4]They utter mere words;
  with empty oaths they make covenants;
so judgment springs up like poisonous weeds
  in the furrows of the field.
[5]The inhabitants of Samaria tremble
  for the calf of Beth-aven.
Its people shall mourn for it,
  and its idolatrous priests shall wail over it,
  over its glory which has departed from it.
[6]Yea, the thing itself shall be carried to Assyria,
  as tribute to the great king.
Ephraim shall be put to shame,
  and Israel shall be ashamed of his idol.

[7]Samaria's king shall perish,
  like a chip on the face of the waters.
[8]The high places of Aven, the sin of Israel,
  shall be destroyed.
Thorn and thistle shall grow up
  on their altars;
and they shall say to the mountains, Cover us,
  and to the hills, Fall upon us.

The reflective note of the preceding passage is maintained in these verses; the opposition to the prophet was persisting, limiting his public ministry, and in the small circle of his friends and allies Hosea reflected on the state of the nation and its career toward destruction. The chronological perspective seems to be a little later now than the crises of 733 B.C. reflected in the preceding chapters, but the calmer times are but a lull before the final storm, as Hosea perceives more clearly than do his contemporaries. These words appear to be Hosea's words, addressed directly to his intimate friends, for God is referred to in the third person (verse 2). And Israel is also talked of indirectly; the nation is being discussed, not addressed, as Hosea traces its path of folly and anticipates its final destruction. This interlude in the prophet's public ministry ranges from a reflection on Israel's beginning to an expectation of its coming end.

(i) *The prophet's words begin with a reflection on the past.* Employing the metaphor of the vine, Hosea recalled how Israel had grown and flourished, bearing a rich harvest of fruit. The metaphor of the vine, in the Hebrew tradition, was normally a positive one; Israel had long been thought of as a vine, planted in the promised land, there to grow and be fruitful (see Ps. 80:8–11). But Hosea transforms the metaphor into one of negative intent: at each stage in its growth, the nation had shrivelled in spirit. Prosperity brought with it only spiritual decline; every moment of growth was accompanied by an increase in the number of altars and pillars that were the furnishings of Baal's alien cult.

Withdrawn briefly from the busy round of public ministry, Hosea begins to understand more clearly than before the true nature of his nation's sickness. What he was observing was not a new phenomenon on the stage of human history; the roots of the decline all around him stretched far back into the early days of his people's history. The general public could still deceive themselves into believing that their history of fruitfulness was a sign of their integrity, but Hosea knew that it was not so. "Their heart is false" (verse 2); past success was a reflection of God's mercy, not of Israel's integrity, but at last the time was coming when the truth would appear. Because their heart was in the wrong place, the people would soon see the destruction of the altars and pillars that expressed publicly the misplaced affections of their hearts.

Hosea's words illustrate the growth and depth of his under-standing. And like the prophet, we need to stand back from time to time to think upon what is happening and to discern the truth from the happy delusion. We will never be able to address the ills of our time unless we see them clearly, with their roots penetrating the past as if to persuade us that antiquity made all things well. The prophet does not particularly like what he sees, but it is better to proclaim the truth than embrace the deceitful delusion.

(ii) *Neither king nor calf offers hope for Israel.* That is to say, neither the human leadership of the nation's king, nor the false comfort of the cult's idolatrous calf, could save the nation in its current crisis. The prophet anticipates the nation's mood in verse 3; the people would come eventually to a recognition of the inability of any human king to save the nation in its time of crisis. But the words, though true, would still be empty words, for though the people would see the incompetence of a king to save, they still would not perceive where their true salvation lay. Perhaps there is an irony in the comment on the calf (verses 5–6). Israel's golden calf, the idolatrous object of worship at the shrine in Beth-aven, would create a national expression of grief when it was despatched to Assyria in partial payment of tribute. They had learned that a king could not help, but they still pinned great hopes on the golden calf!

Hosea, as he reflects on his nation, perceives the obdurate blindness that has characterized it so long. From time to time, in a moment of light, the people have insight and see the folly of the object of their trust. But instead of moving from insight to truth, they merely seek a new object of folly. The message is clear to Hosea: in a time of such fundamental crisis, neither human leader nor misplaced religious faith could bring deliverance. Only a return to God would be effective, but there was no evidence that the capacity to return had survived.

(iii) *The end would inevitably come.* The king, like a fragment of flotsam, would be washed away in the flood waters of judg-ment. The old sanctuaries would be destroyed, thorns and thistles replacing their alien altars. And the nation's shame would be so gross and humiliating that its citizens would invite the mountains and hills to fall on them.

The picture of the falling mountains is striking and dramatic. In southwestern Alberta there is a valley leading west from the prairies into the Rocky Mountains. At the beginning of the twentieth century, there was a small town nestled in the valley; its name was Frank. But in the early morning hours of April 29, 1903, half a mountain broke loose from its moorings. A great wedge of limestone, 2,100 feet high, 3,000 feet wide and 500 feet thick, fell on a part of the town of Frank. Some 90 million tons of rock fell into the valley, instantly killing more than 70 people in less than one hundred seconds. The town is still under rock, the modern highway winding through the rock-field beneath which the human dwellings still remain crushed and buried. It is an ominous valley, reminiscent of death and human vulnerability in the face of nature's force. Hosea envisages a similar scene though with one dramatic difference: the people's recognition of sin, when it finally dawned, would evoke such a sense of shame that they would invite the mountains to fall on them. When one looks at a fallen mountain, it is hard to conceive the depth of shame that would propel a people into seeking such a fate. Yet the prophet's insight is also a telling warning of the shame to which a nation may sink in its flight from God.

THE TUMULT OF WAR

Hosea 10:9–15

⁹From the days of Gibe-ah, you have sinned, O Israel;
 there they have continued.
 Shall not war overtake them in Gibe-ah?
¹⁰I will come against the wayward people to chastise them;
 and nations shall be gathered against them
 when they are chastised for their double iniquity.

¹¹Ephraim was a trained heifer
 that loved to thresh,
 and I spared her fair neck;
 but I will put Ephraim to the yoke,
 Judah must plough,

Jacob must harrow for himself.
¹²Sow for yourselves righteousness,
　　reap the fruit of steadfast love;
　　break up your fallow ground,
　for it is the time to seek the Lord,
　　that he may come and rain salvation upon you.

¹³You have ploughed iniquity,
　　you have reaped injustice,
　　you have eaten the fruit of lies.
　Because you have trusted in your chariots
　　and in the multitude of your warriors,
¹⁴therefore the tumult of war shall arise among your people,
　　and all your fortresses shall be destroyed,
　as Shalman destroyed Beth-arbel on the day of battle;
　　mothers were dashed in pieces with their children.
¹⁵Thus it shall be done to you, O house of Israel,
　　because of your great wickedness,
　In the storm the king of Israel
　　shall be utterly cut off.

After the temporary withdrawal from public ministry reflected in 9:10–10:8, Hosea entered once again the public domain and resumed his prophetic preaching. We do not know for how long the disruption of his ministry lasted, though it was probably only for a short period of time. The scene presupposed in these verses is one of a temporary respite in the international crises of the time: Israel, appearing to recover from its earlier weakness, was building up once again its military strength. And to this nation, recovering both its self-confidence and its military capacity, Hosea addresses once again the word of the Lord. As in the earlier portions of the prophet's book, we are provided here with only a synopsis of his ministry, outlining the new thrust of Hosea's activity.

The summary account of prophetic ministry falls into three sections.

(a) Israel, from ancient times down to the present, had sinned; as a consequence, war would come (verses 9–10). Gibeah has already been a theme in Hosea's preaching (see 9:9); the violence associated with Gibeah in past history had continued in Israel down to the present time, and thus, for this "double iniquity" (verse 10), war must inevitably come as a form of divine chastisement.

(b) The middle section of the passage, verses 11–12, is a small vignette, depicting life as it might have been in the united nation of the chosen people. The metaphorical language is agricultural, though some of the nuances of the imagery are difficult to grasp with precision. The chosen people were like a heifer, but not like the sleek beasts of the dairy or beef herds, simply grazing in the fields or fattening. Rather, they were like a trained beast, useful for threshing and pulling the plough. As a "trained heifer", the chosen people should have broken up the fallow ground and sowed a righteous crop, only then turning to the Lord for those vital rains that would bring the seed to the fulness of harvest.

(c) The reality of Israel's history was altogether different from what it might have been (verses 13–15). They had ploughed indeed, but having sown the seed of iniquity, they reaped a harvest of injustice and lies. The prophet returns again to the theme of war: Israel, having put so much trust in its military might, must inevitably experience the "tumult of war" (verse 14), but it would be a war that led to the nation's destruction. The reference to Shalman's destruction of Beth-arbel (in the northern Transjordan) is elusive; though we cannot now pin down precisely who Shalman was or what he did, the prophet here makes use of a contemporary item of news, well known to his audience, to drive home his point. Just as Beth-arbel has been destroyed in a recent battle, so too would Israel be destroyed.

This portion of the prophet's ministry, though containing similar themes to his earlier preaching, reveals the growth and depth in his understanding with respect to certain issues of the time. Two issues are presented here with remarkable clarity.

(i) *Election.* This was, no doubt, one of the themes of Hosea's reflection during the brief withdrawal from public ministry. Perhaps earlier in his life he had understood election, namely the *chosenness* of Israel, simply in terms of privilege and special status. Israel was God's chosen people. But he had come to understand that election had a purpose, a goal, and that if that goal were not fulfilled, then the election ceased to have any true meaning. In the prophet's metaphorical language, election should have produced a working heifer, not a grazing cow. More precisely, the purpose of Israel's election was to produce a harvest of "righteousness" and "steadfast love" (verse 12); this harvest, in turn, should have been a bounty through which all the nations of the world were blessed (see Exod. 19:5–6). If such had been Israel's history, God's purpose would have been fulfilled, but as Hosea sees all too clearly, Israel had produced a very different kind of harvest (verse 13).

The Church, according to the New Testament perspective (1 Pet. 2:9), is also a body of God's chosen people. And the principles enunciated so clearly by the prophet in ancient times apply equally to the Church. To be the elect is to be chosen for a purpose, as St Peter put it, "that you may declare the wonderful deeds of him who called you out of darkness into his marvellous light." But if the purpose is lost, the point of election concurrently disappears. And Hosea's words to Israel, phrased as they are in the gloomy context of a nation that has forgotten its vocation, are now a solemn injunction to the Church and its membership to examine whether election's purpose remains central to the Church's existence.

(ii) *War.* At precisely the time when his compatriots began to think that war was a more distant reality, Hosea came to perceive its inevitability. The nation as a whole perceived that the immediate military threat had subsided, giving them in turn the opportunity of strengthening their armed forces (verse 13*b*). New military power seemed to make the risk even more distant.

But in Israel the mentality of the Maginot Line prevailed. The great wall in France, constructed in the 1930s at the instigation of war minister André Maginot, extended from the Swiss border in the south to the Belgian border in the north of France. The principal effect of this enormous military line of defence was to create a false sense of security; it had little or no effect on the German flanking manoeuvres in their French campaign of 1940. France quickly fell, though the Maginot Line continued to stand as a symbol of false confidence. So too the tumult of war would soon engulf Israel, making mockery of its new-found confidence in chariots and regiments of infantry.

In all our conflicts, we must beware of the Maginot Line mentaility. Paul urged Timothy to "wage the good warfare" (1 Tim. 1:18), but all who would wage it will do so in vain if their confidence is misplaced. It is the Lord alone who is "mighty in battle" (Psalm 24:8).

THE BANDS OF LOVE

Hosea 11:1–11

¹When Israel was a child, I loved him,
    and out of Egypt I called my son.
²The more I called them,
    the more they went from me;
  they kept sacrificing to the Baals,
    and burning incense to idols.

³Yet it was I who taught Ephraim to walk,
    I took them up in my arms;
    but they did not know that I healed them.
⁴I led them with cords of compassion,
    with the bands of love,
  and I became to them as one
    who eases the yoke on their jaws,
    and I bent down to them and fed them.

⁵They shall return to the land of Egypt,
    and Assyria shall be their king,
    because they have refused to return to me.
⁶The sword shall rage against their cities,
    consume the bars of their gates,
    and devour them in their fortresses.
⁷My people are bent on turning away from me;
    so they are appointed to the yoke,
    and none shall remove it.

⁸How can I give you up, O Ephraim!

How can I hand you over, O Israel!
How can I make you like Admah!
    How can I treat you like Zeboiim!
My heart recoils within me,
    my compassion grows warm and tender.
⁹I will not execute my fierce anger,
    I will not again destroy Ephraim;
for I am God and not man,
    the Holy One in your midst,
    and I will not come to destroy.

¹⁰They shall go after the Lord,
    he will roar like a lion;
yea, he will roar,
    and his sons shall come trembling from the west;
¹¹they shall come trembling like birds from Egypt,
    and like doves from the land of Assyria;
    and I will return them to their homes, says the Lord.

The language of love dominates once again this portion of
Hosea's book. But here it is not the imagery of marital love that is
employed, as in chapters 1–3, but rather that of parental love. As
a parent loved a child, so too God loved Israel intimately, from
the moment of birth and on through the years of later life. And
yet, from the very beginning, this narrative of love is expressed in
a context with various discordant notes. First, the language and
form of the passage imply a quasi-legal setting. Just as, under
Hebrew law, a parent was required to bring a totally delinquent
child to court (Deut. 21:18–21), so too the Lord is bringing to
court Israel, the beloved but delinquent child. Second, though
the divine speech is consistently expressed in the glowing terms of
love, Israel is depicted as perpetually spurning love.

The occasion and setting in which the prophet delivered these
words are difficult to determine precisely. The divine speech,
spoken through Hosea, does not appear to address Israel
directly, nor are there indications of hostile response. And so it is
possible that these words were spoken in the smaller setting of the
prophet in the intimacy of his circle of friends and companions.
And time seems to have moved forward somewhat from the

chronological perspective of the preceding verses. The confidence in military might has disappeared; the coming domination of Assyria seems assured (verse 5*b*). The date is probably around 725 B.C., by which time Shalmaneser V was emperor of Assyria; with the benefit of hindsight, we perceive that these words were delivered just a few short years before the final demise of the northern state of Israel.

The speech begins with a history of divine love and the response to it, from the beginning of Israel's existence down to the time in which Hosea lived (verses 1–7). God had loved Israel from the beginning, yet it seemed that the more he called to Israel in love, the more persistently Israel turned to false faith and vain love. Yet God still loved, leading his people "with cords of compassion, with the bands of love" (verse 4). The language that follows (verse 4*b*) is difficult to translate from the Hebrew; in the RSV the word "yoke" suggests an agricultural metaphor, but it does not seem to fit the context. The verse can be translated: "I was to them as those who lift a small child to their cheek, and I bent down to him, to feed him" (H. W. Wolff); this rendition seems to capture better the sentiment of the passage as a whole. But Israel's persistent refusal of the divine love would inevitably culminate in disaster; the nation would be defeated in war and its citizens would be driven from their homes to foreign countries (verses 5–7).

The judgment, though precipitated by Israel's own actions, sets off a turmoil in the heart of God. How can he simply give up his chosen people? Admah and Zeboiim (verse 8) were cities of sin that God had destroyed in anger (see Deut. 29:23), but could he act in the same way toward Israel? Love overcomes wrath; the story of God's love for Israel would not end, but its final resolution lay beyond the more immediate prospect of judgment. This moving narrative of God's compassion for his people is illuminated by several insights into the nature of divine love.

(i) "God is love" (1 John 4:8); the expression is one of the best known statements in the Bible and it is clearly illuminated in Hosea's narrative. The entire story of Israel, the central theme of the Old Testament, is a love story, but it is not a happy story. God had loved Israel, did love Israel, and would continue to love into the years of the future. But this undying love is never returned by the chosen people, so that the history of divine love becomes a history of tragedy. Only one who has loved deeply can know the grief of love perpetually spurned. And thus we see that the Old Testament's love story, while bearing hope for human beings, is also a story of suffering.

When we say "God is love", we must not say it too glibly, for that fundamental statement carries with it a necessary counterpart: "God is suffering". The love and the suffering are inextricably interrelated: God suffers because he loves and because those whom he loves do not return love. And eventually, in the New Testament, we perceive the suffering of God reach a new climax in the death of Jesus Christ, where the suffering and love of God concurrently mark the countenance of Jesus.

(ii) God's love leads inevitably to internal conflict. "How can I give you up?" he says, yet both justice and common sense would dictate that God abandon Israel. Indeed the law of covenant clearly implies that God was legally bound to abandon Israel. But in the conflict raging within the heart of God, love conquers law. God cannot abandon his people. He can permit the judgment, which is both precipitated by Israel's actions and at the same time a severe revelation of divine mercy, but he cannot stop loving. Thus we perceive that the old saying, "God is love", designates the very essence of the divine being. If God were to cease loving, he would cease to be God; love is his very nature.

(iii) And so the love that suffers and finds its own inner conflict finds eventually a solution. "I will not execute my fierce anger" (verse 9). And love's new goal is positive as well as negative: "I will return them to their homes" (verse 11). The words of hope are addressed to Israel, yet such is their substance that no human being can read them without sharing their deeper hope. If God is so fundamentally a loving deity, cannot all human flesh hope in God? If God continued to love perverse Israel, may he not also love perverse gentiles? Such is the insight of Hosea that extends beyond his own time and place to address every century of human existence.

LIES AND THE REJECTION OF TRUTH

Hosea 11:12–12:14

[12]Ephraim has encompassed me with lies,
 and the house of Israel with deceit;
but Judah is still known by God,
 and is faithful to the Holy One.

[1]Ephraim herds the wind,
 and pursues the east wind all day long;
they multiply falsehood and violence;
 they make a bargain with Assyria,
 and oil is carried to Egypt.

[2]The Lord has an indictment against Judah,
 and will punish Jacob according to his ways,
 and requite him according to his deeds.
[3]In the womb he took his brother by the heel,
 and in his manhood he strove with God.
[4]He strove with the angel and prevailed,
 he wept and sought his favour.
He met God at Bethel,
 and there God spoke with him—
[5]the Lord the God of hosts,
 the Lord is his name:
[6]"So you, by the help of your God, return,
 hold fast to love and justice,
 and wait continually for your God."

[7]A trader, in whose hands are false balances,
 he loves to oppress.
[8]Ephraim has said, "Ah, but I am rich,
 I have gained wealth for myself";
but all his riches can never offset
 the guilt he has incurred.
[9]I am the Lord your God
 from the land of Egypt;
I will again make you dwell in tents,
 as in the days of the appointed feast.
[10]I spoke to the prophets;
 it was I who multiplied visions,

and through the prophets gave parables.
¹¹If there is iniquity in Gilead
    they shall surely come to naught;
 if in Gilgal they sacrifice bulls,
    their altars also shall be like stone heaps
    on the furrows of the field.
¹²(Jacob fled to the land of Aram,
    there Israel did service for a wife,
    and for a wife he herded sheep.)
¹³By a prophet the Lord brought Israel up from Egypt,
    and by a prophet he was preserved.
¹⁴Ephraim has given bitter provocation;
    so his Lord will leave his blood-guilt upon him,
    and will turn back upon him his reproaches.

With the perspective provided by our knowledge of history, we can perceive that, as Hosea's ministry progressed, the nation of Israel came closer and closer to its final end. The ministry which is summarized in these verses took place about 726 B.C.; Shalmaneser V was the new Assyrian emperor, and (as we now know) there were to be only four more years until Israel's final collapse. Hosea, though he did not know precisely the time of the end, was still grasped by the urgency of his task. But the nation of Israel, lulled into a false sense of security by a sudden growth in wealth (verse 8), was still blithely unaware of the critical nature of the time through which it lived.

The theme of this passage is established in the first verse (11:12): it is *lies* and *deceit*. The passage as a whole is difficult to interpret, in part because of the condensed style in which the prophet's ministry has been recorded. But the theme with which the section begins is developed in various ways to bring out the contrast between deceitfulness and truth.

(i) *The false word*. Israel's speech has been a perpetual string of *lies* and *deceitfulness* (11:12); their false speech, compounded with violence (12:1), had carried them away from God into fitful alliances with Assyria and Egypt. The prophet develops his message by means of a series of allusions to the patriarch Jacob (verses 3, 4, 12), but instead of drawing out the splendours of the past,

Hosea elaborates only the deceitfulness of Jacob, whose very name means *deception*. From the moment of birth until the years of manhood, Jacob had practised deceit; so too had Israel, throughout its history and up to the present moment.

The court physician to the English Queen Anne, John Arbuthnot (1667–1735), had a marvellous gift for words in ridiculing the false tempers of his times. In a book entitled *The Art of Political Lying* (1712), he "warns the heads of parties against believing their own lies." Arbuthnot would have found companionship with Hosea, for both perceived the insidious nature of lies; the lies told first to deceive others soon came to be believed by the tellers. The nation of Israel, confronted with Hosea's word, said, "Ah, but I am rich!" (verse 8); the tragedy is that the nation had come to believe its own falsehood and thus blinded itself to its true condition. As with so many sins and crimes, they may rebound on the head of the perpetrator. At a time in Israel's history when the truth was desperately important, indeed survival depended upon it, the truth could not be seen because of the cataracts of mendacity covering the nation's eyes.

(ii) *The true word*. All the while that Israel pursued its own lies, God sent messengers with words of truth. He spoke truth to them through the prophets (verse 10), and by the prophetic word had led forth his people from Egyptian bondage to promised freedom (verse 13). And indeed, even in these last days of the nation's history, the divine word of truth was still being declared by Hosea. But, if the first person narrative of 11:12 should properly be interpreted as the prophet's own words, the prophetic word of truth was "encompassed with lies".

Israel was caught in the battle of words. God spoke to his people words of truth, but the nation spoke only lies. The word of truth was eventually snared by the network of lies. Those who practised only deceit could no longer discern the truth, and so inevitably they pursued the path that led to their own destruction. Jesus said, later on in time, "you will know the truth, and the truth will make you free" (John 8:32). But there can be no freedom for those who refuse to know the truth, and there is no surer way of failing to know the truth than living a life devoted to lies.

(iii) *The final word*. The pursuit of lies and the rejection of truth finally elicited from God a word of judgment (verse 14). It is a harsh word, condemning Israel (Ephraim) to the future it has prepared for itself in the rejection of truth. And it is an ominous word, when viewed in the context of our knowledge of Israel's subsequent history; in only a few years' time, the prophetic word would be experienced by Israel as a painful reality.

But the final word of judgment must not be detached from its context. Such a word is only stated at the end of a long history of the proclamation of God's word of truth. And such a word is finally precipitated by a nation's devoted embrace of a life of lying. The final word of judgment is a word spoken in grief. Though beyond the coming disaster words of grace would be heard once again, the judgmental word would soon be experienced in Israel in all its terrible reality.

THE SENTENCE OF DEATH

Hosea 13:1–16

[1]When Ephraim spoke, men trembled;
      he was exalted in Israel;
      but he incurred guilt through Baal and died.
[2]And now they sin more and more,
      and make for themselves molten images,
   idols skilfully made of their silver,
      all of them the work of craftsmen.
   Sacrifice to these, they say.
      Men kiss calves!
[3]Therefore they shall be like the morning mist
      or like the dew that goes early away,
   like the chaff that swirls from the threshing floor
      or like smoke from a window.

[4]I am the Lord your God
      from the land of Egypt;
   you know no God but me,
      and besides me there is no saviour.
[5]It was I who knew you in the wilderness,

in the land of drought;
6but when they had fed to the full,
they were filled, and their heart was lifted up;
therefore they forgot me.
7So I will be to them like a lion,
like a leopard I will lurk beside the way.
8I will fall upon them like a bear robbed of her cubs,
I will tear open their breast,
and there I will devour them like a lion,
as a wild beast would rend them.

9I will destroy you, O Israel;
who can help you?
10Where now is your king, to save you;
where are all your princes, to defend you—
those of whom you said,
"Give me a king and princes"?
11I have given you kings in my anger,
and I have taken them away in my wrath.

12The iniquity of Ephraim is bound up,
his sin is kept in store.
13The pangs of childbirth come for him,
but he is an unwise son;
for now he does not present himself
at the mouth of the womb.

14Shall I ransom them from the power of Sheol?
Shall I redeem them from Death?
O Death, where are your plagues?
O Sheol, where is your destruction?
Compassion is hid from my eyes.

15Though he may flourish as the reed plant,
the east wind, the wind of the Lord, shall come,
rising from the wilderness;
and his fountain shall dry up,
his spring shall be parched;
it shall strip his treasury
of every precious thing.
16Samaria shall bear her guilt,
because she has rebelled against her God;
they shall fall by the sword,

their little ones shall be dashed in pieces,
and their pregnant women ripped open.

Hosea's active ministry is now drawing toward a close, for the things of which he has spoken are rapidly coming to pass. Called to be a prophet to the northern kingdom, Hosea will soon no longer have a nation to whom he can prophesy. But here we have a summary account of one final stage in his ministry. The date is about 724 or 723 B.C.; the end has almost come. And in the dark days that precede the end, Hosea has little that is cheerful to say. He still desperately wants his people to understand, though, and to shed their delusions and see where they stand.

Ten years earlier, when Tiglath-Pileser was the Assyrian emperor, there had been a momentous crisis, but somehow the nation had survived the events of 733 B.C. And yet in the aftermath of the crisis, they had learned nothing; they had not understood the prophet's word, nor had they perceived the renewed licence of divine mercy. They had simply sinned "more and more" (verse 2), renewing devotedly the images and idols of the cult that contributed to calamity. "Men kiss calves!" (verse 2): Hosea cannot contain his scathing words, powerfully denouncing the misplaced affection of a nation that has forgotten its first love.

Not only had Israel returned to its old idolatrous ways, but in doing so it had forgotten and abandoned the God who had provided so fully in the past (verses 4–6). Such wilful forgetfulness on the nation's part transformed God: the One who had been companion and guardian through the trials of wilderness would become like a dangerous lion, a lurking leopard, a mother bear robbed of her cubs (verses 7–8). And so the prophet comes to declare a terrible statement from God: "I will destroy you, O Israel" (verse 9). All the false sources of confidence, the kings and princes who had promised so much (verses 10–11), would be powerless in the day of God's wrath. For the east wind was blowing (verse 15), a symbol of the approaching armies of Assyria, and it would scorch the frail reed that was Israel. When God had decided that he could no longer exercise compassion (verse 14), there could be no prospect of pity for the chosen people.

Running through this final episode of public ministry prior to Samaria's collapse are two of the most central themes in Hosea's preaching.

(i) International affairs are under God's ultimate sovereignty. Whereas the majority of people in Hosea's time did not see the link between world events and their nation's faith, Hosea saw it clearly. For the populace as a whole, hopes rose and fell as a direct consequence of good or bad news from the international front. They thought that their fate would somehow be determined beyond their borders; they did not see that it rested within the nation and in their relationship with God.

Political theology of Hosea's kind is no more easy to grasp in our day than in the prophet's time. On the one hand, there are those who say that international affairs have no relation at all to theology; mankind makes its own history. On the other hand, there are those who would attempt to unravel the mysteries of contemporary history by reference to the supposed meaning of Old Testament prophets or New Testament apocalyptic writings. But Hosea stands at neither extreme. God is sovereign in human affairs, yet the course of history is determined largely by human actions. From this tension of faith, Hosea perceived not only that Israel's fate would come about at the hands of God, but also that the nation had created, by its actions, its own ill-fortune.

(ii) Hosea also knew that the roots of Israel's failure were to be found in the inner life of the nation. In this passage, he highlights two of the most fundamental flaws: *false religion* (verses 2–3) and *false politics* (verses 10–11). Both appeared to offer comfort and security in perilous times; neither was strong enough to resist the momentum of judgment.

And yet Israel, in its final hours, simply typifies the human race in a time of crisis. Perhaps this cult or that faith can help us. Perhaps this great leader or that great president can avert the looming disaster. From Hosea's perspective, there is no ultimate security apart from God. The meaning of human life cannot be determined apart from God, the giver of life. The future of nations cannot be known apart from God, the sovereign of all nations. The leadership of kings and princes, prime ministers and presidents, cannot deliver, if it has abandoned the divine and fundamental principles of justice.

THE ORPHAN FINDS MERCY

Hosea 14:1–9

¹Return, O Israel, to the Lord your God,
 for you have stumbled because of your iniquity.
²Take with you words
 and return to the Lord;
say to him,
 "Take away all iniquity;
accept that which is good
 and we will render
 the fruit of our lips.
³Assyria shall not save us,
 we will not ride upon horses;
and we will say no more, 'Our God,'
 to the work of our hands.
In thee the orphan finds mercy."

⁴I will heal their faithlessness;
 I will love them freely,
 for my anger has turned from them.
⁵I will be as the dew to Israel;
 he shall blossom as the lily,
 he shall strike root as the poplar;
⁶his shoots shall spread out;
 his beauty shall be like the olive,
 and his fragrance like Lebanon.
⁷They shall return and dwell beneath my shadow,
 they shall flourish as a garden;
they shall blossom as the vine,
 their fragrance shall be like the wine of Lebanon.

⁸O Ephraim, what have I to do with idols?
 It is I who answer and look after you.
I am like an evergreen cypress,
 from me comes your fruit.

⁹Whoever is wise, let him understand these things;
   whoever is discerning, let him know them;
for the ways of the Lord are right,
   and the upright walk in them,
   but transgressors stumble in them.

From a national and political perspective, it seems that the end has now come. The divine judgment, so central a theme throughout the decades of Hosea's ministry, is now in the process of fulfilment. Strictly speaking, it should have been a time in which national hope was finally buried, especially in the light of God's terrible statement in 13:9. Surely now, with the world crumbling around them, Israel must abandon any notion of a future. And surely now, when the prophet's preaching was finally finding its fulfilment in daily events, Hosea must claim: "I told you so!" For in 722 B.C. the capital city of Samaria finally collapsed in the face of the Assyrian foe. What had been foretold was being fulfilled. And yet Hosea's book ends with a final twist which turns the preceding passages of judgment on their tail.

Now that the end is upon Israel, Hosea calls upon his people again: "Return, O Israel, to the Lord God" (verse 1). He gives them a prayer to use (verses 2–3). They must pray for forgiveness, abandon their old dependence on military might and foreign allies, and no longer worship their man-made idols. If they would only pray these words, Hosea says, there may yet remain a hope for the future. He then proclaims the words of divine compassion (verses 4–8), which might be announced in response to repentance. This final divine speech of the book is penetrated by the language of love, its words and imagery powerfully evocative of the love poetry of the Song of Solomon. To the people who would say: "In thee the orphan finds mercy", God would respond: "I will love them freely" (verse 4).

The prophet's words are not a final call to repentance urged in the hope of avoiding catastrophe. Rather, they are a call to repentance which penetrates beyond the current catastrophe to a dim and uncertain future. The catastrophe was the end of Israel as a nation state; indeed, to this day, the only historical remnant of that once proud state is the small community of Samaritans who still survive in the modern state of Israel. But Hosea sees beyond the immediate curtain of earthly reality. Just as earlier he had seen a new marriage beyond the nation's divorce (chapter 3), so now he sees a new chapter of love in the long story of Israel's relation to its God.

For all the gloom that has dominated the prophet's ministry, Hosea's book ends on a note of love. His vision of God outstrips conventional theology and law: God continues to love even when the divine love has long been rejected. And his vision of God reaches beyond the historical events of his time; when at last all his contemporaries understood that Israel had no future, suddenly Hosea perceived that there was a future after all. For love, in the last resort, cannot be restrained. God's love cannot die, despite the persistent efforts of mankind to bring it to an end.

And we have only grasped Hosea's message fully if we leave this book with this message of love firmly in the forefront of our mind. It is a book written long ago, but it was specifically written down so that the future generations could understand its message, as the *postscript* (verse 9) so clearly states. To those who recognize that they are as orphans in this world, there comes still the word of God proclaimed by Hosea: "I will love them freely".

INTRODUCTION TO THE BOOK OF JOEL

AUTHORSHIP, DATE AND CIRCUMSTANCES

The prophet, after whom this short book is named, is called simply "Joel son of Pethuel" (1:1). Although the name *Joel* is quite common in the historical narratives of the Old Testament, nothing further is known of Joel son of Pethuel beyond the scant information provided in his book. He was, in all probability, a citizen of Jerusalem in Judah, which is the focal point of the book's substance. He may have been a priest or cult-prophet, as some scholars have supposed, but of this there can be little certainty. He was a prophet, at least for a short period of his otherwise unknown life, as is indicated by the explicit statement that his speech was none other than the "word of the Lord". And it may be assumed that Joel was a person of some education, for his poetry has literary power and his words reflect familiarity with the writings, or sayings, of other prophets. Beyond these brief scraps, we can have no certainty about the person and biography of Joel.

Given the uncertainty about the man, it follows that there must also be uncertainty as to the date of his short prophetic ministry. The opening verse of the book does not specify the period, as is commonly the case in the other prophetic books; the interpreter is left to speculate on the date on the basis of what few historical allusions exist in the text. During the long history of interpretation of this book, Joel's ministry has been set in the ninth century B.C., the seventh century, the sixth century, and as late as the fourth century! Such extraordinary discrepancies in the various proposals as to date give some indication of how elusive and ambivalent are the internal dating criteria. Of recent proposals on the chronology of the book, perhaps the most convincing are those that would set the prophet's ministry in the last two decades of the sixth century B.C.; if such a conclusion were correct, the prophet's ministry would have taken place in Jerusalem relatively early in the period after the Exile. But there can be no certainty, and perhaps it would be wise to remember John Calvin's words concerning Joel: "as there is no certainty, it is better to leave the time in which he taught undecided; and as we shall see, this is of no great importance."

Though the date of the prophet's ministry remains shrouded in mystery, the event which prompted the ministry, from the human perspective at least, is perfectly clear: it was the horrifying experience of a locust plague. The prophet describes in vivid terms the recent experience of the devastation caused by locusts (1:2–2:17) and takes that historical reality as the launching point of his prophetic ministry. But again, there are no adequate external records that would allow us to determine the precise year in which this particular invasion of locusts took place.

That the prophet describes a real infestation of the land by locusts need not be doubted, though there was a tendency among the older interpreters to understand the tale of the locusts to be merely symbolic or allegorical. Not only in ancient times, but also in the modern era, Jerusalem and the surrounding land have been vulnerable to the ravages of locusts. In the spring of 1915, Jerusalem, Palestine and Syria were subjected to terrible devastation as a consequence of an influx of locusts (reported by John Whiting in the *National Geographic Magazine* for December, 1915). At the end of February, great clouds of locusts began flying into the land from a northeasterly direction, so that "attention was drawn to them by the sudden darkening of the bright sunshine." They came in enormous numbers, settling on the fields and hillsides. There they laid their eggs in vast numbers (it was calculated that some 60,000 could come from the eggs planted in thirty-nine square inches of soil, and that figure involved a 30% loss rate!) Once hatched, the new broods started crawling across the ground, at a rate of 400 to 600 feet per day, devouring every scrap of vegetation in their path. While the plague of 1915 was exceptionally bad, similar plagues were not infrequent; even in 1915 the year 1865 was still remembered in Jerusalem as the "year of the locusts" because of the plague in that year!

The principal theme of the prophecy is the "Day of the Lord", an expression which occurs with frequency throughout the short book. It is a phrase used also by other prophets, but no other writer devotes his attention so comprehensively to the theme as does Joel. In general terms, the Day of the Lord is the day on which God's judgment of evil persons and nations is executed and his reign of righteousness established.

In developing this theme, Joel's vision and words have an elastic capacity, stretching the normal constraints of time, so that the present, the immediate future, and the distant future are all condensed as if contained within a small capsule of time. The focus on the present is prompted by the plague of locusts, which evokes in Joel's mind the approaching judgment of God. The threat, although it may symbolize future judgments of a more general nature, is real enough in the prophet's time; locusts could literally destroy the staples of life and reduce people to starvation and death. And so Joel calls upon his people to repent (2:12–17); after the passage of an undetermined period of time, it appears that the people have responded to the prophet's message and judgment has been averted (2:18–27).

But the turning aside of impending judgment does not eliminate the Day of the Lord; that day lies still in the future. In the prophet's vision of a more distant future, he now perceives more clearly the dual character of the day: for those that knew and worshipped God, it would be a day of blessing and restoration, but for the enemies of God, a day of destruction and desolation. Thus the immediate and positive response of the people to the prophet's message bodes well for the future of the faithful, but a judgment day still must come.

Joel thus addressed his own generation and future generations, though no doubt, to his audience at that time, the chronological perspective of the future proclamation could scarcely be understood. And indeed, in the light of the New Testament, the prophet's future vision has within it stages of chronological development. His prophecy of an outpouring of the Spirit of God

(2:28–29) is interpreted by St. Peter, in his Pentecost sermon, as being fulfilled in the birth of the Christian Church (Acts 2:17–21). Yet the concluding part of the book, concerning the final judgment of nations and beyond that a new world, remains even today in the realm of eschatology.

Thus Joel was a man of his own times, yet also a man for all future generations. Reading the immediate signs of his own age, he summoned his people to repentance, and they responded. Yet the threat of disaster, so vividly exemplified in the locust plague, was in a sense an ever-present threat. Wherever and whenever evil prospered, the Day of the Lord must always be at hand. Although that day may be delayed, inevitably it must some day come to pass. And though the Day of the Lord would be a fearful time for the practitioners of evil, both persons and nations, it would nevertheless be a time of hope. For beyond that day the prophet sees a vision, albeit distant and without clear substance, when the years lost to the locust would be remembered no more.

THE PLAGUE OF LOCUSTS

Joel 1:1–12

¹The word of the Lord that came to Joel, the son of Pethuel:

²Hear this, you aged men,
    give ear, all inhabitants of the land!
Has such a thing happened in your days,
    or in the days of your fathers?
³Tell your children of it,
    and let your children tell their children,
    and their children another generation.

⁴What the cutting locust left,
    the swarming locust has eaten.
What the swarming locust left,
    the hopping locust has eaten,
and what the hopping locust left,
    the destroying locust has eaten.

5Awake, you drunkards, and weep;
 and wail, all you drinkers of wine,
because of the sweet wine,
 for it is cut off from your mouth.
6For a nation has come up against my land,
 powerful and without number;
its teeth are lions' teeth,
 and it has the fangs of a lioness.
7It has laid waste my vines,
 and splintered my fig trees;
it has stripped off their bark and thrown it down;
 their branches are made white.

8Lament like a virgin girded with sackcloth
 for the bridegroom of her youth.
9The cereal offering and the drink offering are cut off
 from the house of the Lord.
The priests mourn,
 the ministers of the Lord.
10The fields are laid waste,
 the ground mourns;
because the grain is destroyed,
 the wine fails,
 the oil languishes.

11Be confounded, O tillers of the soil,
 wail, O vinedressers,
for the wheat and the barley;
 because the harvest of the field has perished.
12The vine withers,
 the fig tree languishes.
Pomegranate, palm, and apple,
 all the trees of the field are withered;
and gladness fails
 from the sons of men.

This book begins in a simpler fashion than do many other prophetic books. We are told the prophet's name, Joel son of Pethuel, but nothing is said with respect to the time and circumstances in which he lived (in contrast to the books of Hosea and Amos). Yet the most important information has survived: "the word of the Lord" (verse 1) indicates clearly that the substance of this book is prophecy, namely the divine word mediated to the chosen people through God's prophet. That word, as it will be expressed, has independent merit and significance without respect to the specific time and place in which it was first delivered.

The enduring nature of the prophet's message is brought out clearly in the first words that he speaks (verses 2–3). He summons both the old men and the people in general to listen to what he has to say and he tells them in turn to repeat it to their children, who will repeat it to their children, so that the message will be passed down from one generation to another. The message, as will be clear in a moment, was prompted by a particular and momentous event; its significance, however, extended beyond the event and was to be recalled in future ages. Already we begin to grasp the prophet's purpose. He had an extraordinary experience in his own lifetime, but the meaning of that experience was to be passed on for the benefit of those yet unborn. The prophet's role was thus didactic as well as prophetic; he wanted to teach something, and the reader of his book must search diligently for the essence of his teaching.

Next, the prophet presents in summary form the event which prompted his preaching and teaching: a plague of locusts had come and devoured every scrap of natural produce in the land (verse 4). The event is elaborated in greater detail later in the prophet's preaching, but initially he simply declares the facts in powerful lines of poetry. The various terms used in this verse have been the source of great debate: *cutting locust, swarming locust, hopping locust* and *destroying locust*. The precise entomological significance of each Hebrew word is uncertain and hence the debate. Are four different kinds of locust intended? Or do the words refer to the different stages in the development of one species of locust, from hatch to larva, and then from pupa to imago? In a sense, such questions miss the mark, for the lines are poetic and are intended to communicate the devastation and completeness of the locust plague. But the lines are more likely to designate the developing stages of the locust from the egg. The various accounts of locust plagues in Palestine indicate that when the flying insects come, they do not eat, but simply bury their eggs in the ground. But then, following the hatch some weeks later, the developing insects are voracious, devouring everything in their path. The hatch often takes place in May and June.

Having declared the event, the prophet then addresses various groups of persons, summoning them to lament because of the disaster that has befallen them. The language which the prophet now uses is similar to that of a messenger whom a king might send out in times of national crisis, summoning the citizens to attend a national liturgy of lamentation. Indeed, this characteristic of the prophets language has prompted some interpreters to suggest that the Book of Joel was indeed the text for such a national liturgy. But this interpretation is unlikely; the prophet has adapted the language to his own purpose. He is God's messenger, summoning the people not to liturgy, but to learning. They are to reflect on the crisis, learn from it, and teach its message to subsequent generations. Three groups of persons are addressed in the following verses, and the character of the first group, in particular, indicates the dramatic form of the prophet's speech.

(i) *Drunkards* (verses 5–7). In ironic language, the prophet summons the drunkards and "winos" to lament the nation's disaster. Faced with such a calamity, many a man with a tendency to tipple would have sought solace in a cup of wine. But of course the nature of the crisis was such that the grape crop would have been destroyed and there would be no more wine. The powerful "nation" that destroyed the fruit was none other than the army of locusts that had marched over the land, devouring all grapes and figs in its path. And the poetry has a powerful element of realism to it, for many modern accounts of locust plagues have observed that the insects have eaten not only fruit, but also bark, leaving white and naked trees behind them.

It is nevertheless odd that the prophet's invitation to lamentation should begin with an address to drunkards. It may have been done simply for poetic effect, but equally the choice may be indicative of the character of society in Joel's time. Heavy drinking may have become the norm of his society, and the effect of the plague would be to curtail that drinking, not as a consequence of moral revolution, but simply by virtue of a diminishing supply of alcoholic beverages!

(ii) *A young woman bereaved* (verses 8–10). The second address may be to Jerusalem and its Temple, but the language likens its sorrow to that of a young woman in grief, whose fiancé has died. Yet the consequence of the plague is that the offerings normally brought to the Lord's Temple in Jerusalem are no longer available. The priests and ministers, whose duty it was to give the offering to God as a sign of the nation's thanksgiving, were now in mourning for they had nothing to offer. The prophet illustrates clearly how the loss of crops and fruit has penetrated the entire economy, not least the worship of the Temple. Those staples of life which were the gift of God and the blessing of the land could no longer be given to God: there was nothing left to give.

(iii) *The farmers* (verses 11–12). Finally the farmers are addressed. All their crops and fruit have perished; all their hard work and tilling of the soil has been in vain. Everything has gone, lost to a voracious army of locusts whose appetite has no limits and whose taste has no discrimination; anything edible has been eaten.

So far the prophet has not revealed the meaning of the dreadful crisis. He has alerted his audience to listen and learn; he has declared the disaster, and summoned various segments of society to lament. And they are to lament not only their immediate and personal loss; the failure of food supply was so complete that not even the proper pursuit of worship in the Temple was possible.

Yet the seed of the prophet's thought may perhaps be detected. The produce of the promised land was the gift of God to his people, not simply the end result of hard work and good farming. Hence, for one who thought about the current crisis, the elements of an enigma were present: if God's gifts were gone, then God must have some hand in the crisis. As Lord of nature, he controlled the locust no less than the seed in the ground or the fruit on the vine. So there was something to be learned from all this; the hand of God must be in it, if only its purpose could be discerned. And all must learn the lesson, the pious and impious alike, the drunkard as well as the priest who had lost those staples central to their existence, and the faithful farmer who normally fed the society to which he belonged.

A PLAGUE PORTENDING DOOM

Joel 1:13–20

13Gird on sackcloth and lament, O priests,
    wail, O ministers of the altar.
Go in, pass the night in sackcloth,
    O ministers of my God!
Because cereal offering and drink offering
    are withheld from the house of your God.

14Sanctify a fast,
    call a solemn assembly.
Gather the elders
    and all the inhabitants of the land
to the house of the Lord your God; *
    and cry to the Lord.

15Alas for the day!
For the day of the Lord is near,
    and as destruction from the Almighty it comes.
16Is not the food cut off
    before our eyes,
joy and gladness
    from the house of our God?

17The seed shrivels under the clods,
    the storehouses are desolate;
the granaries are ruined
    because the grain has failed.
18How the beasts groan!
    The herds of cattle are perplexed
because there is no pasture for them;
    even the flocks of sheep are dismayed.

19Unto thee, O Lord, I cry.
For fire has devoured

the pastures of the wilderness,
    and flame has burned
        all the trees of the field.
²⁰Even the wild beasts cry to thee
    because the water brooks are dried up,
and fire has devoured
    the pastures of the wilderness.

Now the prophet's invitation to the nation to engage in lamentation takes on a more precise focus. Joel asks that a national crisis be recognized and that the associated rituals begin. He addresses the invitation to both the religious and the secular leaders of his country (verses 13–14), and then provides the reason for the lamentation (verses 15–18), before engaging in the first act of prayer with which the occasion begins (verses 19–20).

(i) The invitation to initiate a period of national lamentation is addressed to two groups of people. First, the priests and ministers responsible for the worship of the Temple are addressed. They are told to put on sackcloth, and wear it day and night; this rough garment of mourning would be in stark contrast to the standard splendid attire of the priests who participated in the great temple rituals. But clothing in worship was symbolic; there was no reason for the priests to dress with the symbols of holiness and thanksgiving, for the normal services had ceased in the absence of supplies for the offerings. The sackcloth symbolized poverty, both of life and of spirit. In addition to the priests, Joel also addressed the elders (verse 14); they were the civic leaders of the nation who were responsible for the people as a whole. It was the elders who had the civil authority to proclaim a time of national fasting and sorrow, and it was they who could summon all their fellow citizens to engage in an act of contrition towards God. So the formal invitation has been delivered to the people by the prophet, acting in his role as the spokesman of God.

We have seen in our own time such occasions of crisis that a nation has been given by its leaders a summons to stop and reflect. It is appropriate for a nation to pause and take stock when disaster has overtaken it, or looms on the horizon. But it is important, when engaging in national contrition, to see things correctly. It was too late, and in any case pointless, to declare a national "curse the locust" day throughout the nation. The day of the locust, in Joel's time, symbolized something; only if the underlying meaning of the locust plague could be determined could a day of national lamentation have any lasting significance.

(ii) Thus, after delivering a call for a national assembly of lament, Joel declares the reason for his call. It is not the havoc created by the locust that prompts his call; it is rather the "Day of the Lord" that is close at hand (verse 15). But the devastation created by the locusts was nevertheless a portent of that coming day. The encounter with the locusts was, as it were, a brush with disaster, a reminder that a day of more awful horror was close at hand. And when Joel referred to the "Day of the Lord", his audience knew that to which he referred, for Amos (5:18) and other prophets had talked of the fearsome judgment that would characterize the Day.

Now we begin to see the prophet's mission and strategy. All the citizens of Judah had observed the devastation wrought by the locusts; they had no need of a prophet to tell them how bad things were. They needed no call to lament what *had* happened; they were already stricken with grief at their loss. But the people did not perceive, as did Joel, that the devouring locusts were only the forerunners of a greater threat lying just over the horizon of their history. If they only looked back to what had been lost to the locust, they would miss the significance of what had happened to them. It was that which was still to come that gripped the prophet; it was a national lament to avoid further disaster for which he called. In summoning his people to observe this deeper significance in recent events, he observes not only that food and fellowship have been excised from the life of the Temple, but also that the world of nature itself is in a state of shock. The fields and farm buildings have failed in their function; the poor sheep and cattle are torn between perplexity and dismay, for the meadows in which they were accustomed to graze are but a wasteland. The perplexity of the beasts serves as a pointer to human observers; they too should reflect on the meaning of the events they have seen.

(iii) Finally, the prophet utters a prayer, though it contains only despair. He joins his voice in harmony with those of pasture, forest, and wild animals, in expressing grief at the terrible state of the land. But his grief is greater than that of the world of nature, for his eye has seen more, namely that beyond the burned pasture and parched waterbrooks lies a darker and more awesome threat. So he says: "Unto thee, O Lord, I cry."

Though Joel's cry has little substance, we can learn from it nevertheless. He does not yet say to God, "Help!" Nor does he yet implore his people to turn from their evil and repent. For the moment, it is enough that he has seen the horror of the locust, and discerned in that event the spectre of the coming Day of the Lord. And having seen all that, he can only cry out. It is a sign of his walk with God that he can perceive the divine word in the events around him. And it is a sign of his profoundest hope that, when faced with disaster, he spontaneously cries out to God.

THE COMING DAY OF THE LORD

Joel 2:1–11

¹Blow the trumpet in Zion;
   sound the alarm on my holy mountain!
Let all the inhabitants of the land tremble,
   for the day of the Lord is coming, it is near,
²a day of darkness and gloom,
   a day of clouds and thick darkness!
Like blackness there is spread upon the mountains
   a great and powerful people;
their like has never been from of old,
   nor will be again after them
   through the years of all generations.

³Fire devours before them,
   and behind them a flame burns.
The land is like the garden of Eden before them,
   but after them a desolate wilderness,
   and nothing escapes them.

⁴Their appearance is like the appearance of horses,
   and like war horses they run.

⁵As with the rumbling of chariots,
  they leap on the tops of the mountains,
like the crackling of a flame of fire
  devouring the stubble,
like a powerful army
  drawn up for battle.
⁶Before them peoples are in anguish,
  all faces grow pale.
⁷Like warriors they charge,
  like soldiers they scale the wall.
They march each on his way,
  they do not swerve from their paths.
⁸They do not jostle one another,
  each marches in his path;
they burst through the weapons
  and are not halted.
⁹They leap upon the city,
  they run upon the walls;
they climb up into the houses,
  they enter through the windows like a thief.

¹⁰The earth quakes before them,
  the heavens tremble.
The sun and the moon are darkened,
  and the stars withdraw their shining.
¹¹The Lord utters his voice
  before his army,
for his host is exceedingly great;
  he that executes his word is powerful.
For the day of the Lord is great and very terrible;
  who can endure it?

The prophet now declares a further oracle from the Lord, in which he weaves together the horrors of the past and dark anticipations of the future. The principal theme of this passage is the Day of the Lord; the theme brackets the substance of the oracle, being introduced in verses 1–2 and concluding the narrative in verse 11. But the central substance of the text seems at first to revert to the locust plague (verse 3–10); on closer inspection, however, it becomes clear that the language of the locust plague, which had so recently been experienced, is now being employed to describe vividly the coming judgment day.

Thus the note of alarm with which the message begins (verse 1) anticipates the future, rather than referring back to the past. Choosing his words with care, the prophet paints a picture of a city about to be beseiged. The city is Jerusalem, or Zion; the watchmen on the city's walls are instructed to blow their trumpets, thereby to alert all the inhabitants to the impending danger of attack. The trumpet blasts warn the citizens of an advancing army, but on this occasion, it is not merely an enemy that approaches; rather it is an army of an apocalyptic character, whose approach indicates the nearness of the fearful Day of the Lord. The Day is described as one of darkness and gloom, and the approaching regiments appear to be as a dark blackness, gradually enveloping the hills around Jerusalem. The apocalyptic character of the event is highlighted by the uniqueness of the event, for which there has been no precedent and which would never be repeated beyond the terrible Day.

Gradually the prophet's language changes; he continues to describe the coming apocalyptic army, but his language is now of such a kind as to evoke memories of the recent locust plague. Thus, the connection between the past horror and the coming judgment, in the prophet's teaching, becomes clear. The recent locust invasion, horrifying enough in itself, was but a foreshadowing of a more awful event to come; and if the total disaster of the past were but a token of the future, how much more terrible the Day of the Lord must be!

The focus in the description of the apocalyptic army, portrayed as if it were a locust plague, is upon its comprehensive destruction and the unalterable course of its march. The language of these verses (3–10) is constantly reminiscent of other descriptions of locusts engaged in destructive rampage. Their capacity to ravage is like a brush fire, the flames leaping ahead to seek new fuel, leaving behind them a trail of spot fires as the brush is steadily burnt to the ground. Just as a line of locusts marches steadily in ranks across a garden land, leaving behind it a wilderness without vegetation, so too the apocalyptic army's advance defoliates the land. And so the awesome description continues: a totally unstoppable force, orderly and sinister, treads steadfastly across the land, missing no corner, conquering all resistance, overcoming every defensive barricade, so that even the cosmos seems to tremble, and the light of sun and moon are obscured.

The power of the prophet's preaching emerges not only from the poetry, which is penetrating in its use of language, but also in the associations it calls forth in the memories of his listeners. They had recently experienced the real devastation of the locust; now, in language evocative of that memorable nightmare, they were being warned of a still more awful event, the Day of the Lord, which was about to break into the sequence of time and history. And as the prophet described the Day, it had an other-worldly character to it; it was not unlike their recent encounter with the trauma of the locust, yet somehow it would be unspeak-ably worse, beyond the normal descriptive capacity of human speech.

For all the awesomeness of the prophet's description and the apparent inevitability of the coming Day, the passage begins nevertheless with a ray of hope, though it is a hope that has not yet been given substance. The hope is to be found in the instruc-tion in verse 1 that an alarm and a warning be sounded; it is true that, despite the warning cry, the coming army seems invincible, yet if the warning were heeded perhaps it would not be too late. For that which was coming was the Day of the Lord; the only one to whom appeal could be made that the Day be averted was the Lord himself.

As we reflect upon this part of the prophet's message so many centuries after it was delivered, its urgency may seem very remote from our modern world. Yet there is a sense in which the Day of the Lord is always at hand, always threatening, and thus always urging us to delay its apparently inevitable advent. Centuries later, in the mysterious writing of St. John, he too was to use the language of locusts to warn of apocalyptic disaster (Rev. 9:1–10). It is not language that can be literally interpreted and forced into the strait-jacket of future events. Rather, it is a projection of the potential for apocalyptic disaster that lies always within the pres-ent capacity of human beings and human nations. As members of the human race, we have developed an extraordinary capacity for evil on a phenomenal scale. We have already perpetrated in our own century actions of near apocalyptic character; we have hoarded the weapons of the apocalypse, awaiting as it were some demonic impulse to unleash their power. The point of the prophet was not so much to predict some future event, as it was to see the possibility of such a future in the present. And likewise the peculiar frenzy of our own age, the obsession with trying to relate ancient prophetic "predictions" to the calamities of modern history, may miss the point of the prophets entirely. For the future lies mysteriously within us, within our immediate present. And the "Day of the Lord" will be what we, as members of the human race, make it. The ruthless pursuit of evil may indeed make it a "day of darkness and gloom", yet there is hope in the thought that the future belongs to One whose nature it is to have mercy and patience. The divine will does not change the nature of the future, for human evil can still create its own apocalypse, but it does make it possible for the future to be changed. And that was the message which Joel wished to convey to his own generation, as much as to future generations.

A CALL TO REPENTANCE

Joel 2:12–17

12"Yet even now," says the Lord,
    "return to me with all your heart,
  with fasting, with weeping, and with mourning;
13   and rend your hearts and not your garments."
  Return to the Lord, your God,
      for he is gracious and merciful,
    slow to anger, and abounding in steadfast love,
      and repents of evil.
14Who knows whether he will not turn and repent,
      and leave a blessing behind him,
  a cereal offering, and a drink offering
      for the Lord, your God?

15Blow the trumpet in Zion;

sanctify a fast;
call a solemn assembly;
16   gather the people.
Sanctify the congregation;
    assemble the elders;
gather the children,
    even nursing infants.
Let the bridegroom leave his room,
    and the bride her chamber.

17Between the vestibule and the altar
    let the priests, the ministers of the Lord, weep
and say, "Spare thy people, O Lord,
    and make not thy heritage a reproach,
    a byword among the nations.
Why should they say among the peoples,
    'Where is their God?'"

In the preceding verses, the prophet had drawn a dark picture of impending doom; he had warned of a fearsome army bearing down upon the city of Jerusalem, bent upon its destruction. And the approaching foe seemed all but invincible; the only faint ray of hope to which the prophet alluded was the cry of warning which the city's watchmen were to utter. Now the prophet turns his words to a more positive purpose. He calls his people to repentance, for therein lay the only hope of averting the threat of disaster. As one reads the invitation to repentance, it is crucial to bear in mind the background against which the call is given, for it is that apocalyptic threat which imparts such urgency to the words now under consideration. The prophet's words on repentance can be seen from three perspectives, following the inner structure of the passage now under examination.

(i) *The invitation to repentance* (verses 12–14). The message begins with a quotation of God's own words: "return to me with all your heart" (verse 12). And then the prophet adds his own exhortation, urgently pressing the people to return to God. It is important to stress this sequence. Earlier, Joel had warned of the horror of the imminent Day of the Lord; now it is the same Lord, master of the apocalyptic hosts, who takes the initiative in inviting his people, through his prophet, to turn back from their evil ways and return to their true faith in God. And the prophet's own words of encouragement explain the reason for this extraordinary sequence of events: it is in God's very nature to be gracious, merciful, long-suffering and full of love towards his people. Judgment is a consequence of the stubborn resistance of people, persistently refusing to return to God; in a sense it is always self-induced. The will of the Judging God is always that his wrath be turned aside; it may be turned aside when those who have turned away from God return to the path of faith. And where there is true repentance, God himself will "repent"; that is, he will turn back the tide of judgment and reveal again the face of his mercy. When that happened, the normal blessings of life would be restored, sufficient in quantity that the traditional offerings of thanksgiving could be resumed once again (verse 14*b*).

In these words, the prophet provides us with a fundamental insight into the nature of God. Though we hear much from the Old Testament prophets about the judgment of God, it is wise to recall that such judgment runs contrary to his basic character, which is always to love and to have mercy. The true nature of the divine character is seen in the initiative God takes in issuing the invitation to repent; there was no legal requirement for him to act thus, only the powerful pressure of love. At a later point in history, it was the same love and mercy that brought God into the world in the person of Christ, and the same invitation was issued, a call from the heart of God that men and women return to him whose nature it is to have mercy.

(ii) *The act of repentance* (verses 15–16). The prophet perceived clearly that it was not enough simply for him to declare the word inviting repentance; there must also be action of such a kind as to impress upon the people the urgency of their situation, and also to encourage them to repent with true feeling. So again he calls for the trumpet blast. This time, it is not to warn of the approach of the apocalyptic army (see 2:1), but rather to call all the people together in a solemn national assembly.

The nation (in practical terms, the citizens of Jerusalem) were to convene in a great public assembly; in so doing, they were to abstain from eating, for the assembly was to be a general and open action of repentance. By ritual washings, the people were to cleanse themselves for the occasion, the outer cleanliness symbolizing an inner desire for purity. The entire nation were to be present, including the elders, who were the national leaders of the people. Children and infants were to be brought along; though they could hardly be held responsible in any way for the crisis, their future nevertheless was intimately related to the outcome. Even the newlyweds, who more than most could offer an excuse for absence, were to attend the assembly; if they were to have any hope of a future together as husband and wife, it would depend on the consequence of this solemn national fast.

Again we can learn from the prophet's call to action. There are times when we prefer to think of religion as an intensely personal matter, and certainly repentance is often thought of in these terms. Yet an assembly of persons creates a new awareness of the dimensions of crisis. There were in the crowd individuals, who individually had sinned and individually must be repentant. Yet there is a collective guilt that emerges from the actions of a society as a whole; the evil of a people, no less than that of an individual, must be repented. But more than that, in the collective gathering a new kind of awareness emerges: if there is to be a future, if judgment is to be turned aside, all the people must act. Their collective reflection on sin, prodded by the physical pangs of hunger, created an awareness of the crisis and of the need for collective action which no single individual sitting in his room could possibly have grasped. And those of us who prefer our solitude, who hate the great gatherings and the multitudes of people, must learn to recognize that there is an insight gained, and an action possible, in that great assembly which cannot be had in private.

(iii) *The prayer of repentance* (verse 17). Finally, the prophet speaks the words of a prayer; they are spoken in the first instance by Joel, but they are issued for the use of the priests in the national assembly of repentance. The prayer has two parts to it: (a) first, the Lord is asked to spare his people, that is to exercise his mercy in response to the act of repentance by the people and to turn aside the tide of judgment. (b) Second, a further reason is stated as to why God should act thus in mercy; it was so that his people should not be made a "reproach" amongst other nations. The second part of the prayer is not simply a request that they be spared the ignominy of being humiliated in the eyes of foreigners. Rather, it alludes to the fundamental purpose of Israel: the chosen people were to have been a vehicle through whom God was revealed to other nations. If, in judgment, they were over-whelmed, people would only ask: "Where is God?" They would assume that the God of Israel had no real existence, and thereby the divine purpose in the world would be thwarted.

All prayer of repentance must have this double character, if it is to be true and wholesome. Certainly, in repenting, we must pray to be spared, but that prayer alone can easily become selfish. We must also pray for the larger goal, namely that through God's mercy in sparing us, the divine purpose may continue. For as it was God's will to be revealed to all nations through Israel, so too may his mercy be known through the life of one who has been forgiven, and thus has been marked by the divine compassion.

THE ANSWER TO PRAYER

Joel 2:18–27

18Then the Lord became jealous for his land,
    and had pity on his people.
19The Lord answered and said to his people,
    "Behold, I am sending to you
    grain, wine and oil,
    and you will be satisfied;
and I will no more make you
    a reproach among the nations.

20"I will remove the northerner far from you,
    and drive him into a parched and desolate land,
his front into the eastern sea,
    and his rear into the western sea;
the stench and foul smell of him will rise,
    for he has done great things.

21"Fear not, O land;

    be glad and rejoice,
       for the Lord has done great things!
²²Fear not, you beasts of the field,
       for the pastures of the wilderness are green;
    the tree bears its fruit,
       the fig tree and vine give their full yield.

²³"Be glad, O sons of Zion,
       and rejoice in the Lord your God;
    for he has given the early rain for your vindication,
       he has poured down for you abundant rain,
       the early and the latter rain, as before.

²⁴"The threshing floors shall be full of grain,
       the vats shall overflow with wine and oil.
²⁵I will restore to you the years
       which the swarming locust has eaten,
    the hopper, the destroyer, and the cutter,
       my great army, which I sent among you.

²⁶"You shall eat in plenty and be satisfied,
       and praise the name of the Lord your God,
    who has dealt wondrously with you.
And my people shall never again be put to shame.
²⁷You shall know that I am in the midst of Israel,
       and that I, the Lord, am your God and there is none else.
And my people shall never again be put to shame."

In the preceding passage, the prophet had called upon his people to congregate in a national assembly of lament. The recent plague of locusts had intimated to the prophet a more awful threat, namely the proximity of the Day of the Lord, which would be a day of judgment upon the chosen people for their evil. In calling for a national assembly, the prophet urged his fellow citizens to pray that God would spare them from judgment and turn aside disaster (2:17). With verse 18, a new section of the book begins. Between these two sections, during an unspecified period of time, one must suppose that Joel's warning was heeded, that a national assembly was convened, and that the people prayed to God that they might be spared. The remainder of the book of Joel contains a series of prophetic oracles, in which are contained the divine response to the people's prayer. The assembled people, in other words, had been truly repentant and the immediate threat of a judgment day had been averted. But God's response to the repentant's prayer, as is so common in the books of the prophets, addresses not only the immediate future, but also the more distant future. It is the immediate future that is in view in verses 18–27, but beyond that the dim outlines of more distant ages begin to emerge.

It is possible that the oracle contained in verses 18–27 (and perhaps some of the following passages) was actually delivered by the prophet in the national assembly for which he had called. It was not uncommon on such occasions, after the penitence and mourning, for God to address a word of promise to the assembled people through the mouth of his prophet. If such were the case, we may perceive clearly that the Lord's answer to the people's prayer was in the form of a promise: deliverance and blessing would come, and on those grounds the people should rejoice. This divine response to the people's lament illuminates several important dimensions of prayer in the relationship between God and his people.

(i) *The Lord answered* (verse 19): these words specifically introduce the divine response to the prayer which Joel had urged the priests to employ in the national assembly (verse 17). But it is important to notice the processes of change which had taken place before the answer to prayer could be given. The most significant change was in God, as described in verse 17; the same God who, through his prophet, had warned the people of impending doom, now had pity on his people. The words of verse 18 describe the re-emergence of "jealous" love and deep compassion. But the change in God's attitude in turn presupposed the fundamental change in the people, the reality of which had been demonstrated in the national assembly of repentance.

The essence of Israel's faith was a relationship with their God of covenant; prayer was one of the means of communication which gave expression to that relationship. When the relationship failed, the whole faith was in danger of collapse; Israel's sin, as Joel had made so clear, invited the divine response of judgment.

The act of national repentance was an act of conscious turning from evil and returning to God. Only in seeking again the intimate relationship with God, was prayer once again possible. And prayer could be answered, because it was addressed to the One with whom the restored relationship was sought.

Upon reflection, it becomes clear that the divine response to prayer really only presupposes one change, not two. God's love continued always for his people, but as they turned from him, it was manifest in wrath. As they turned back to him, seeking again the intimate relationship that had been lost, they rediscovered the compassion that was always in the heart of God. But the crucial point is the centrality of *relationship* in the meaning of prayer. As prayer is a form of communication, one can only pray to the God to whom one turns; and the corollary of prayer, namely the divine response, is only possible in the context of relationship. Thus, the people's repentance and plea for the relationship to be restored were the basis that made possible the answer to prayer that now follows.

(ii) *The substance of God's response*. The specific substance of God's response to the people's prayer is contained in verses 19–20 and 24–27. And it is instructive, in reading the response, to note the manner in which God's answer parallels the crisis from which the people sought deliverance. Grain, wine and oil had failed in the locust plague (1:10), and so grain, wine and oil would be restored (2:19). They had prayed not to be made a reproach among the nations (2:17), and so they would not be made a reproach (2:19). The northerner (verse 20), in context, probably refers both to the past experience of locust plague, and to the anticipated judgment of a foreign enemy advancing upon the city. The locust plague in Joel's time had probably come from the north (as it did in 1915: see John Whiting, in the *National Geographic Magazine*, referred to in the Introduction) and, from the north, the prophet had no doubt anticipated the arrival of the apocalyptic army, as had other prophets before him (Jer. 4:6). This threatening northern foe, whether pest or person, would be turned aside and destroyed (verse 20). The harvests that had failed in the time of the locust (1:10–17) would be converted in the future to abundant harvests of grain and wine and oil (verses 24–25). Those who had formerly suffered from a shortage of food (1:16) would "eat in plenty and be satisfied" (verse 26). And so, in this catalogue response to prayer, the years lost to the locust would be restored, and more importantly the judgment foreshadowed by the locust plague would be averted.

The crucial aspect to this detailed response to the people's prayer lies not so much in the listed details of future blessings as in the significance to which those details would point. Because God answered prayer, and because the blessings of covenant life would be restored, the people would know once again that God was present in the midst of Israel. And, in the final perspective, this is the most significant part of the entire response. It would be good that life's blessings would be restored in plenty, but best of all would be the restoration of the relationship with God and the knowledge of his presence. It is important to grasp this point; prayer, if we are not careful, may be debased into a kind of shopping list, submitted to God for approval and provision. The response of God may indeed make bounteous provision which, in turn, may promote the notion of prayer for material blessings. But, at base, the response to any prayer is the gift of the divine presence, the knowledge of God in the midst. And of that central issue we can learn from this experience in the life of ancient Israel.

(iii) *The response to prayer* (verse 21–23). In the midst of the account of God's response to the people's prayer, there is contained this short hymnic passage in which the people are invited to respond to God's bounty. Indeed, verses 21–23 contain in part further detail of God's blessing, but their central feature is the threefold invitation to respond to the God who answers prayer. The words are addressed to the *land* (verse 21), to the *beasts of the field* (verse 22), and to the *sons of Zion* (verse 23). (a) The land, which had been devastated by the former plague (1:10), is invited to exchange fear for gladness and rejoicing, for God had acted in such a way as to restore its fulness. (b) The beasts of the field, which had been dismayed and perplexed when the pasture failed (1:18), are called upon to fear no more, for the pastures would be plentiful. (c) The "sons of Zion" (an expression which may designate the people actually involved in the national assembly of repentance) are called on to rejoice; the life-giving rains, upon which all crops depended, would be sent once again. In the language of poetry, the prophet addresses the entire nation, inanimate and animate alike; as all had suffered, so all would be blessed and thus participate in the response of thanksgiving.

Thanksgiving and rejoicing are an essential part of the response to God's provision, for they are an expression of that fulness of life in which God too may rejoice. C.S. Lewis once wrote that God did not need thanksgiving from his people, as if he were "like a vain woman wanting compliments, or a vain author presenting his new books to people who had never met or heard from him." Rather, thanksgiving emerged from the full lives of those whom God blessed and thus fulfilled in him the richness of the relationship granted to his people.

FUTURE BLESSINGS

Joel 2:28–32

28"And it shall come to pass afterward,
    that I will pour out my spirit on all flesh;
  your sons and your daughters shall prophesy,
    your old men shall dream dreams,
    and your young men shall see visions.
29Even upon the menservants and maidservants
    in those days, I will pour out my spirit.

30"And I will give portents in the heavens and on the earth, blood and fire and columns of smoke. 31The sun shall be turned to darkness, and the moon to blood, before the great and terrible day of the Lord comes. 32And it shall come to pass that all who call upon the name of the Lord shall be delivered; for in Mount Zion and in Jerusalem there shall be those who escape, as the Lord has said, and among the survivors shall be those whom the Lord calls."

Following the oracle containing the promise of an answer to prayer (verses 18–27), there is now a further oracle of promise.

Like the one it follows, it pertains to the future from the time perspective of Joel, but now it is a more distant future that is envisaged. The word *afterward* in the opening line of verse 28 indicates that its substance refers to a time beyond the immediate restoration of blessing anticipated in the preceding prophecy. Yet it clearly refers to both an intermediate and indeterminate future; what is described here will take place "before the Day of the Lord comes" (verse 31). The Day of the Lord, which the prophet had earlier foreseen as an imminent threat to Judah (2:1–2), has now receded to a more remote horizon. And whereas that day had loomed with menace for Judah, now its threat seems to be directed more to the other nations of the world (chapter 3). But before that still distant and apocalyptic time, the prophet speaks of an intermediate time, filled with the promise of further blessing.

The verses describing this intermediate period have become so central to the meaning of the New Testament writings, and indeed to the history of the Christian Church, that there is grave danger of reading these verses too quickly with "Christian eyes", thereby failing to grasp their significance in the first Jewish context in which they were uttered. It may be helpful to examine the two levels of meaning in turn.

(i) In their initial context, these words were addressed by Joel to his fellow citizens in Judah and Jerusalem. They were a people who had just passed through a grave crisis in their national existence; indeed, though a promise of restoration had already been given (2:18–27), the actual condition of the people to whom Joel spoke was still that of the devastation and poverty which followed the locust plague. To these people, the prophet brings a word from God.

A time was coming when God would "pour out" his spirit in abundance. The word *spirit* is used in the Old Testament with various nuances; in this context, it is vital to note that the spirit is linked intimately with prophecy. The spirit of God was the power of God, in general a life-giving power; in this specific context, the spirit of God is that divine power which would enable persons to prophesy. And prophecy, in turn, was the declaration of the word of God to the people of God, in various modes. It is stated that this outpouring of the spirit would be upon "all flesh"; again, the context determines the sense of the phrase, and here it clearly means all the chosen people (Israelites, or Jews) of the future age to which reference is made. This specificity of reference is made clear by the following words, indicating that "all flesh" pertained to sons and daughters, old and young men, male and female servants. The prophecy does not have, in the first instance, any universal reference beyond the chosen people. It does, nevertheless, break down some of society's fundamental divisions, those between male and female, young and old, masters and servants. The first part of the prophecy, then, declares an abundant outpouring of the spirit, such that many different persons would prophesy; the implication is that as a consequence of the abundant declaration of God's word in prophecy, new life would be breathed into the people as a whole. And, if it is correct to date the Book of Joel to the latter part of the sixth century B.C., then the words were announced in a time when the declaration of the prophetic word was becoming increasingly rare; in contrast, the future time to which Joel refers would be marked by an abundance of prophetic declarations. Thus, this first part of the message was filled with future promise; the preceding prophecy had indicated that the real drought would be followed by abundant rains, and now the prophet indicates a further development when the drought of God's word would be ended by the abundant rainfall of the spirit.

Then the prophet looks still further into the mists of the future: before the Day of the Lord finally came, extraordinary natural events would take place, including an eclipse of the sun and a partial eclipse of the moon. In those portentous and threatening days, there would be nevertheless deliverance and security for those who called upon the name of the Lord.

Precisely what meaning would have been drawn from these words by Joel's audience cannot be ascertained. They would have understood that the Day of the Lord, which until so recently had seemed on the verge of breaking into their own time and history, was now more distant. That Day, nevertheless, was still coming. And they would have understood that the Day, which until so recently had offered only threat and judgment, had been in some fashion transformed; though still pregnant with threat and disaster (see chapter 3), it would be a time in which security could be found. And preceding all the future threat, there would be a gracious outpouring of God's spirit, with all its promise of new life. While such words as these could hardly have been transformed by Joel's audience into an eschatological timetable, they would have seemed full of future promise. And though, from the perspective of a later point in history, we may see that the future of which Joel spoke was not a period close to his own time, that chronological perspective could hardly have been grasped at the time the words were uttered. So the principal thrust of these words, at the time of their first delivery, was to impart a general hope for the future.

(ii) Reading this part of Joel's prophecy from the perspective of the New Testament, we are entitled to read into it a new level of meaning, beyond what would have been the explicit understanding of the words in the prophet's time. These words are frequently quoted and alluded to in the New Testament writings (e.g. Mark 13:24; Rom. 10:13), but their most central exposition is provided in the sermon of St. Peter delivered on the Day of Pentecost (Acts 2). The sermon takes the prophecy of Joel as its central text (Acts 2:17–21), developing the meaning of the prophecy with respect to the significance of Jesus, but also with respect to the phenomena of the spirit that marked the Day of Pentecost on that occasion (Acts 2:1–4). The spirit of prophecy made possible a new and extraordinary declaration of the word of God in many languages, so that the new gospel could break the barriers of speech and understanding.

Thus we may perceive, from the perspective of the New Testament, that Joel (perhaps quite unconsciously) spoke of the "Birthday of the Church" in these words declared several centuries earlier than the time to which they referred. To those whose lives had been devastated by the years of the locust was afforded a glance of a future work of God in the world, a turning point in human history, in which God's spirit would be freely given. And within the Church, we may look back to that Day of Pentecost with gratitude and wonder. To the contemporaries of Joel, looking forward in time, Joel's message offered hope for the present as much as the future. And for us, looking back in time, it is nevertheless the present and future hope implicit in these remarkable words from the prophet Joel that we must seek to grasp.

THE VALLEY OF JUDGMENT

Joel 3:1–12

1"For behold, in those days and at that time, when I restore the fortunes of Judah and Jerusalem, 2I will gather all the nations and bring them down to the valley of Jehoshaphat, and I will enter into judgment with them there, on account of my people and my heritage Israel, because they have scattered them among the nations, and have divided up my land, 3and have cast lots for my people, and have given a boy for a harlot, and have sold a girl for wine, and have drunk it.

4"What are you to me, O Tyre and Sidon, and all the regions of Philistia? Are you paying me back for something? If you are paying me back, I will requite your deed upon your own head swiftly and speedily. 5For you have taken my silver and my gold, and have carried my rich treasures into your temples. 6You have sold the people of Judah and Jerusalem to the Greeks, removing them far from their own border. 7But now I will stir them up from the place to which you have sold them, and I will requite your deed upon your own head. 8I will sell your sons and your daughters into the hand of the sons of Judah, and they will sell them to the Sabeans, to a nation far off; for the Lord has spoken."

9Proclaim this among the nations:
Prepare war,
    stir up the mighty men.
Let all the men of war draw near,
    let them come up.
10Beat your ploughshares into swords,

and your pruning hooks into spears;
   let the weak say, "I am a warrior."

[11]Hasten and come,
   all you nations round about,
   gather yourselves there.
Bring down thy warriors, O Lord.
[12]Let the nations bestir themselves,
   and come up to the valley of Jehoshaphat;
for there I will sit to judge
   all the nations round about.

The focus of Joel's prophecy now turns still further towards the future. He had spoken to Judah of God's answer to prayer and the coming deliverance from the immediate crisis (2:18–27); beyond that, he had spoken of further blessings God had in store for the world, which would be experienced *before* the final advent of the awful "Day of the Lord" (2:31). Now the prophet's attention turns to focus on a still more distant future, a time of judgment upon the nations, yet also a time of restoration of Judah and its capital city of Jerusalem (3:1).

The theme of this part of the prophet's message is the "Valley of Jehoshaphat", introduced in verse 2 and rounding off the message in verse 12. The word *Jehoshaphat* is a name; indeed, it was a personal name of one of the Hebrew kings, though here it has the appearance of being a geographical name. But no such place is literally known (later tradition identified the location with the Valley of Kidron, east of Jesusalem, but that is simply tradition); rather, the meaning of the name indicates the significance of the place. *Jehoshaphat* means: "the Lord judges". The valley would be the place in which God's judgment would be exercised against the world's evil nations as a part of the divine activity associated with the "Day of the Lord".

The message as such has a number of component parts. (a) The prophet declares that the nations will be brought to the valley for judgment, to be conducted on the basis of their behaviour towards the chosen people and their land (verse 1–3). (b) There then follows a further message, addressed specifically to the people of Tyre, Sidon and Philistia, indicating the nature of the judgment that would come upon them (verses 4–8). The focus of the general theme is here narrowed, and it may be that these verses were originally a part of a separate message, introduced at this point to illustrate the theme of "boy and girl" mentioned in verse 3. (c) The prophet returns to the main theme, depicting the manner in which the nations would be summoned to the Valley of Judgment. They would be summoned as if for battle, but the ensuing battle, as they would discover in the valley, would be the final war in which they were to be judged by God (verses 9–12).

Though the theme of future cataclysm runs throughout these verses, it is clear nevertheless that the prophet envisages the judgment of human nations always in terms of their actions and character. Such events do not merely happen; they are in a sense created by their victims. Those who have shaped the human history of evil are to become eventually the victims of that same history.

(i) The exploiters would be exploited on the judgment day; the oppressors would be oppressed. The nations summoned to the valley would be those that had exploited God's land and oppressed his people. The land had been divided up and sold for profit; the people had been traded as common slaves. There had been no sense of the sanctity or value of human life; boys were sold into slavery to provide payment for a prostitute, and young girls bartered for the price of a drink. A moment's gratification or superficial pleasure was sufficient ground for the disposal of young lives into years of hardship and the loss of freedom. Tyre, Sidon and Philistia are introduced as specific examples of the crimes committed; their coastal ports on the Mediterranean Sea were the avenues through which such inhuman commerce was conducted. The loot of the land was traded through the market place, and its populace sold as slaves to the Greeks and other foreigners.

And yet the essence of the prophet's declaration is one not only of judgment, but also of justice. The exploiters and oppressors of the world would one day live to see their deeds haunt them and return upon their own heads. It is not easy to understand precisely how the prophet envisaged this balancing of the accounts in future ages, yet his theme takes up one of the most perpetual puzzles of human history. There are constant injustices done in the affairs of human beings and human nations, yet there never seems to be any calling to account. Century after century, nations are destroyed, their people are exploited, their children sold into slavery, and yet so far as we can perceive there is no justice or day of reckoning; the "enslavers" of this world never seem to be called to give account of their actions. While Joel does not provide a rational resolution to this perpetual problem, he does affirm a faith in ultimate justice: the Day of the Lord will not only be a time of restoration (3:1), but also a day on which justice will finally, and in some mysterious fashion, be executed.

(ii) There is a distinctive element of surprise and shock associated with the final judgment of the nations (verses 9–12). In dramatic poetry, the prophet employs words that are in the conventional style of a summons to holy war. And the language has its own ironic twists. Where the prophets in earlier times had spoken of an age when nations would be called upon to convert the instruments of war into instruments of peace (Isa. 2:4 and Mic. 4:3), Joel reverses that language. In summoning the nations to the valley, he urges them to convert their agricultural implements into weapons (verse 10). But, when the nations were assembled in the valley, fully equipped for battle, they would receive a shock; they would find there the Judge of all the nations, and in their hands they would be holding the incriminating evidence of their own history of violence. Like Pavlov's dog, conditioned to respond to a stimulus, they would turn out in response to the call to battle, only to discover that they were to be judged for their warfare and violence.

We become what we have been, our characters conditioned by the actions of a lifetime. Likewise a nation's actions shape and mould its character, making it the sum of its history. And yet, in the irony of Joel's words, we begin to see that those very reflexes, shaped by a lifetime of response, will one day bring us, as a natural response to a summons, to the "Valley of Judgment". The only escape from such valleys is to be found earlier in Joel's message: it is only repentance which may turn us from evil towards a new future. It is only a conscious setting aside of those actions which shape and condition our character which can set us on a new path, leading away from the "Valley of Judgment".

JUDGMENT AND PROMISE

Joel 3:13–21

[13]Put in the sickle,
    for the harvest is ripe.
Go in, tread,
    for the wine press is full.
The vats overflow,
    for their wickedness is great.
[14]Multitudes, multitudes,
    in the valley of decision!
For the day of the Lord is near
    in the valley of decision.
[15]The sun and the moon are darkened,
    and the stars withdraw their shining.
[16]And the Lord roars from Zion,
    and utters his voice from Jerusalem,
    and the heavens and the earth shake.
But the Lord is a refuge to his people,
    a stronghold to the people of Israel.
[17]"So you shall know that I am the Lord your God,
    who dwell in Zion, my holy mountain.
And Jerusalem shall be holy
    and strangers shall never again pass through it.
[18]"And in that day
the mountains shall drip sweet wine,
    and the hills shall flow with milk,
and all the stream beds of Judah shall
    flow with water;
and a fountain shall come forth from the house of the Lord
    and water the valley of Shittim.
[19]"Egypt shall become a desolation
    and Edom a desolate wilderness,
for the violence done to the people of Judah,

because they have shed innocent blood in their land.
²⁰But Judah shall be inhabited for ever,
and Jerusalem to all generations.
²¹I will avenge their blood, and I will not clear the guilty,
for the Lord dwells in Zion."

The prophet's message concludes with further perspectives on the "Day of the Lord", which has been the principal theme throughout this short book. He describes first how the "Valley of Judgment" has become the "Valley of Decision" (or the "Valley of Verdict", verse 14). The scene described in verses 13–14 appears to be on the eve of the "Day of the Lord". With the nations gathered in the valley in response to the summons to war, now another summons to war is delivered; it is given not to the assembled nations, but rather (one must suppose) to the heavenly host who are to undertake God's judgment. This divine army is invited to "put in the sickle" (verse 13) and cut down, as if a harvest of grapes, the assembled armies of the nations whose weapons included converted ploughshares and pruning hooks (verse 10). The metaphor is that of an abundant grape harvest: as the dense clusters of grapes are cut from the vines and then trampled in the press, so too would the soldiers of sin be cut down and trampled in the "Valley of Judgment and Verdict". And this awesome trampling of judgment would be a consequence of the evil done by those nations, as declared in the verdict of the divine Judge.

Yet the slaughter of verses 13–14 is still only the precursor of the Day of the Lord; the day itself is described in verses 15–17. The day as such is the time at which persons shall recognize once again that God is the Lord; his city, the earthly symbol of the heavenly presence, would once again be a holy city. And beyond the Day, there lay a new, indeed renewed, future. The promised land would once again flow richly with all God's bounty, whereas the lands of evil nations would remain perpetually as desolate wildernesses, symbols of the consequence of doing violence to God's people and land.

It is important, at the conclusion of Joel's short message, to grasp the central themes he conveyed not only to his own generation, but also to future generations.

(i) For all his focus on the future, we would surely be mistaken to view the prophet's words simply as predictions of coming events. It is true that many of the events of which he spoke did indeed come to pass, yet it is not so much the inevitability of events that Joel stressed, but the "alterability" of the future. The locust plague, which prompted his ministry in the first place, made him believe that the Day of the Lord would come in his own time, but he called for national repentance. The people repented and the Day was averted. And all thinking about the Day of the Lord should have this balance. There are contemporary prophets among us who, through sermons and paperback books, would have us believe that the "Day" is now almost upon us as a predicted event that cannot be changed. We should be more true to Joel's purpose if we sought not simply to discern the future, but rather to change the future by present action. Repentance, whether for individuals or nations, is always a path that may lead us to see the other side of God's wrath, namely the countenance of love.

(ii) The Christian perspective on the Book of Joel automatically evokes in our minds the promise of God's spirit and the fulfilment of that gift on the Day of Pentecost, the Birthday of the Christian Church. Yet we should be wise to remember the context in which that promise was made; the Day of Pentecost can only be understood properly in the context of the "Day of the Lord" and of the nations. If, as Christians believe, the spirit was given not only to Jews, but also to Gentiles (the citizens of the "nations"), then those among the nations who received God's spirit have assumed some responsibility for turning their own nations aside from the path that leads to the "Day of the Lord". Like Joel, we have received a message, a call to repentance, a summons to faith and action of such kind that that "Day", which is in a sense implicit in the heart of every person and nation, may yet be put off in God's mercy, as it was in the time of Joel.

INTRODUCTION TO THE BOOK OF AMOS

Amos was a contemporary of the northern prophet Hosea. And although Amos was a citizen of the southern state of Judah, he ministered, as did Hosea, to the northern kingdom of Israel; on the historical context of the two prophets, see further the Introduction to the Book of Hosea. Amos and Hosea, despite being contemporaries and ministering in the same context, were very different persons. The messages they delivered were each shaped by their distinctive personalities and thus provide us with two different insights into the same period of Israel's history in the latter half of the eighth century B.C. Whereas the focus in the Book of Hosea is to be found in the love of God, it is the righteousness and justice of God that are central to the message of Amos. And whereas Hosea may have been the more profound theologian, Amos perceived more clearly the social implications of the faith of Israel. The two books should be studied concurrently, for taken together they provide a balanced and broad perspective on the theology of the classical Hebrew prophets.

AMOS, THE MAN AND THE PROPHET

As with the Book of Hosea, so in the Book of Amos we are provided with a certain amount of biographical information about the prophet himself. The name *Amos* (literally "load, burden") is used of no other person in the Old Testament, nor is the prophet referred to beyond the confines of the book named after him; we are thus entirely dependent on the nine short chapters of the book in garnering all the information that has survived concerning this remarkable prophet.

His home was a place called Tekoa, situated in the southern kingdom of Judah. The word *Tekoa* designated both a village and a territory. The village was located some twelve miles south of

Jerusalem, and the territory extended from there some twenty miles eastward, to the northwestern shores of the Dead Sea. While the village of Tekoa (which survives in the name of the modern Arab village, Tekua) was at an elevation of more than 2,700 feet above sea level, the wilderness of Tekoa sank some 4,000 feet to the east, into the great rift filled by the Dead Sea. It was a formidable region, a "waste and howling wilderness". More than any other modern writer, that distinguished Scottish geographer and biblical scholar, Sir George Adam Smith, captured the atmosphere of the place:

> When you climb the hill of Tekoa, and, looking east, see those fifteen miles of chaos, sinking to a stretch of the Dead Sea, you begin to understand the influence of the desert on Jewish imagination and literature. It gave the ancient natives of Judaea, as it gives the visitor of today, the sense of living next door to doom; the sense of how narrow is the border between life and death; the awe of the power of God, who can make contiguous regions so opposite in character. The desert is always in the face of the prophets, and its howling of beasts and dry sand blow mournfully across their pages the foreboding of doom.

> (From *The Historical Geography of the Holy Land*, 1894)

This was the place of Amos' home and work, and one suspects, from the substance and shape of his writings, that it profoundly influenced the prophet's perception and vision.

Despite the substance of the book, Amos protests that he was neither a prophet nor a prophet's son (7:14). He meant, in part, that he was neither a full-time prophet, nor a professional prophet, as others were. In fact, we are told three things about his normal professional pursuits. (i) He was a *shepherd* (1:1), though the Hebrew word thus translated is not the common word for *shepherd*. It designated, rather, someone who was in the sheep-business, who owned or managed large flocks of sheep. (ii) He was also a *cattleman* (again, a rare Hebrew word is used in 7:14), probably having responsibility for large herds in addition to flocks. (iii) And he was a fruit-farmer of sorts, growing and harvesting a rather bitter fruit from a type of fig-mulberry tree that grew in the vicinity of the Dead Sea, in eastern Tekoa (7:14). Amos, in other words, was involved in mixed farming; and it was probably the demands of business that took him on travels from his home in Tekoa to the northern state of Israel. It was in Israel, not Judah, that he functioned briefly as a prophet.

The details of his prophetic ministry remain somewhat obscure, as does the time of his vocation. It is possible that his entire ministry as a prophet lasted for only a week or two, more likely a little longer, perhaps if 1:1 is interpreted in a certain way, two years. But in trying to come to grips with Amos, the prophet, we should see him first and foremost as a layman, indeed a businessman, who for a short period of his life was called on to serve as a prophet in what was, for him, a foreign country. He brought with him to his task not only the strength of character shaped by his native Tekoa, but also a clear perception of Israelite society which few native residents could have obtained. And in the performance of his duties, he was a man of obedience to the divine call and resolute courage in the face of opposition.

THE MESSAGE OF AMOS

The preaching of the prophet Amos is dominated by his aware-ness of the righteousness and justice of God. When he visited Israel, in the north, he perceived a country which was, on the surface at least, strong in economic and military terms. There was no shortage of money; law and order appeared to rule in society. But Amos had the capacity to see beneath the surface. He knew that the true health of a society could not be measured merely in the terms of economic prosperity, but must be assessed from the moral pulse of the nation. And in moral terms, he perceived a nation on the verge of collapse, with great gulfs separating the rich from the poor, merchants from customers, priests from people, and judges from the innocent accused. Power and wealth were in the hands of a few, and the populace was oppressed and exploited.

His analysis of the social sickness inherent in Israel's society prompted inevitably the declaration of divine judgment. Any society that had departed so far from the fundamental norms of justice, that had abandoned so radically the covenant precepts of its own constitution, invited by its every action the intervention and judgment of the righteous God of Covenant. And thus, at a cursory reading, the Book of Amos is a gloomy work, constantly shadowed by the clouds of judgment. Yet the real gloom lies not in the proclamation of judgment, but rather in the social evils that invited, indeed demanded, such judgment. Justice is not only essential to the proper functioning of human society, but is also required by God.

The social evils in Israel were compounded by the hypocritical veneer of religion with which the perpetrators of social injustice sought to veil their acts. Thus we find in Amos not only a critique of social injustice, but also a scathing assault on formal religion that has lost its heart and become little more than a shell of hypocrisy.

There is only a little by way of positive hope in the Book of Amos; it is expressed in a short passage at the end of the book (9:11–15), which many scholars do not consider to be authentic to the prophet. The doubt is extended by some to the less positive hope expressed in the immediately preceding verses (8c–10). Whether the book ends in gloom, or with a flicker of hope, it was to other prophets that the full development of a future hope was left. Yet perhaps the saddest aspect of the Book of Amos is not the tone of doom throughout its pages, but the perennial relevance of its message beyond its own world and time. For human society in the modern world has changed very little from that which Amos encountered, and his message continues to speak to each succeeding generation with the same immediate relevance and urgency.

THE LORD ROARS

Amos 1:1–2

[1]The words of Amos, who was among the shepherds of Tekoa, which he saw concerning Israel in the days of Uzziah king of Judah and in the

days of Jeroboam the son of Joash, king of Israel, two years before the earthquake. ²And he said:
"The Lord roars from Zion,
    and utters his voice from Jerusalem;
the pastures of the shepherds mourn,
    and the top of Carmel withers."

The book begins, in a manner common to the prophetic works, with some introductory information; these first two verses are the equivalent to the title page and preface in a modern book. They provide the information which will set the appropriate perspective within which to read the chapters that follow: we are told about the key figure in the book, Amos, about the time in which he served as a prophet, and about the essential message.

(i) *Amos, the "prophet"*. The key figure in the book is Amos; we will be told a little more about him in 7:14–15, but here just enough is stated to set the stage. He is not technically described as a prophet; indeed, later on he will deny any professional status of prophethood. Here he is described simply as one of the shepherds of Tekoa (see further the Introduction), a person engaged in the agricultural and farming world. Amos is a layman, not one employed in ministry as a professional.

He is, nevertheless, one who is engaged in ministry, for the words which he speaks constitute a message from God. He will talk about that "which he saw concerning Israel"; although these words could describe visionary experience, in this context they are more general. Amos will speak his God-given word concerning what he has seen of Israel and its relationship to the Lord. And it should be noted that he will speak "concerning Israel"; as a Judean, he will speak as a foreigner in the state of Israel, giving them a message that would be unpopular at the best of times, and exceptionally difficult for a foreigner to deliver in an alien land.

Amos thus illustrates, from the very beginning of the book named after him, one of the forms of vocation. He is a man called to serve God, but from a human point of view his background and circumstances are hardly ideal. There were lots of professional prophets around, no doubt well trained for the task, but the onus of this particular ministry fell upon Amos, an amateur. There were numerous nationals, surely, who could have been called on to minister, but a foreigner is given the job. A search committee, charged with nominating a person to serve as prophet in Israel, would hardly have chosen Amos, but God did choose him. And Amos must have been quick to see the problems, but he had been called, and so he responded in obedience.

(ii) *The date and circumstances*. The historical period is speci- fied by reference to the reigns of two kings: Uzziah, king of Judah (783–742 B.C.) and Jeroboam II, king of Israel (786–746 B.C.). This general period in the history of the chosen people was one marked by the external signs of success: prosperity, a degree of peace between nations, and continuity in the governments of Israel and Judah. But the calm on the surface of Israel's life belied the nation's inner health. All was not well in matters of justice and humanity, as the prophet's preaching will make clear.

The date is further specified by reference to a catastrophe in the natural world. Amos ministered "two years before the earth- quake." The phrase may mean that the prophet had a short ministry which took place two years before the earthquake; alternatively, the implication may be that the ministry extended over the period of two years prior to the earthquake (see RSV footnote: *during [the] two years*).

Earthquakes were not unknown in the territory occupied by the states of Israel and Judah, a consequence of the geological formation of the land around the great rift of the Jordan Valley and the Dead Sea. The historian Josephus informs us that there was a great earthquake in that part of the world in 31 B.C., which culminated in the death of some 30,000 people. Evidence of that earthquake was found in the cracked walls and cisterns of the community buildings at Qumran, on the west flank of the Dead Sea, which were excavated some twenty years ago. Other than the biblical information, we do not have hard data on the earth- quake referred to in Amos. Yet it was clearly a terrible event, perhaps resulting in thousands of deaths; several centuries later, it is still recalled vividly by the prophet Zechariah (14:5).

The reference to the earthquake, however, is probably in- tended to imply more than chronology. In his preaching, Amos alludes to the divine use of earthquakes as a form of judgment (see 8:8 and 9:1–6). Thus, in the beginning of the book, reference is made to a prophetic ministry *before* the earthquake; the event itself, when it actually happened, proved to be a sign that the citizens of Israel had paid little attention to the message of Amos.

(iii) *The message of Amos.* The prophet's message is given in summary form in verse 3, which contains a quotation of the prophetic words. The essence of his ministry will be this: "the Lord roars from Zion" (verse 2). The verb *roars* is a strange one to use with God as its subject, and there has been much debate as to the precise significance of the word. The immediate sense is illuminated by one of the prophet's own metaphors: "the lion has roared; who will not fear?" (3:8). The message which the prophet will declare, in other words, will not contain the pastoral cadences of words from the divine Shepherd; rather, it will ring with terror. The words will contain the tone of ferocity and terrifying strength. And, as any will know who have heard lions roaring in the quiet hours of the night, the divine words will send a tingle of fear down the spines of those who hear them.

Amos' status as a foreign prophet emerges clearly in these summary words. The Lord roars from *"Zion"*, his voice is from *"Jerusalem"*, the two terms being synonymous in context. Only a foreign prophet in Israel would speak this way, referring to the capital city of Judah and its Temple in Jerusalem; again, the words are hardly designed to elicit warm support from northern audiences, but they would certainly have made people listen. And when the people listened, they would not like what they heard, for there was to be little cheer in Amos' message. Drawing metaphors from pastoral and natural settings (verse 2*b*), the prophet indicates that a drought is coming. It is probably not a literal drought of which he speaks, but rather a drying up of the wellsprings of spiritual and social life in the northern kingdom.

And so the book of Amos begins on a note which is both informative and intimidating. It is infomative with respect to time and place, and the ministry of the prophet which is about to begin. It is intimidating by virtue of its intimation of the character of the message which will follow: "The Lord roars from Zion".

THE DEEDS OF DAMASCUS

Amos 1:3–5

³Thus says the Lord:
"For three transgressions of Damascus,
   and for four, I will not revoke the punishment;
because they have threshed Gilead
   with threshing sledges of iron.
⁴So I will send a fire upon the house of Hazael,
   and it shall devour the strongholds of Ben-hadad.
⁵I will break the bar of Damascus,
   and cut off the inhabitants from the Valley of Aven,
and him that holds the sceptre from Beth-eden;
   and the people of Syria shall go into exile to Kir,"

                    says the Lord.

The first example we are given of the prophet's preaching is contained in a long passage extending from 1:3 to the end of chapter 2. It is probable that this extensive passage should be viewed not only as the introductory passage in the book, but also as the inaugural message in the prophet's ministry. As we read through this larger section, we are being afforded an insight into the beginning of Amos' prophetic work. And if we are to grasp its power we must imagine that, like the prophet's first audience, we have never heard of this man before and we are curious to know what he has to say.

The entire section (1:3–2:16) is comprised of a series of oracles, or messages, addressed to various nations and peoples. Although each oracle is self-contained with respect to its message, the effect of the prophet's preaching emerges from the collection as a whole and the sequence in which they are delivered. There cannot be certainty as to whether 1:3–2:16 was delivered originally as a single address or a series of addresses; in either case, we must attempt to perceive the impact of the whole section on the prophet's audience, and especially of the final oracle addressed to Israel (2:6–16).

Each of the messages is structured in a similar fashion. It begins with the prophetic formula: "Thus says the Lord". That is fol-

lowed by a stereotyped expression, "for three transgressions...for four..."; the expression is poetic, and despite the
numbers, usually only one transgression is stated explicitly. The
expression of condemnation is followed by a statement of coming
judgment and concludes with another prophetic formula: "says
the Lord."

The first message is addressed to Damascus, here representing
Israel's neighbouring state on its northern border. The crime of
Damascus is that of having "threshed Gilead with threshing
sledges of iron" (verse 3). The language is metaphorical; the
threshing sledge, in the ancient world, was a heavy wooden
sledge with iron protrusions on its base. It was dragged by oxen
across the cut harvest, separating thereby the grain from the
chaff. The metaphor implies cruel treatment by the armies of
Damascus toward the citizens of Gilead, a region in northern
Transjordan that belonged traditionally to Israel. The prophet
was alluding no doubt to a recent historical event, well known to
his audience, in which a newly powerful Damascus had invaded
Israel's territory and committed atrocities.

For such inhumane action, Damascus would be judged and
punished. Its royal household would be destroyed, its reign terminated, and its citizens would leave their homes for foreign
exile. Some years later, after the prophet's ministry, the Assyrian
emperor, Tiglath-Pileser III, recorded in his "Annals":

I destroyed 592 towns of the 16 districts
of the country of Damascus, rendering them
like hills over which the flood had passed.

The passage of time turned Amos' words into a terrible reality.
But if we are to grasp their primary significance, we must think of
them in terms of the people who first heard the spoken message.

(i) Initially, the prophet's message would be well received.
Amos may have been a foreigner in Israel, but his opening words
would be heard with delight in a nation where little love was lost
for Damascus. Damascus was a neighbour to Israel, but also an
enemy. And the events in Gilead had fanned the flames of hate
for a neighbour that flickered perpetually. So Amos is off to a

good start; if he continues in this fashion, he may well become a star in the dim heaven of Israel's prophets. It is his intention to win approval at the beginning of the speech, though neither the audience nor the reader understands yet what is the prophet's ultimate purpose.

(ii) One of the most fundamental of Amos' assumptions becomes clear in this opening prophecy. It is that his God is Lord not only of the chosen people, but also of the world's gentile nations. Amos, an alien prophet in a northern land, has no parochial conception of God in his mind; all the world's nations stand responsible before God for what they have done. The deeds of Damascus, no less than those of the chosen people, fall within the divine purview.

As we read the later prophets, we will see that this international vision became the common property of the prophetic tradition. But Amos was among the pioneers of this wide-ranging theology. He grasped the notion of a God who could not be confined, whose power was not limited to a particular people in a particular place; the Lord of Israel was the God of the nations. And yet we may too easily accept such thinking as a commonplace, without having grasped it for ourselves. The vision of God common at that time was restricted to the chosen people and their nations; it was not so much wrong as inadequate. And just as easily we can confine God to the Church, shrinking the deity into conformity with moulds of our little minds. Amos would have us break the moulds and see a larger vision of God.

(iii) God's hatred, as expressed here, is directed especially against the sins of cruelty. The actions of Damascus in Gilead, referred to only in metaphor, had betrayed no concern for human life. It is at first curious that the prophet does not condemn the invasion as such, but only the behaviour of the invaders. And yet the condemnation reaches immediately to the heart of the matter. The possession of territory passes back and forth among the nations of the world, but in the last resort territory is less important than the way in which people and nations act towards one another.

From the time of Amos to the twentieth century, territorial struggles have continued. No doubt, from the mundane perspective of human politics, many of the territorial struggles have been legitimate ones. But nothing can justify the abandonment of esteem for human life; nothing can vindicate the acts of cruelty perpetrated in the name of territory. Life is more valuable than land, love is of more worth than a plot of earthly soil. And the words of Amos remind us vividly of the wrath of God against all who espouse the ideals of terrorism and cruelty.

THE MESSAGE TO GAZA AND TYRE

Amos 1:6–10

6Thus says the Lord:
"For three transgressions of Gaza,
  and for four, I will not revoke the punishment;
because they carried into exile a whole people
  to deliver them up to Edom.
7So I will send a fire upon the wall of Gaza,
  and it shall devour her strongholds.
8I will cut off the inhabitants from Ashdod,
  and him that holds the sceptre from Ashkelon;
I will turn my hand against Ekron;
  and the remnant of the Philistines shall perish,"

says the Lord God.

9Thus says the Lord:
"For three transgressions of Tyre,
  and for four, I will not revoke the punishment;
because they delivered up a whole people to Edom,
  and did not remember the covenant of brotherhood.
10So I will send a fire upon the wall of Tyre,
  and it shall devour her strongholds."

After damning Damascus, Amos now turns his attention to two other states, Gaza and Tyre. Gaza was a city, though here it represents the small Philistine state in the southeastern corner of the Mediterranean, situated between Egypt and the promised land. Tyre, a great coastal port on the eastern Mediterranean, was a Phoenician city-state, situated to the northwest of Israel. These two states now become the focus of the divine words of complaint and judgment delivered by the prophet.

The complaints laid against each of these small states are virtually identical, with only minor variation in the wording. Both states had been responsible for engaging in the slave trade, for selling people "to Edom" (verses 6–9), either to serve there in Edom as slaves, or to be traded in Edom onto the international slave market. Although it is not specifically stated, the condemnation implies a "raiding" technique, where small military bands raided an unprotected village and carried off "a whole people" (viz. the entire population) to be sold as slaves.

Both states were ideally located to promote such inhumane activity and both states had sufficient power to carry it out. Gaza, which has been called "the outpost of Africa, the door of Asia", was a great trading centre, straddling the north-south trade routes between Egypt and Palestine, and east-west trade routes between Edom in the interior and the Mediterranean Sea. And the citizens of Gaza and its neighbouring cities were the Philistines, who since early in the biblical period had been noted for their military strength.

Tyre was a wealthy and powerful city-state on the Mediterranean coast about a hundred miles northwest of Jerusalem. The city itself was divided in two, one part on the mainland, and one part on a small rocky island just off-shore; the capacity of the city to resist military threat gave it great self-confidence in the world of nations (see also Ezek. 26:1–28:10). And even later in the course of history, Tyre was known for its trade in slaves (Ezek. 27:13).

These two states, because of their active participation in the trading of human slaves, would suffer God's judgment. The Philistine cities and their inhabitants would perish; Tyre would be ravaged by fire. (Only a few years later, Gaza and the Philistine cities were to suffer the same fate as Israel, being overrun by the Assyrians in 732 B.C. Gaza was rebuilt, then destroyed again in 720 B.C. Indeed, the history of Gaza is one of resilience and destruction. During World War I, General Alenby's troops bombarded Gaza; when they entered the city on November 7, 1917, they found it a ruin. And in more recent conflicts between Israel and Egypt, "the Gaza Strip" has been a frequent field of violence. Tyre, on the other hand, was to survive longer than did Gaza after the time of Amos. Despite numerous setbacks and attacks, particularly on the mainland part of the town, Tyre did not finally fall until the time of Alexander the Great in the fourth century B.C. Perhaps ironically, after Alexander's capture of the city in 332 B.C., 30,000 of Tyre's inhabitants were sold as slaves.)

Slavery and trading in slaves, so powerfully condemned in these divine oracles, seem to be as old as human history. And although in the western world we like to think of slavery as a thing of the past, it was a part of our history until very recently. Even in our own century, it continues to be present. In the United Nations "Declaration of Human Rights" (1948) a provision was made prohibiting slaves and slave-trading. And again in 1956, the United Nations adopted a convention on the abolition of slavery. But the United Nations has condemned wars, and wars are still with us; likewise, the noble conventions have not done away with slavery, though the trade and practice are less evident than they used to be.

Yet we miss part of the prophet's thrust if we think only of the legal and technical aspects of slavery. Amos is concerned with fundamental aspects of human behaviour and human rights. He condemned Damascus, in the first oracle, for cruelty. He condemns Gaza and Tyre for their unconscionable trading in human liberty. The freedom of others was held by them to be of no value in the pursuit of profit and power. And, in principle, any human activity which seeks its own gain and advancement through the curtailing of the liberty of our fellow human beings falls under the same divine condemnation declared so forcefully by Amos against Gaza and Tyre.

EDOM AND AMMON

Amos 1:11–15

[11]Thus says the Lord:
"For three transgressions of Edom,

and for four, I will not revoke the punishment;
because he pursued his brother with the sword,
and cast off all pity,
and his anger tore perpetually,
and he kept his wrath for ever.
[12]So I will send a fire upon Teman,
and it shall devour the strongholds of Bozrah."

[13]Thus says the Lord:
"For three transgressions of the Ammonites,
and for four, I will not revoke the punishment;
because they have ripped up women with child in Gilead,
that they might enlarge their border.
[14]So I will kindle a fire in the wall of Rabbah,
and it shall devour her strongholds,
with shouting in the day of battle,
with a tempest in the day of the whirlwind;
[15]and their king shall go into exile,
he and his princes together,"

says the Lord.

The prophet's panoramic survey of the evil of nations continues. Having disposed of Gaza and Tyre, both lying on the Mediterranean coast, Amos now turns his attention to two nations lying to the east of the great rift valley containing the Jordan and the Dead Sea, namely Edom and Ammon. Edom lay to the east and south of the Dead Sea, between the Arabah and the great desert of the interior. Ammon lay further to the north, directly to the east of Israel's territory and beyond the River Jordan. As with the previous nations referred to in the prophet's international survey, these two states are condemned for crimes against humanity.

(i) Edom is condemned for acts of cruelty, undertaken in anger, against people for whom ties of kinship should have been felt. According to the ancient biblical traditions, the Edomites were the descendants of Esau, Jacob's twin brother; thus, in theory at least, a degree of humanity should have marked Edom's behaviour toward the chosen people. But apparently such was not the case. We do not know precisely which incident the prophet refers to in verse 11, for there was a long history of animosity between Edom and both Israel and Judah. (See further the Book of Obadiah, immediately following Amos, in which the entire prophetic message is directed against Edom.)

Because of the cruelty and bloodlust of the Edomites in the pursuit of their "brother" (viz. the Israelites), a fire of judgment would overwhelm the great cities of Edom, namely Teman and Bozrah. After the prophet's time, Edom was to be conquered by the Assyrians and to pay tribute to the emperor, Tiglath-Pileser III. Still later, in the fifth century B.C., the Edomites were totally conquered and evicted from their traditional homeland by the Nabateans, who invaded from the desert.

The crime of Edom, as specified here, has three distinct dimensions to it.

(a) *Cruelty*. Edom cast off all restraint and abandoned pity in its use of the sword against enemies. The Edomites exemplified the dehumanizing process that is an inevitable consequence of the perpetual pursuit of war and violence. Ordinary people, their morals and pity stunted by the context of conflict, abandon themselves to the urges of cruelty that lie deep within the human heart. The actions of the Edomites have been repeated in every century of human conflict; such cruelty has been practised, by both partners in warfare, throughout two world wars in our own century and in the numerous wars since 1945, as the abundant literature on war so abundantly demonstrates. And yet the prophet's condemnation of cruelty is as much an indictment of all war and violence, for it is in the pursuit of warfare that there are released in human behaviour the demons of cruelty.

(b) *Fratricide*. The Edomites are condemned for the pursuit of a "brother". In the immediate context of the message, the allusion is to ancient links between Edom and Israel. But in the larger context, we perceive that all human cruelty has a dimension of fratricide to it. All human beings, all men and women, are linked by a common bond of humanity; all are the offspring of God. And the exercise of cruelty against a fellow human being breaks the bond of common humanity and is ultimately a crime against the Creator of all mankind.

(c) *Anger*. "Anger is a short madness," the Latin poet Horace wrote in his first volume of *Epistles*, but it is of the long and cherished forms of anger that Amos speaks. Edom "kept his wrath for ever" (verse 11). And a carefully preserved wrath is a reservoir of poison. It destroys generation after generation, injecting its venomous love of violence and cruelty into the children of the future, so that the world will never know peace. And that which Amos so roundly condemned must still be condemned. The legacy of anger holds no promise for the future. The nation or people that retains its identity and goals only by fanning the flames of anger creates its own joyless future. No less, the individual who daily stokes the fires of anger within invites inevitably the devouring fire of God (verse 12); only the rediscovery of mercy can quench the fires of anger, and only the experience of forgiveness can avert the flames of destruction.

(ii) Ammon's sin was also one of gross and inhuman acts (verse 13). In marauding bands, the Ammonites invaded the neighbouring lands of Gilead. There they committed atrocities, ripping open the bellies of pregnant women and slaughtering both mother and unborn child. It would be comforting, perhaps, if the language could be interpreted in a metaphorical manner, but it should probably be interpreted literally. The Assyrian Emperor, Tiglath-Pileser I, had been praised by his chroniclers in the eleventh century B.C. for the ruthless murder of pregnant women and the children of their wombs. Indeed, only a few years after the ministry of Amos, an Israelite king, Menahem, was to commit the same terrible crime (2 Kings 15:16). The act was criminal even by the most minimal standards of human decency, but it was an act employed with a ruthless military purpose. Not only were the enemy killed, but the next generation was in part eliminated, and such would be the terror following these acts that women would fear to become pregnant.

Rabbah, the nation's capital, would be burned down for this crime, and the king and princes of the nation would go into exile.

Amos declares God's judgment and total opposition to the heartless acts of the Ammonites.

Ammon's sin, like that of Edom, is an example of mankind's inhumanity to fellow human beings. And yet, for all the horror of Edom's acts, those of Ammon are even more reprehensible. They employed their violence against the defenceless and the unborn. And for all the macho bragging with which they must have celebrated their violent deeds, those Ammonites have survived in history as the exemplars of cowardice. Upon those without defence, they raised their bloodthirsty swords. And Amos is convinced that such cowards must stand under the judgment of God.

MOAB AND JUDAH

Amos 2:1–5

¹Thus says the Lord:
  'For three transgressions of Moab,
    and for four, I will not revoke the punishment;
  because he burned to lime
    the bones of the king of Edom.
²So I will send a fire upon Moab,
    and it shall devour the strongholds of Kerioth,
  and Moab shall die amid uproar,
    amid shouting and the sound of the trumpet;
³I will cut off the ruler from its midst,
    and will slay all its princes with him,"

                       says the Lord.

⁴Thus says the Lord:
  "For three transgressions of Judah,
    and for four, I will not revoke the punishment;
  because they have rejected the law of the Lord,
    and have not kept his statutes,
  but their lies have led them astray,
    after which their fathers walked.
⁵So I will send a fire upon Judah,
    and it shall devour the strongholds of Jerusalem."

(i) The crime of Moab consisted in the desecration of the remains of the dead. Moab was a small state lying to the east of the Dead Sea; its neighbour, immediately to the south, was the state of Edom (see 1:11–12), and from time to time there was war between the two states. The prophet knew no doubt of a recent war or raid of Moab into the territory of Edom (Amos' home in the territory of Tekoa looked across the Dead Sea to the shores of Moab). During this battle, the Moabites had broken open the tomb of a former king of Edom and burned his bones, turning them into lime. (Although the language is poetic, it is nevertheless descriptive, the calcium in the human bones being turned, by burning, into lime, or calcium oxide.)

Compared with the other crimes described in these chapters, that of Moab may seem at first to be relatively harmless. After all, one cannot do damage to the dead, and the king whose bones were burned had long since left this life. And yet, for all our modern standards of judgment, the actions of the Moabites must be viewed as a reprehensible crime, its effect being upon the living, not the dead. We know from various archaeological excavations, for example those at Ras Shamra and Tell Mardikh in Syria, that particular care was taken of the remains of the dead. In the ancient cities of Ugarit (modern Ras Shamra) and Ebla (modern Tell Mardikh), the kings had special areas of burial, their tombs linked to great mortuary palaces by means of tunnels. And the care and worship of deceased kings seems to have played a significant role in these ancient religions.

Thus we begin to see that the crime of Moab was something like what we would call sacrilege. It was, on the one hand, the destruction of the bones of the deceased; on the other hand, it was the destruction of objects held sacred and precious in the eyes of the Edomites. It was a wanton crime: it reaped no benefits for Moab, but simply increased the agony of defeat for Edom. It desecrated that which they held sacred.

This oracle, coming from the mouth of a Hebrew prophet, is particularly interesting for the light it sheds on Amos' view of foreign faith. Clearly the prophet must have viewed the Edomites not only as pagans, but as violent people (1:11–12). Yet they were, nevertheless, human beings; both their dead kings and their own feelings of faith deserved a degree of respect. Certainly God could call for judgment on Edom for bloodthirsty deeds (1:12), but Moab had no right thus to behave against their neighbours, the Edomites.

In a way, the crime of Moab illustrates a theme running through all the other crimes specified in these oracles to the nations: it is the total lack of any respect for the lives, feelings and faith of others. And if we are to learn from the ancient oracles, we must learn the value of other lives, their feelings and their faiths, and their value in the eyes of God. It is instructive that, although Amos declares an oracle of judgment against the Edomites, here he vocally proclaims their fundamental privileges as members of the human race.

(ii) Now the prophet comes to an oracle concerning Judah (2:4–5). His Israelite audience, who up to this point must have delighted in the prophet's proclamations of judgment against various foreign enemies, would have had somewhat mixed feelings at this point. On the one hand, their delight would have continued; despite the ties of history and ancestry, there was little love in Israel for the citizens of Judah. And Amos was, after all, a prophet from Judah; the declaration of this oracle against his native country would prove beyond doubt that he was not prejudiced, that he could see fault at home as well as abroad. On the other hand, the new direction in the prophet's preaching must have produced in the audience at least a tweak of anxiety. If Amos could condemn Judah, might he not also have something to say about Israel?

The crime of Judah is specified in verse 4; it is of a quite different kind from the crimes specified for the preceding gentile nations. Judah had rejected the divine *torah*, or "law of the Lord"; the people of Judah had refused to live by the divine imperatives entrusted to them. They exchanged the truth for lies, and then believed their own lies in going far astray from the path in life which God had assigned to them. And so for Judah, as for the other foreign nations, the fire of judgment was declared: even the strongholds of Jerusalem would be devoured (as indeed they were in the war with Babylon, 586/7 B.C.).

At first sight, the crime of Judah seems far less grave than those of the other nations, and therefore the penalty appears excessively harsh. It is not said of the people of Judah that they engaged in the slave trade, that they were excessively cruel, that they slaughtered pregnant women and unborn children, or even that they had committed sacrilegious acts. They had simply "rejected the law of the Lord", an act which, in our modern democratic societies, would be the right and privilege of every person. We live now in an age of freedom of religion, or freedom to have no religion.

But we cannot project back into ancient Judah the ethos of our own age. Judah was a nation of the chosen people. They had been granted great privilege, but also great responsibility. The privilege brought with it a certain freedom, but it was not a freedom to abandon the faith. For they had been called to be a special nation, through whom all the earth's nations should be blessed (Gen. 18:18). And, as Amos' other oracles to the nations so clearly demonstrate, the gentile nations of the world were desperately in need of light; their criminal acts revealed the downward slide of all nations that know nothing of the fundamental principles of justice and righteousness. To these nations, Judah should have stood as a witness, a demonstration of the principles of justice and righteousness, but it had failed. And its failure was both culpable and reprehensible; culpable, because Judah had been given much but had returned nothing, and reprehensible, because the atrocities of the nations must lie in part on the conscience of Judah in its failure to witness to them of the righteousness of God.

The analogy between Judah and the Christian Church is a frightening one. If Judah, through its failure to fulfil its God-given mission, is aligned with those nations who had committed human atrocities, where must the Church be placed in its relation to the world? Insofar as it has failed in its mission, it must surely be aligned with Judah, with Moab, with Ammon and the rest. Which is to say that the Church cannot escape its responsibility for a share in the atrocities of our age, ranging from war to holocaust. It is easy to protest, "We didn't do those things!" And yet the failure in responsibility, the failure to fulfil the calling of God, results inevitably in sharing in the guilt for the evil of our times.

THE EVIL OF ISRAEL

Amos 2:6–16

⁶Thus says the Lord:
"For three transgressions of Israel,
   and for four, I will not revoke the punishment;
because they sell the righteous for silver,
   and the needy for a pair of shoes—
⁷they that trample the head of the poor into the dust of the earth,
   and turn aside the way of the afflicted;
a man and his father go in to the same maiden,
   so that my holy name is profaned;
⁸they lay themselves down beside every altar
   upon garments taken in pledge;
and in the house of their God they drink
   the wine of those who have been fined.

⁹"Yet I destroyed the Amorite before them,
   whose height was like the height of the cedars,
   and who was as strong as the oaks;
I destroyed his fruit above,
   and his roots beneath.
¹⁰Also I brought you up out of the land of Egypt,
   and led you forty years in the wilderness,
   to possess the land of the Amorite.
¹¹And I raised up some of your sons for prophets,
   and some of your young men for Nazirites.
   Is it not indeed so, O people of Israel?"

says the Lord.

¹²"But you made the Nazirites drink wine,
   and commanded the prophets,
   saying, 'You shall not prophesy.'

¹³"Behold, I will press you down in your place,
    as a cart full of sheaves presses down.
¹⁴Flight shall perish from the swift,
    and the strong shall not retain his strength,
    nor shall the mighty save his life;
¹⁵he who handles the bow shall not stand,
    and he who is swift of foot shall not save himself,
    nor shall he who rides the horse save his life;
¹⁶and he who is stout of heart among the mighty
    shall flee away naked in that day,"

says the Lord.

For some time, the prophet's audience has listened with delight as Amos has hammered the nails of judgment into the coffins of neighbouring nations. But now the hammer must fall at home, "for three transgressions of Israel, and for four"; precisely the words that sounded the knell for the nations, now introduce the crime and punishment of the chosen people in the north. Amos has softened his audience by parading before them the sins of others; now they must see and acknowledge their own sins.

The prophet begins by elaborating upon the transgressions of Israel (verses 6–8). He does this in greater detail than he did for the other nations, for he has now arrived at the focal point and purpose of his ministry. The catalogue of crime is followed by a brief rehearsal of God's gracious acts on Israel's behalf, highlighting thereby the ingratitude of the people and the folly of their ways (verses 9–12). The Lord had destroyed the Amorites, Israel's predecessors in the promised land, despite their phenomenal stature and extraordinary strength. Before that, he had freed his people from Egyptian slavery and led them safely through all the trials of the wilderness years. And in addition, he had given to his nation two special groups of people: the Nazirites, whose austere vows held before their fellow citizens the simple faith of former days, and the prophets, through whom the word of God was declared. But even these two groups, whose presence was a sign of God's grace in the community, were set aside. The Nazirites, whose special vows prohibited them from drinking alcoholic beverages (see Num. 6:1–3), were forced to drink liquor. The prophets were banned from speaking in God's name.

And so, of necessity, God's judgment must also fall upon Israel. When judgment came, it would permit no reaction, as the people would be pressed down by its weight. The swift warriors, for all their fleetness of foot, would be unable to escape it; the strength of the strong men would be powerless in the face of judgment's force. With these and similar words (verses 13–16), Amos describes the coming judgment of Israel. And there seems to be a terrible inevitability about it all, for he issues no call to repentance, nor does he reveal any prospect of hope. The inevitability of the judgment and its severity require that we go back toQexamine Israel's crimes (verses 6–8). The nation's transgressionsappear to fall into three distinct, but interrelated, areas.

(i) *The abuse of law.* "They sell the righteous for silver, and the needy for a pair of shoes". On first reading, the words may seem to imply only the general exploitation of the upright poor, but the language employed alludes to something more specific. The *righteous* person, in this context, is the one who, in a court of law, should be declared innocent, or "not guilty". But the courts had been perverted: silver changed hands, from the hands of the rich to those of the corrupt judges, so that the innocent person was declared guilty. And it did not take much to pay off a corrupt judge; the price of a "pair of shoes" (or sandals), in the Hebrew expression, was an idiom for something very cheap (the idiom requires clarification, given the cost of shoes in our own time). Thus, for just a few pennies, the wealthy could divert the course of justice to serve their own cause.

The corruption or integrity of the judiciary, in any country, may serve as an accurate barometer of a nation's inner health. The judiciary exercises real power, but its decisions presuppose truth in the courts and integrity in the character of judges. In Israel, lies were accepted in the courts and the integrity of the judges was for sale; the criteria of justice had been exchanged for motives of personal profit and gain. The abandonment of justice in Israel, which was a state founded by the God of all truth and justice, was the first ground for the coming judgment.

(ii) *The abuse of the poor*. The rich and powerful in Israel trampled "the head of the poor into the dust of the earth" (verse 7). The motives in the exploitation of the poor were the same as those underlying the perversion of the law: personal profit and gain. The rich desired greater wealth, the powerful more power, and to gain their ends all the normal constraints a society establishes to protect its weaker and poorer members were to be cast aside. In the charge toward greater wealth and power, the poor and weak were trampled underfoot.

No doubt Amos, a foreigner in Israel, perceived the true state of Israel's society more clearly than did the nation's own citizens. Living within a society, it is easy to turn a blind eye to what is going on, to accept as normal the perpetual practice of exploitation. But Amos, visiting Israel from the wilderness of Tekoa, saw very clearly the exploitation that marred society in the northern state; not liking what he saw, he denounced it. This is the second ground upon which judgment must come to Israel.

(iii) *The abuse of religion*. "A man and his father go in to the same maiden". The reference is not to general laxity in sexual mores, nor even to incestuous behaviour of some kind, but rather to the sexual activity associated with the cult of Baal, so abhorred by the prophet Hosea. In the pursuit of the fertility faith, men lay with the temple's prostitutes, abandoning thereby the strictures of their own more ancient faith. And in addition to sexual laxity, they participated in the drunken orgies at the altars of fertility; having left behind the sobriety of the ancient covenant faith, they abandoned themselves to the alcoholic delusions of the false cult. And all this indulgence was perpetrated to the further exploitation of the poor, whose garments were purloined and whose wine offerings were imbibed by the licentious elite of Israel's establishment.

As Amos describes the scene, Israel was a very corrupt society; it is surprising that the locals had not seen its corruption, that it took a foreigner to point it out to them. Yet we are all inclined to a kind of local blindness. We can see poverty in Bombay, but not at home. We like to think of the abuse of power in the Soviet Union, but think that it does not exist in our nation. And perversion of the true faith is always more evident in other denominations or religions than it is in our own. But worst of all, we can always detect abuses in the actions of others more easily than we can in our own actions. Amos held up a mirror to Israel, so that they could see their own society and their own image and he asked: "Is it not indeed so, O people of Israel?" (verse 11). And if we are to learn from the oracles of Amos, we must let his words serve as a looking glass for our own lives.

"THE LORD HAS SPOKEN"

Amos 3:1–8

[1]Hear this word that the Lord has spoken against you, O people of Israel, against the whole family which I brought up out of the land of Egypt:
[2]"You only have I known
  of all the families of the earth;
 therefore I will punish you
  for all your iniquities.

[3]"Do two walk together,
  unless they have made an appointment?
[4]Does a lion roar in the forest,
  when he has no prey?
 Does a young lion cry out from his den,
  if he has taken nothing?
[5]Does a bird fall in a snare on the earth,
  when there is no trap for it?
 Does a snare spring up from the ground,
  when it has taken nothing?
[6]Is a trumpet blown in a city,
  and the people are not afraid?
 Does evil befall a city,
  unless the Lord has done it?
[7]Surely the Lord God does nothing,
  without revealing his secret
  to his servants the prophets.
[8]The lion has roared;

who will not fear?
The Lord God has spoken;
who can but prophesy?"

We move now to the second main section of the book of Amos, chapters 3–6. Unlike the first section (chapters 1–2), in which a degree of thematic unity was provided by the collection of oracles addressed to various nations, the second section is somewhat less cohesive. It is a collection of oracles or prophetic sayings, many of which may be preserved only in summary form; taken together, these chapters provide in outline form the main themes of Amos' ministry.

The first eight verses contain two messages, perhaps initially independent: (a) verses 1–2, and (b) verses 3–8. Each message provides, from a different perspective, the background and purpose to the prophet's work. They are addressed to the audience in Israel to elicit from them a recognition of why it is that Amos must prophesy and what is to be the substance of his prophecies.

(i) *Israel's election.* The people of Israel, to whom Amos speaks, are described as "the whole family which I brought up out of the land of Egypt" (verse 1). The brief clause summarizes an entire history of divine liberation and purpose. The people who, long ago, had been slaves in a foreign country, with no future set out before them, had been liberated from that slavery and led out from that alien land. This extraordinary act of mercy had taken place because God had "known" Israel in a special way (verse 2a); that is, his special love and his election of this people had resulted in a particular act of mercy.

For all the words of grace running through the opening oracle, it ends nevertheless in a peculiar way: "I will punish you for all your iniquities" (verse 2b). The force of the words is seen in the context. God's choice of Israel implied not so much privilege, as purpose. The nation's past did not give it a licence to sin, but imposed a special imperative to live in righteousness. Thus the prophetic declaration of God's impending punishment of Israel's sin is made all the more dramatic by setting it in the context of Israel's privileged past. Israel had accepted the privilege, but had ignored the purpose in its redemption. And thus Amos the prophet is sent to declare the beginning of a new chapter in the history of God's dealings with Israel.

In his teaching on masters and servants, Jesus enunciated clearly the principle which is implicit in the prologue to Amos' preaching: "Every one to whom much is given, of him will much be required" (Luke 12:48). A great deal had been given to Israel: redemption from slavery, a special relationship with God, and a new land. The great gift implied great requirements: to love and to serve God, to be a holy nation, to represent God's righteousness amongst the nations of the world. But none of these requirements had been met, in the prophet's view; only the nation's iniquities could be clearly seen. And therefore he must announce the coming of judgment.

It was not easy for Israel to grasp that its election implied God's purpose and its own responsibility; the sense of privilege emerging from the past had an anaesthetic effect, dulling the senses and blunting the will to service. It is no more easy for the Church and its membership to escape from Israel's bind. The awareness of redemption from past bondage, the privilege of relationship with God, the gift of a "new land" in our human lives, all these things (signs of grace in and of themselves) may so swell the pride of privilege that the sense of responsibility is lost. But "to whom much is given, of him will much be required."

(ii) *The prophet's vocation.* The second introductory message (verses 3–8) demonstrates the cause-and-effect character of the vocation of Amos. The prophet employs a series of illustrations, the majority drawn from the world of nature with which his country background had made him so familiar, each illustrating the *linkage* between certain kinds of events. His language is rhetorical and persuasive, rather than philosophical and logical. When two people walk together (in the dangerous wilderness may be implied), they do so because they have made an appointment. The fierce roar of the lion in the forest indicates it has pounced on its prey. With these and other illustrations, Amos presses the relation between causes and effects. All the illustrations would be readily acknowledged by his audience; the bird does not fall snared to the ground unless a trap has been set. And indeed the prophet's purpose is to gain the acknowledgment of his audience with respect to the simple illustrations, so that they will also see his point at the end. The climax is this: "the Lord has spoken; who can but prophesy?" (verse 8).

As the lion's roar naturally causes fear in those who hear, so the Lord's speech necessarily requires that Amos declare it as a prophet. But the prophetic saying is not simply a dispassionate statement; there are undertones of terror echoing in his words. The lion's roar evokes fear, implying that God's word will also be frightening. And one of the illustrations of cause and effect, apparently placed harmlessly in the sequence of illustrations, is foreboding of danger: "Does evil befall a city, unless the Lord has done it?" The simple analogies from the world of nature are suddenly made more serious by an example that demonstrates the sovereignty of God over nations and cities.

But the most striking part of this second portion from the introduction to the prophet's preaching is the implied simplicity of Amos' response to God's calling. That is not to say that the man may not have engaged in a deep personal struggle when he heard God's call, though of this we know nothing. All we know is that God called, and Amos answered; God spoke, and Amos declared the word of the Lord. In this, Amos has become an exemplar of the proper and obedient response to all vocation.

THE SINS OF SAMARIA

Amos 3:9–15

⁹Proclaim to the strongholds in Assyria,
  and to the strongholds in the land of Egypt,
 and say, "Assemble yourselves upon the mountains of Samaria,
  and see the great tumults within her,
   and the oppressions in her midst."
¹⁰"They do not know how to do right," says the Lord,
   "those who store up violence and robbery in their strongholds."
¹¹Therefore thus says the Lord God:

"An adversary shall surround the land,
  and bring down your defences from you,
and your strongholds shall be plundered."

[12]Thus says the Lord: "As the shepherd rescues from the mouth of the lion two legs, or a piece of an ear, so shall the people of Israel who dwell in Samaria be rescued, with the corner of a couch and part of a bed."

[13]"Hear, and testify against the house of Jacob,"
  says the Lord God, the God of hosts,
[14]"that on the day I punish Israel for his transgressions,
  I will punish the altars of Bethel,
and the horns of the altar shall be cut off
  and fall to the ground.
[15]I will smite the winter house with the summer house;
  and the houses of ivory shall perish,
and the great houses shall come to an end,"

says the Lord.

Samaria was the capital city of the northern state of Israel; it had been built by King Omri, and by Ahab his successor, in the ninth century B.C. The city was built on a hill, rising some 300 feet above the level of the surrounding plain, and the plain in turn was encircled by further hills. Encompassing the city were the great fortification walls, within which the splendid palaces constructed by Omri and Ahab were located. It was a city that impressed upon its visitors both power and wealth, but when Amos came to the capital of Israel, he saw it in a different light. We have three of his messages, in summary and condensed form, in these verses, each providing us with different insights on the prophet's preaching in the city of Samaria.

(i) *The strongholds of Samaria* (verses 9–11). In the manner of a king sending heralds to a foreign country, Amos speaks as if he were sending messengers to Egypt and Assyria. (Note: the Hebrew text reads *Ashdod*, a Philistine town near the border with Egypt; RSV, in translating *Assyria*, follows the Septuagint, or Greek version. Ashdod is the more probable reading, for Amos has already referred to that city, but makes no other reference to Assyria.) The figurative messengers are specifically sent to the *strongholds* of these foreign lands and there they make their proclamation: the garrisons of distant strongholds are invited to assemble on the hills around the plain of Samaria, there to witness an extraordinary scene.

The foreign observers examine the stronghold of Samaria; for all its formidable military strength, what they notice are the actions going on within the defensive walls. The inner life of the stronghold of Samaria is one of chaos and disorder. The "great tumults" may be drunken and disorderly orgies of excess. The "oppressions" are no doubt the acts of injustice and exploitation to which Amos has already referred (2:6–8). The archaeological excavations of Samaria have revealed great storehouses in the palace complex; perhaps the prophet mocks these structures in saying that the citizens of Samaria "store up violence and robbery" (verse 10).

The scene is thus one of a great amphitheatre; on stage is the garrison of the stronghold of Samaria, and looking on are the garrisons of foreign forts. What the observers saw must have appalled every ounce of military fibre they possessed, for the great walls of a fortress offered little protection if there was rottenness within the ramparts. And then the scene played out on the stage of the amphitheatre is interrupted: a voice declares (and it is God's voice) that the land would be surrounded, the defences brought down, and the stronghold plundered.

It is a dramatic scene, painted in words, of a city prepared for the enemy without, not knowing that the true enemy lies within. And the enemy within so weakens the heart of the city that, ironically, it will be unable to withstand the assault of the enemy outside. The words are addressed to Samaria's leaders simply as a declaration of coming collapse; no call for repentance is stated, though it is implied by the very presence and ministry of the prophet. But his words serve as a warning to examine all our strongholds. Great walls offer no protection if the lives of those within are weakened with corruption.

(ii) *Samaria ravaged* (verse 12). The previous declaration that strongholds would be plundered is now strengthened by a further statement indicating the totality of the city's collapse.

Drawing upon the experience of his life in the sheep business, Amos employs a startling simile to indicate the completeness of the coming destruction of Samaria. He would have had numerous shepherds looking after his sheep in the grazing lands of Tekoa, and each shepherd would have been accountable for the specific number of sheep entrusted to his care. If a sheep were lost, it must be accounted for. And in particular, if a sheep were to be ravaged by a lion, then the shepherd must bring to his master the remains of the carcass, the meatless ears or the left-over bones, as evidence of the cause of death (see Gen. 31:39).

Amos applies this simile to Samaria, but not without irony. Little was left of a sheep devoured by a lion, only useless bits and pieces. And yet Amos says that in this manner the citizens of Samaria would be "rescued"! (The last part of the verse, referring apparently to a "couch" and a "bed", is extremely difficult to translate and the precise meaning remains obscure. The translation of RSV, nevertheless, provides clearly enough the general sense of the verse.) The coming destruction of Samaria, which Amos declares so forcefully, would be virtually complete (as indeed it was in the Assyrian invasion in 722 B.C.)

(iii) *Altars and homes destroyed* (verses 13–15). Now the emphasis falls upon the extent of the destruction that will befall Samaria. The altars, upon which no doubt pagan sacrifices had been offered, would be destroyed. (Note: there is debate as to whether the mention of "Bethel" is a reference to a god of that name, or to the Israelite shrine at the town of Bethel, some distance south of Samaria near the border with Judah.) The "summer houses" and "winter houses" were the seasonal residences of the rich; though their very existence symbolized wealth, they would offer no security on the day of judgment. The "houses of ivory" were buildings richly adorned with ivory inlay and furnishings (see 1 Kings 22:39). In the archaeological excavation of Samaria, a storeroom was uncovered in which there were found some two hundred ivory plaques, offering physical evidence of the wealth of the city in and before the time of Amos. But all the signs of wealth and power would mock the citizens of Samaria when the city's day of judgment dawned.

THE COWS OF BASHAN

Amos 4:1–3

[1]"Hear this word, you cows of Bashan,
  who are in the mountain of Samaria,
who oppress the poor, who crush the needy,
  who say to their husbands,
  'Bring, that we may drink!'
[2]The Lord God has sworn by his holiness
  that, behold, the days are coming upon you,
when they shall take you away with hooks,
  even the last of you with fishhooks.
[3]And you shall go out through the breaches,
  every one straight before her;
  and you shall be cast forth into Harmon,"

says the Lord.

To catch the power of this passage, one must imagine an analogous scene in the modern world. Think, for example, of a distinguished English businessman invited to address a gathering of the Women's Institute in a Scottish country town. All the ladies and dignitaries of the district have assembled to hear him. He stands up and begins his address: "Now listen to me, you herd of Highland cows!" And in the speech that follows, he berates his audience for their moral behaviour and their excessive imbibing of alcoholic beverages. This is essentially what Amos did in a gathering of Samaria's elite women.

The expression "cows of Bashan" designates a breed of cattle famous for their fatness and beef. (The cows did not necessarily come from Bashan, the high and fertile plateau lying east of the Sea of Chinnereth, or Galilee. Rather, just as we refer to Herefords or Aberdeen Angus, Bashan cows are a special breed employed in beef herds.) It was a most insulting expression to employ in a speech to assembled females, designed to evoke not only attention, but wrath. (Curiously enough, a few commentators have claimed that no insult was intended by the words, suggesting that such forms of address were traditional with oriental poets, indicating "voluptuously endowed maidens". But such an interpretation surely misses the point, not only of the form of address, but also of the scathing critique which follows.)

Having grasped the attention of his audience, the prophet now comes to the point of his message. His point is to condemn and to announce the consequent judgment of God. He condemns these women for oppressing the poor and, by implication, for drinking too heavily. The judgment, expressed in the language of a solemn oath taken by God, would take the form of being dragged away, either to death or to exile. Parts of the translation of both verses 2 and 3 are difficult; some would translate the Hebrew expressions in verse 2 by "ropes" and "harpoons", rather than "hooks" and "fishhooks". The translation *Harmon* is also of uncertain meaning. But despite the uncertainty as to detail, the overall sense still remains clear. Those whose lives of luxury had been lived at the expense of the poor would be dragged off into judgment. For all the unpleasantness of this short passage, it is instructive in a number of ways with respect to the perspectives and message of Amos.

(i) The prophet implies that exploitation can be done "at arms' length". The women demanded of their husbands: "Bring!" And no doubt the husbands, in order to satisfy their wives' thirst for alcohol, engaged in further exploitation of the poor to provide the necessary funds. But the women were as guilty as their husbands. One does not have to dirty one's hands in the actual business of exploitation; someone else can do it, someone else can engage in the dirty work. It is possible to delegate dirty deeds, but it is not possible to avoid their guilt.

(ii) In these times of appropriate sensitivity as to the manner in which men and women are addressed, the prophet's language in these verses might seem at first to mark him irrevocably as a "male chauvinist". And yet, curiously, almost the opposite is true. It was precisely because Amos perceived women's importance and responsible place in society that he addressed them in this manner. They were responsible, along with the men, for the future of the society to which they belonged. The health of the nation depended upon their integrity and their righteousness. And thus the failure of these women from the upper ranks of

Israel's society deserved to be condemned, for it was a failure which was contributing to the downfall of the society as a whole.

If Amos was prejudiced, it was against evil, not women. This passage is not the equivalent, as some have suggested, of the famous pamphlet of John Knox, published in 1558: *The First Blast of the Trumpet against the Monstrous Regiment of Women* (though, to be fair to Knox, "regiment" in his title means "rule", and he was thinking of the hurt done to Protestant Scotland by a Catholic queen rather than of women in general). Amos' words are indeed a trumpet blast. And later, he will blast an equally strident note specifically against the villainy of *men* (6:1–7). And perhaps the majority of his ministry should be viewed as being addressed to the citizenry as a whole, male and female alike.

Standing before God, there is no fundamental difference between men and women. Both are made in the image of God. To both should be accorded full human rights and privileges. But, as Amos reminds us, both must be responsible for their moral behaviour. The exploitation of the poor, or the indulgence in excessive drinking, is no less a crime for being committed by a male or a female.

"PREPARE TO MEET YOUR GOD"

Amos 4:4–13

⁴"Come to Bethel, and transgress;
    to Gilgal, and multiply transgression;
  bring your sacrifices every morning,
    your tithes every three days;
⁵offer a sacrifice of thanksgiving of that which is leavened,
    and proclaim freewill offerings, publish them;
  for so you love to do, O people of Israel!"
                                    says the Lord God.

⁶"I gave you cleanness of teeth in all your cities,
    and lack of bread in all your places,
  yet you did not return to me,"
                                    says the Lord.

7"And I also withheld the rain from you
  when there were yet three months to the harvest;
I would send rain upon one city,
  and send no rain upon another city;
one field would be rained upon,
  and the field on which it did not rain withered;
8so two or three cities wandered to one city
  to drink water, and were not satisfied;
yet you did not return to me,"

                                              says the Lord.

9"I smote you with blight and mildew;
  I laid waste your gardens and your vineyards;
  your fig trees and your olive trees the locust devoured;
yet you did not return to me,"

                                              says the Lord.

10"I sent among you a pestilence after the manner of Egypt;
  I slew your young men with the sword;
I carried away your horses;
  and I made the stench of your camp go up into your nostrils;
yet you did not return to me,"

                                              says the Lord.

11"I overthrew some of you,
  as when God overthrew Sodom and Gomorrah,
  and you were as a brand plucked out of the burning;
yet you did not return to me,"

                                              says the Lord.

12"Therefore thus I will do to you, O Israel;
  because I will do this to you,
  prepare to meet your God, O Israel!"

13For lo, he who forms the mountains, and creates the wind,
  and declares to man what is his thought;
who makes the morning darkness,
  and treads on the heights of the earth—
the Lord, the God of hosts, is his name!

It is probable that the prophet's tactless talk to the leading ladies
of Samaria resulted in his disbarment for a while from the capital
city. Now he is in the south of the northern state, probably at

Bethel or Gilgal (verse 4). Both towns contained important sanctuaries, and both are the focus of his new preaching; the setting of
this condensed sermon, however, is more likely to be Bethel,
where later the prophet was to get into hot water once again (see
7:10–17).

Amos has now turned his attention from the ladies of Samaria's
establishment to the people of Israel as a whole. And yet he
chooses a particular occasion on which to address them. There
appears to be a great pilgrim festival going on, involving the
sanctuaries at both Bethel, in the south of Israel, due north of
Jerusalem, and at Gilgal, lying further to the east in the Jordan
valley near Jericho. One must envisage the pilgrim crowds,
cheerful and jostling, as they partook of the celebratory rituals at
the two ancient sanctuaries of Israel's faith. They would have
offered sacrifices and contributed their tithes; they would have
been addressed as an assembly by the officiating priests. It was a
happy time, celebrating Israel's most ancient traditions, restoring
a feeling of well-being in the nation as a whole. As in our own
celebration of Christmas or Easter, the mood would be infectious, affecting faithful and unfaithful alike; during the pilgrim
festivals, all the world seemed slightly brighter for a few days.

Amos, the visiting businessman from the southern state, observes this happy scene and is compelled by God to use it as a
further setting for his prophetic ministry. The crowds are ready-
made, there for the asking, but the message he will declare to
them will not make Amos the hero of the day. His opening
declaration is in the form of a priestly invitation to participate in
the celebrations: "Come to Bethel . . . to Gilgal". But it is a
parody of the priestly pronouncement, for it sours the supposedly
cheerful nature of the occasion: "Come to Bethel, and
transgress".

Following the parody of the invitation to worship, there follows
a series of five oracles (verses 6–11), each of which concludes in
the same manner: "yet you did not return to me, says the Lord."
The language of this section has suggested to many scholars that
the words are not the authentic sayings of Amos, but are a later
editorial insertion in his book. While such a view is possible, it is

not probable, though the words in a strict sense may not be those of Amos. That is, the prophet may take the familiar words of a part of the pilgrim liturgy and adapt them to his own purpose. (There are close parallels between this section of Amos and such texts as Lev. 26, Deut. 28, and 1 Kings 8:33–37.) But whereas the pilgrim liturgy would normally focus upon the blessings of God upon Israel, it is the curses of God that Amos draws into his lampoon of the normally cheerful liturgy.

Each of the five oracles, or adaptations of liturgical curses, refers to a judgmental act of God which might have led to the people's repentance, but in each case they did not return to God. Hunger and famine had no effect on them (verse 6). Drought did nothing to help them see the situation they were in (verses 7–8). Blight and mildew ruined their produce, but did not open their eyes (verse 9). Plagues and military disasters were absolutely ineffective (verse 10). Even when disasters overwhelmed them, in proportion to the troubles that engulfed Sodom and Gomorrah, Israel did not perceive its precarious situation.

And so Amos declares: "Prepare to meet your God, O Israel" (verse 12). Even in this pronouncement there is irony, for the purpose of the pilgrim festivals was to enable the people to meet God anew. But the prophet does not expect a happy reunion; the encounter he intimates would be one of judgment. And his final words to the pilgrims indicate that the God they must meet is the powerful creator of heaven and earth, one who is well able to fulfil his proclamation of judgment (verse 13).

There are two aspects of Amos' address that are particularly striking and relevant beyond their time.

(i) The prophet chooses the high point in the nation's liturgical life to reveal the low point in their spiritual existence. From a psychological perspective, it is an effective technique. At the great festivals, everybody celebrates, even those who give little thought to the substance of the faith throughout the normal weeks of a year. Those who have no real grounds for confidence are caught in the infectious enthusiasm of the confident congregations. And when the nation celebrates, thinking all is well, Amos stands up and punctures the balloon of cheerful celebration.

One must imagine a Christmas service, the congregation sing-
ing lustily, "O come, all ye faithful". But when Amos stood to
preach, his text would be: "O come, all ye faithless". He takes the
familiar words, reversing their sense, thereby drawing back the
drapes of hypocrisy that so easily shroud the great celebrations.
The relevance of this portion of Amos may become crystal clear if
we reflect on it at Christmas or Easter. In our own great festivals
of faith, are there really grounds for confidence? Or should we
look within, searching the moral and spiritual life to determine
whether we can, with integrity, join in the festival occasion?

(ii) The prophet's five oracles (verses 6–11) remind us that
life's experiences of trouble may function as signposts. Of course,
not every encounter with difficulty is necessarily an explicit divine
sign, though it may be used nevertheless as an occasion for
introspection. Many things had happened to Israel: drought, crop
failure, defeat in war, disaster after disaster. And yet not once,
the prophet implies, had the time of trouble caused sufficient
thought on Israel's part for the people to see that they had long
since ceased to walk in God's path. The prophet's words ring out
like a sorry epitaph on the nation's history: "yet you did not
return to me," he says five times. It never hurts, and frequently it
helps, to reflect upon the dramatic events of our lives, to consider
the road we are taking, to ask if it is still the road in which we
walked when first we embraced the faith with joy.

A FUNERAL LAMENT

Amos 5:1–17

¹Hear this word which I take up over you in lamentation, O house of
Israel:
²"Fallen, no more to rise,
    is the virgin Israel;
forsaken on her land,
    with none to raise her up."

³For thus says the Lord God:
"The city that went forth a thousand

shall have a hundred left,
and that which went forth a hundred
shall have ten left
to the house of Israel."

⁴For thus says the Lord to the house of Israel:
"Seek me and live;
⁵ but do not seek Bethel,
and do not enter into Gilgal
or cross over to Beer-sheba;
for Gilgal shall surely go into exile,
and Bethel shall come to naught."

⁶Seek the Lord and live,
lest he break out like fire in the house of Joseph,
and it devour, with none to quench it for Bethel,
⁷O you who turn justice to wormwood,
and cast down righteousness to the earth!

⁸He who made the Pleiades and Orion,
and turns deep darkness into the morning,
and darkens the day into night,
who calls for the waters of the sea,
and pours them out upon the surface of the earth,
the Lord is his name,
⁹who makes destruction flash forth against the strong,
so that destruction comes upon the fortress.

¹⁰They hate him who reproves in the gate,
and they abhor him who speaks the truth.
¹¹Therefore because you trample upon the poor
and take from him exactions of wheat,
you have built houses of hewn stone,
but you shall not dwell in them;
you have planted pleasant vineyards,
but you shall not drink their wine.
¹²For I know how many are your transgressions,
and how great are your sins—
you who afflict the righteous, who take a bribe,
and turn aside the needy in the gate.
¹³Therefore he who is prudent will keep silent in such a time;
for it is an evil time.

¹⁴Seek good, and not evil,
　　that you may live;
　and so the Lord, the God of hosts, will be with you,
　　as you have said.
¹⁵Hate evil, and love good,
　　and establish justice in the gate;
　it may be that the Lord, the God of hosts,
　　will be gracious to the remnant of Joseph.

¹⁶Therefore thus says the Lord, the God of hosts, the Lord:
　"In all the squares there shall be wailing;
　　and in all the streets they shall say, 'Alas! alas!'
　They shall call the farmers to mourning
　　and to wailing those who are skilled in lamentation,
¹⁷and in all vineyards there shall be wailing,
　　for I will pass through the midst of you,"

　　　　　　　　　　　　　　　　　　　says the Lord.

Funerals, in ancient Israel, were times of great lament and mourning. At the death of Jacob, Joseph and his company lamented his passing in seven days of mourning (Gen. 50:1;); likewise, when Saul died, the funeral occasion extended for a week (1 Sam. 31:13). In this new section of the prophet's preaching, the message is shaped as if it were a final oration delivered alongside the grave. The passage begins with the words of lamentation (verses 1–3) and ends in the same way (verses 16–17). In between are words intermixed with hope and helplessness, but the stench of death permeates the whole, casting a pall even upon the invitation to "seek the Lord and live" (verses 4, 6, 14). The more cheerful words at the centre of this address are like fragrant flowers, yet their fragrance is deceptive; as the flowers of a wreath laid beside the grave, they are wrapped in the black crepe of mourning.

We cannot be certain, but it is probable that Amos delivered this address (here given in summary form only) on the same occasion as the preceding one; there occur once again the references to the pilgrim centres at Bethal and Gilgal (verse 5). And it may be that Amos has once again adapted the occasion to his purpose. If the pilgrim festival was one that extended over seven days, his funeral lament may have been designed to evoke from his audience the seven days of lament observed after death. Thus, by his words, he subtly transforms the festal week to a funerary week.

The opening words of the lament as such (verses 2–3) are sombre in their implication; the lament is for Israel, but normally one only employs the lament *after* the death has occurred. And yet the words are addressed to an assembled crowd of Israelites, apparently alive and kicking. Like some macabre dream, the whole scene takes on the shades of unreality. A great crowd of happy pilgrims constitutes the audience, yet Amos is lamenting their death as if it had already happened.

The prophet's address seems to brighten a little in verses 4–7. He invites his audience to "seek the Lord and *live*", even though the very form of his address implies they are *dead*. But the words are tainted with irony; the pilgrims think that they are indeed seeking the Lord, turning to him in his sanctuaries. And so, with a powerful word-play at the end of verse 5, Amos condemns the sanctuaries of their false seeking; it is not easy to convert the Hebrew word-play into English but is something like this: "Gilgal to the gallows, Bethel is bedevilled." The people must indeed seek the Lord, but in the places where they are seeking they will find nothing.

The progress of the prophet's address is interrupted, somewhat strangely, by two verses (8–9) which do not seem to fit the context at all. They appear to be some lines from a hymn, in which God is praised for his creation of the stars and the constellations (Pleiades and Orion), indeed for his power and control over all the created order. When one reads verses 1–17 as a piece of literature, these verses clash with the context, but when we try to understand Amos' speech in the festal setting in which it was delivered, they may begin to make sense. The hymnic words may have been a portion of a hymn sung by the festival crowds at Bethel or Gilgal, the words as familiar to the crowds as are those of our Christmas and Easter hymns. And here Amos quotes the familiar words, establishing the power of the God of whom he speaks over creation, and therefore over life and death.

The prophet then contrasts the creative power of God with the crassness of mankind (verses 10–13). The people have hated the truth, but practised evil avidly. They have exploited the poor to accumulate wealth for themselves, they have taken bribes, they have ignored the pleas of the needy. But these words are not merely another prophetic denunciation of evil; their context determines the manner in which they are to be read. Normally, at a funeral, the oration would dwell on the life and accomplishments of the deceased, recalling achievements and endearing aspects of the life now ended. Amos though, in declaring Israel's funeral oration, changes what is normal. To paraphrase verse 11: they built great houses, but did not live long enough to dwell in them, they planted splendid vineyards, but did not survive to sample the wine.

Again Amos speaks positively (verses 14–15), this time without irony and perhaps with a ray of hope. If they would only seek good, and not evil, there might yet be a chance to rise from the grave and live again. But though these verses contain some of the most fundamental moral truths of Israel's faith, they are spoken with little assurance. The "may be" is too powerful. For immediately Amos continues to the conclusion of his address (verses 16–17), in which the double "alas" of lament is sounded as the end of Israel's funeral.

This mournful funeral oration of Amos is one of his darkest passages. Read as literature, it would be bleak enough. But when one reads it against the cheerful setting of its delivery, in the context of Israel's happy holiday crowds, it is even more morose. He would surely have been condemned as a "killjoy", one with no sense of occasion. Perhaps such sermons have to be preached, some might have said, but must they be given on the festival days? Would we be happy to hear such miserable words at Easter or Christmas? Surely the funeral lament is not the proper form of address for the festive occasions!

And yet, though Amos may have been tactless, he was a man of integrity. For his people were like the company and crew of the Titanic: they danced cheerfully in the ballroom, full of the joys of life, but Amos could see only the iceberg. In a sense they were all

as good as dead, yet still Amos must warn. And still his warning
rings out, not to crush and spoil all festive moments, but rather to
plead for that moment of introspection, in which we may look
beyond the external celebrations and inquire if all is well within.

FLEEING THE LION, BUMPING INTO THE BEAR

Amos 5:18–27

¹⁸Woe to you who desire the day of the Lord!
   Why would you have the day of the Lord?
  It is darkness, and not light;
¹⁹   as if a man fled from a lion,
    and a bear met him;
  or went into the house and leaned with his hand against the wall,
    and a serpent bit him.
²⁰Is not the day of the Lord darkness and not light,
   and gloom with no brightness in it?

²¹"I hate, I despise your feasts,
   and I take no delight in your solemn assemblies.
²²Even though you offer me your burnt offerings and cereal offerings,
   I will not accept them,
  and the peace offerings of your fatted beasts
   I will not look upon.
²³Take away from me the noise of your songs;
   to the melody of your harps I will not listen.
²⁴But let justice roll down like waters,
   and righteousness like an everflowing stream.

²⁵"Did you bring to me sacrifices and offerings the forty years in the
wilderness, O house of Israel? ²⁶You shall take up Sakkuth your king,
and Kaiwan your star-god, your images, which you made for yourselves; ²⁷therefore I will take you into exile beyond Damascus," says
the Lord, whose name is the God of hosts.

The mournful message in the form of a funeral lament is now
followed by an equally dismal declaration addressed to the
people as a whole. Although we cannot be sure, these verses may
also reflect a setting in the festal celebrations at Bethel, and like

so many other portions of the prophetic books, they are probably a condensation of several addresses delivered by Amos to his assembled audience. The passage as a whole is divided into three sections, each one, perhaps, being the kernel of an originally independent message.

(i) *The Day of the Lord* (verses 18–20). The sermon is one of woe, but its text is one which would initially have elicited hope in the ears of the congregation. The "Day of the Lord" is a common theme in the prophets; indeed, we have already seen that it is a central theme in the Book of Joel. Although we cannot pin down the precise content of the phrase as it would have been understood by the prophet's audience, that content was clearly positive. And on the festival days, the phrase would have been understood with both past and future connotations. They recalled in the past the great days of the Lord's activity, the day of redemption from Egypt and the day of the giving of the law at Mount Sinai. The recollections of the ancient days of the Lord held hope for the future. In the coming year there would be hope, and further down the corridors of time the Day of the Lord was anticipated in which God would bring final victory to his people. The Day of the Lord, in Israel's religion, was a day to desire.

"Woe to you who desire the day of the Lord" (verse 18): thus does Amos open his sermon, shattering in his first words all happy delusions held about the future. For the day they all desired would turn out to be darkness, not light, misery without joy. Then, by means of a series of similes, he illustrates not only the negative characteristics of the coming day, but also the surprise with which it would be encountered. A man fleeing from the dangerous lion bumps into the equally dangerous bear. Or a person entering his house, thinking himself to be safe at last from the terrors outside, leans against the wall and is bitten by a venomous snake.

The prophet is concerned to show not only the danger of the Lord's coming day, but also the element of surprise and fear with which it would be encountered. Just when one thinks one has escaped a mortal danger, the true and deadly danger appears. Amos, like a surgeon, is attempting to cut away the tumours of false confidence and future hopes that endanger the health of his patients. Given the trials of present circumstance, the people created the delusion of a coming day in which there would be no more sorrow and difficulty. They engaged in a natural and perpetual human tendency: they sought to make the present more bearable by projecting a happy day into the future. And in principle it is not such a bad thing to do, for the present is unbearable enough for many people.

And yet Amos was not being unkind in destroying the delusion of a future happy day; his was indeed a severe form of charity, but the people's notion must be destroyed because it was a delusion. The Day of the Lord would be a day of judgment for those who did not know God in integrity and truth. And thus one can only look forward to the coming Day of the Lord when the present day is lived in God's light and truth.

In a multitude of ways we recreate for ourselves the delusions of Amos' congregation. Sometimes it is in a general manner; finding the present unbearable, we live in the future, waiting for a happier day to dawn. For others, a curious consolation in the future is found by espousing one of the modern varieties of eschatology, those various systems which purport to know the future directions of world events and their outcome in the plan of God. But all too often these obsessions with future days emerge from an unwillingness to cope with the present day; and, as Amos would have it, in fleeing from the lion of the present, such persons will bump into the bear of the future.

(ii) *Unacceptable worship* (verses 21–24). These four verses contain God's words, spoken by the prophet; the "I hate" refers not to the prophet's opinion, but to the divine perspective from which he speaks. The feasts, the assemblies, the sacrifices and offerings, the songs and choral music, all these things are hated and despised by God. Rather than the clamour of the congregation's worship (and the great festival days may still be implied here), God desires of his people justice and righteousness.

There has been great debate amongst the scholars as to whether these verses establish that Amos was unalterably opposed to Israel's cult and forms of public worship. Taken out of context, the passage certainly might seem to support such a view, and no doubt Amos, as a Judean, must have had reservations about parts of Israel's worship, just as a member of the Church of Scotland might have reservations about aspects of worship in the Church of England. But to puzzle over whether or not Amos was for or against the sacrificial cult of Israel is in a sense to miss the point. His real focus is on that knowledge of God which issues in righteous living and just dealings. With respect to essentials, namely the knowledge of God and the impact of that knowledge upon human living, formal worship is a secondary matter. To put it another way, the most splendid worship in the world, the finest liturgies with the best choirs, are totally irrelevant *if* the congregation have ceased to know the God whom they worship. The prophet does not engage so much in a critique of worship as such, but rather in a critique of worship in which there is no true knowledge of God.

The principle propounded by Amos continues to apply to all worship; if the knowledge of God is absent, it becomes but a hollow shell. Yet the principle may extend beyond worship. Karl Barth, in his farewell lecture at the end of the 1961-62 academic year, adapted Amos' words to theology and theologians, reminding us all of the necessity of examining our enterprise:

> I hate, I despise your lectures and seminars, your sermons, addresses, and Bible studies, and I take no delight in your discussions, meetings and conventions.

In any supposedly Christian activity, if the knowledge of God is absent and if righteousness and justice do not flourish, the activity may be in vain.

(iii) *The judgment of exile* (verses 25–27). These verses have been described as being among the most difficult in the entire book of Amos, and yet despite the many difficulties of detail, the general sense remains clear.

During the forty years in the wilderness, the Israelites did not offer to God the normal sacrifices and offerings; their circumstances in life made such formal worship impossible. Now, the prophet implies, the Israelites have perverted their faith by taking up the idolatrous standards of two Assyrian astral deities, Sakkuth and Kaiwan. The consequence of losing the purity of the ancient faith and perverting it in modern times would be the nation's exile "beyond Damascus" (implying exile in Assyria).

Again, what the prophet stresses are the priorities. Israel has got them all wrong, adding the objects of Assyria's faith to its own forms of elaborate worship. The real priorities could be seen by reflecting on the wilderness period. In those days there was hardship and uncertainty; in those days there was not sufficient wealth even to offer the sacrifices that later were to become the norms of public worship. But at least, in those days, the people knew God; their heart was in the right place. Amos would have us examine the plethora of activities that have become our daily lives and ask if the priorities are still correct.

NO SECURITY IN SAMARIA

Amos 6:1-7

¹"Woe to those who are at ease in Zion,
   and to those who feel secure on the mountain of Samaria,
 the notable men of the first of the nations,
   to whom the house of Israel come!
²Pass over to Calneh, and see;
   and thence go to Hamath the great;
   then go down to Gath of the Philistines.
 Are they better than these kingdoms?
   Or is their territory greater than your territory,
³O you who put far away the evil day,
   and bring near the seat of violence?

⁴"Woe to those who lie upon beds of ivory,
   and stretch themselves upon their couches,
 and eat lambs from the flock,
   and calves from the midst of the stall;
⁵who sing idle songs to the sound of the harp,
   and like David invent for themselves instruments of music;
⁶who drink wine in bowls,
   and anoint themselves with the finest oils,

but are not grieved over the ruin of Joseph!
⁷Therefore they shall now be the first of those to go into exile,
and the revelry of those who stretch themselves shall pass away."

Earlier in the book we were provided with an example of the prophet's condemnation of the "cows of Bashan" (4:1–3), namely the wealthy women of Samaria. Now the prophet's attention is turned to the rich and powerful men of Samaria. Like their female counterparts, they are to be condemned for their pride, their easy living and heavy drinking at the nation's expense. The scene that is reflected in these verses is the capital city once again; Amos has returned to Samaria from the great religious centres in the south of Israel that are presupposed in the preceding passages.

The prophet's condemnation of "notable men" has two parts to it, each introduced by the word "woe". Each part of his message focuses upon a different aspect of the failure of the nation's leading citizens.

(i) *A false sense of security* (verses 1–3). The first line, with its reference to Zion (Jerusalem), has been the source of suspicion to some commentators. Amos is a prophet in the northern kingdom, and thus one would not expect a reference to Zion in Judah; hence, some would say that the first line is an editorial addition from a later age. But such need not be the case; in these verses, Amos' view is international and several foreign cities are referred to. And what he says applies in principle to all "notable men", though the prophet's focus is on those of Samaria, the capital of Israel.

The message of woe is addressed to those who feel secure, and who are therefore at ease, but whose sense of security is based on false grounds. Now we begin to see why both *Zion* and *Samaria* are mentioned in the first verse; both are capital cities, both are constructed on a hill, and both were thought by their inhabitants to be impregnable. The chief citizens of Samaria were secure in the knowledge of the military strength of their position, but not in any deep-seated trust in God.

The prophet, to make his point, then refers to other great cities. *Calneh* was in the far north of Syria, a little north of the modern city of Aleppo. Hamath was also in northern Syria, on the banks of the River Orontes. Gath was one of the Philistine cities on the southeastern seaboard of the Mediterranean Sea. The purpose in the prophet's reference to other cities is the subject of some debate. Does he mention them because they have been destroyed, and are therefore an example of what will happen to Samaria? Or are they examples of prosperous gentile cities, indicating to Samaria that it is just another prosperous city with no special status in the world of cities? Verse 2*b* suggests the latter interpretation. Samaria's strength and supposed security are no greater than those of other great cities; there is no special status, no special reason for prosperity, and therefore no certain guarantee for the future of the city.

The notable men of Samaria exemplify the elite of this world, powerful and influential, basing their sense of security in the invincibility of the city which they control and in which they reside. The city symbolizes human strength and achievement; its location is strong and fortified. And, for such people, their world was centred in Samaria: "this is *the* city, and we are *the* men." But a position in the city, and the life of influence that it brought, were no sure ground of confidence. The notable men were curiously parochial in their thinking, not knowing the world's other cities with their own self-confident notables. They did not understand that "here we have no continuing city" (Heb. 13:14), that no lasting security was to be found in any city, but only in God.

(ii) *A false sense of values* (verses 4–6). The false sense of security led inevitably to a way of life based upon a false premise. Thinking themselves to be safe, come what may, they concluded that they could live as they pleased. The security of the city provided the environment for luxurious and loose living; the citizens did not believe that their manner of life would in any way affect the city's safety.

The prophet sounds almost ascetic as he sketches in the manner of life of Samaria's leading men. At their great dinners, they reclined on rich couches inlaid with ivory panels. They feasted on lamb and veal, accompanied by their own songs of idleness. They drank "wine in bowls"; some have claimed that the "bowls" were sacrificial bowls, so that they were committing sacrilege. But it is more probable that the phrase indicates quantity. Not pausing to pour the wine into cups or goblets, they drank straight from the bowl, as in our own day some will drink straight from the bottle. These diners took every care of themselves, anointing themselves with oil, but cared not a whit for the "ruin of Joseph" (verse 6), namely the shambles to which their nation had degenerated.

Though no doubt there was a strong streak of asceticism in Amos' character, shaped perhaps by the wilderness of his home in Tekoa, it is not simply a critique of luxurious living that is presented here. The entire picture of the indulgent banquet is set in perspective by the final clause: the notable men wine and dine, "but are not grieved over the ruin of Joseph [Israel]" (verse 6*b*). Their sense of values was totally out of perspective. They were "notable men" precisely because to them had been entrusted responsibility for their city and nation. Their raison d'etre was to ensure that their people did not end up in ruin. But they knew nothing of responsibility and had no thought for the persons entrusted to their care. They cared only for themselves and the perks that power could provide. Their world of experience was circumscribed by the immediate goal of sensual pleasures, the happy company of wine-bibbers drowning out the sounds of ruin beyond their feast. Their values were directed entirely to themselves, having no room for their fellow citizens or for God.

(iii) *A statement of judgment* (verse 7). The prophet's condemnation of the city's notable men concludes with an announcement of their coming judgment. Soon the revelry of Samaria's social elite would be exchanged for a passage into exile. Even in the declaration of judgment, Amos retains an ironic tone. These notable men would not lose their pre-eminence in judgment; they would be privileged in passing first into exile when the time came.

The judgment fits the crime. Those who had a false sense of security would have it shattered as they left behind them the city walls that promised so much before the journey into exile began. Those who had a false sense of values and cared not at all for the ruin of their people would find those values stripped away in the enforced ruin of exile. Human security and the goal of personal pleasure cannot stand up in the day of divine judgment. Only a life that is rooted in God and lived in the service of fellow human beings may face coming days of hardship with courage and integrity.

THE NATION'S COLLAPSE

Amos 6:8–14

> 8The Lord God has sworn by himself (says the Lord, the God of hosts):
> "I abhor the pride of Jacob,
>   and hate his strongholds;
>   and I will deliver up the city and all that is in it."
>
> 9And if ten men remain in one house, they shall die. 10And when a man's kinsman, he who burns him, shall take him up to bring the bones out of the house, and shall say to him who is in the innermost parts of the house, "Is there still any one with you?" he shall say, "No"; and he shall say, "Hush! We must not mention the name of the Lord."
>
> 11For behold, the Lord commands,
>   and the great house shall be smitten into fragments,
>   and the little house into bits.
> 12Do horses run upon rocks?
>   Does one plough the sea with oxen?
>   But you have turned justice into poison
>   and the fruit of righteousness into wormwood—
> 13you who rejoice in Lo-debar,
>   who say, "Have we not by our own strength
>   taken Karnaim for ourselves?"
> 14"For behold, I will raise up against you a nation,
>   O house of Israel," says the Lord, the God of hosts;
>   "and they shall oppress you from the entrance of Hamath
>   to the Brook of the Arabah."

These verses bring to a conclusion the second principal section of the Book of Amos (chapters 3–6), in which were contained a selection of the themes and messages employed by the prophet in his ministry in Israel. This concluding passage contains a final collection of short messages, perhaps extracts from longer sermons and memorable sayings, which bring to an end the larger section to which they belong with various insights concerning Amos' work. Each short message may be examined separately.

(i) *Pride leads to collapse* (verse 8). The message is introduced with a solemn divine oath, emphasizing the certainty of the specified outcome. God has sworn upon his honour that the city of Samaria, together with all its citizens, will be delivered to judgment. The root of the city's fall is to be found in pride, which in turn finds its basis in a foolish confidence in the strength of its "strongholds", or military fortifications. Such pride and confidence in human ability, declares Amos, are hated by God, and that which God hates must be destroyed.

(ii) *Even survivors will not survive* (verses 9–10). This tersely written scene is difficult to understand, given the shortage of detail. It seems to presuppose a post-war scene, in which the survivors of war come home only to be ravaged by the outbreak of plague. The survivors of war return to their homes, there to die, the victims of disease. And then the distant relatives come, together with the undertaker, looking for the corpses to dispose of them decently. But as they search the houses for bodies, they talk in hushed tones; the plague is perceived to be an act of God, and the body hunters whisper nervously for fear of God hearing and acting in wrath again. It is a frightening depiction of coming disaster, indicating not only the comprehensive character of the nation's collapse, but also the dawning awareness that its origin is to be found in an act of God.

(iii) *Destruction at the Lord's bidding* (verse 11). This short verse indicates not only that the residences of Samaria and Israel would be destroyed, but reinforces the fact that the Lord would be the destroyer. Though our familiarity with the prophetic writings makes this notion seem a commonplace, it was perhaps one of the most difficult things for Amos to communicate to his audience. *God* would be the author of their destruction, not some foreign power, and the destruction would be complete and final.

Although the message is clear enough, it would have been hard to grasp precisely because it seemed so alien to the comforting notion of God that prevailed at the time.

(iv) *Perversion of the natural order of things* (verse 12). By means of two pointed questions, Amos illustrates in a didactic manner the way in which Israel has perverted the divine and natural order of the world. "Do horses run upon rocks? Does one plough the sea with oxen?" In each case, the automatic response would be "No"! The very questions are foolish. Yet the folly of the question brings out in turn the folly of the situation which prompted the posing of the questions. The pure juice of justice had been made into poison, the fruit of righteousness changed into "wormwood". To do this was the utmost folly and inevitably invited disaster. Amos shared the Wisdom perspective on the world. The order of creation was pertinent to the order of human society; the observation of the principles of justice and righteousness in human society preserved that society within the harmony of the created world as such. The abandonment of justice and righteousness was folly, replacing order with chaos, purity with poison. And the implication of the two questions, to which the answer is so obvious, is that Israel should have known better.

(v) *Military victories will not avert military defeat* (verses 13–14). There is a word-play in verse 13 which makes the sense difficult to grasp in English. The words are the statements of confidence employed by Amos' audience. They refer to two cities, Lo-debar and Karnaim, which had probably been recently captured for Israel during Jeroboam II's period of military expansion. (Lo-debar was to the south of the Sea of Chinnereth, Karnaim to its east in Bashan.) And the people refer to these places, scenes of recent military victories, as symbols of their current military strength. But *Lo-debar* also means "thing of nought" and *Karnaim* means "horns" (symbols of a bull's strength). Perhaps the prophet implies: "you who by bullish strength have captured nothing." If, in a later age, Robin Hood and his men had captured Nottingham, Amos would have called it "Nothingham".

The reality, with which Amos punctures Israel's military confidence, is that God was preparing a nation which would oppress Israel "from the entrance of Hamath to the Brook of Arabah" (verse 14), that is from the northern extremity of the kingdom to its southern limit. Israel's false confidence in military might was based upon victories in two regional skirmishes, but they would soon lose the coming war.

THREE VISIONS

Amos 7:1–9

[1]Thus the Lord God showed me: behold, he was forming locusts in the beginning of the shooting up of the latter growth; and lo, it was the latter growth after the king's mowings. [2]When they had finished eating the grass of the land, I said,

"O Lord God, forgive, I beseech thee!
How can Jacob stand?
He is so small!"
[3]The Lord repented concerning this;
"It shall not be," said the Lord.

[4]Thus the Lord God showed me: behold, the Lord God was calling for a judgment by fire, and it devoured the great deep and was eating up the land. [5]Then I said,

"O Lord God, cease, I beseech thee!
How can Jacob stand?
He is so small!"
[6]The Lord repented concerning this;
"This also shall not be," said the Lord God.

[7]He showed me: behold, the Lord was standing beside a wall built with a plumb line, with a plumb line in his hand. [8]And the Lord said to me, "Amos, what do you see?" And I said, "A plumb line." Then the Lord said,

"Behold, I am setting a plumb line
in the midst of my people Israel;
I will never again pass by them;
[9]the high places of Isaac shall be made desolate,
and the sanctuaries of Israel shall be laid waste,
and I will rise against the house of Jeroboam with the sword."

The last three chapters of the Book of Amos constitute the third major section of the book. Like the second section, this last section contains various types of material, often in condensed form, probably reflecting different occasions in the prophet's ministry. The most prominent substance of this section of the book is the account that is provided of five visions which the prophet had. Three are recorded in these opening verses; the fourth is in 8:1-3 and the fifth begins in 9:1. The vision accounts contain references to Amos in the first person, as if he had recorded them in a diary, or dictated them to a disciple. We do not even know whether all the visions were employed in the prophet's public ministry, or whether they were simply a part of his own spiritual development. It is certainly the case that as we read the visions in sequence we can perceive the development in Amos of a growing understanding with respect to God's coming action towards Israel. The time at which these visions were experienced cannot be determined with any precision. It would be a mistake, nevertheless, to think of this third section of the book as introducing a new period in what was after all a relatively brief ministry. The substance of this section seems to contain material from parts of the ministry with which we are already familiar from chapters 3-6; the general setting of the prophecies in these three concluding chapters is provided by the ministry of Amos in the capital city of Samaria and in the cult city of Bethel.

(i) *The vision of the locusts* (verses 1-3). The prophet observes the Lord preparing a plague of locusts. If we assume that the visionary experience is related to that which Amos actually saw in his travels in Israel, the time of year would be late spring. The first spring crop of hay had been taken from the fields and the second crop was beginning to sprout. The vision was thus one of promise and disaster; the second crop offered promise of provision, but the seething locusts threatened to destroy it all. (On locust plagues in Palestine and their threat to the whole land, see further the Introduction and Commentary on the Book of Joel.)

The substance of the vision is followed immediately by the prophet's prayer (verse 2). He sees perfectly clearly that the

locusts are not a fluke of nature, but are an act of divine judgment, the consequence of Israel's sin. And so he prays: "forgive!" And to his plea, he adds words directed towards the divine
compassion: "How can Jacob [viz. Israel] stand? He is so small!"
In response to the prophet's plea, God changes his mind and
cancels the locust plague.

(ii) *The vision of fire* (verses 4–6). In the second vision, Amos
sees God calling for a fire of judgment to come upon the land, and
he sees the fire begin. The intensity of the fire is illustrated by its
"devouring the great deep". A fire that "devours" water cannot
be extinguished, and in the vision it is already beginning to
consume the land. Whereas the first vision presupposed late
spring, the second vision appears to reflect the hot mid-summer
months; during those months, the risk of a quickly burning grass
fire was high. Again, Hosea prays that God would stop the fire in
its path, and again God responds to the prayer.

(iii) *The vision of the plumb line* (verses 7–9). In the third
vision, Amos sees the Lord standing beside a wall, perhaps the
city wall of Samaria, with a plumb line in his hand. The plumb line
was used by a builder both in the construction of a wall, to see that
it was straight, and also in the examination of old walls, to see
whether, for safety's sake, they should be demolished. The Lord
stands beside a wall that has been constructed correctly; he is
using the plumb line to see whether it has retained its correct
alignment. This time, the vision involves dialogue. The Lord asks
Amos what he sees, and he responds, "A plumb line." Then the
symbolism is interpreted for the prophet: God is setting the
plumb line against the chosen people to see if they are still
"straight", but they are not. Just as a dangerously leaning wall
must be demolished for safety's sake, so too must Israel be
destroyed because of its crooked alignment (verse 9).

These three visions have a good deal in common with respect to
substance and form, and yet it is the progression and development of thought that is most notable by the end of the third
visionary account. The first two represent classic cases of prophetic intercession. The Lord intimates coming judgment; the
prophet prays, prompting the divine pity, and the judgment is

averted. Thus the first two visions are illuminating with respect to both God and his prophet. God is holy and thus must judge a sinful people; on the other hand, God is merciful and may be swayed in his action by the prayers of his prophet. The prophet, seeing the impending disaster in the visions, is immediately prompted to pray for mercy; he too is moved by compassion.

But in the third vision, time has passed and nothing has changed in Israel. Early judgments have been averted, but Israel has not changed its evil ways. (Perhaps one may assume a period of the prophet's preaching, as reflected in chapters 1–6, had intervened between the first and third visions.) And so, when Amos perceives the third vision and the threat of destruction, he no longer prays to God that it be averted. And God, whose compassion has already been demonstrated in the first two visions, does not indicate that the judgment of the third vision will be set aside.

The sequence of visions demonstrates the fundamental compassion of both God and his prophet. Neither wish for the judgment of Israel. Both have sought to avert it. But there comes a point of no return; it is Israel, in its dedicated pursuit of evil, that pushes Amos beyond the capacity to intercede and precipitates God into final commitment to judgment. It is a sobering picture, appropriately filling in the nuances of the general prophetic portrait of a God of judgment. Judgment only comes when the long line of compassion is finally exhausted. Judgment is never a capricious act, never a spontaneous occasion of wrath, but always the final result of mercy refused and compassion rejected. Judgment, in other words, is always invited by the persons judged. And if, when it is finally perceived, it brings terror to its recipients, it must not be forgotten that it is a source of final grief to God, its compassionate author, and Amos his prophet.

AMOS AND THE ENCOUNTER WITH AMAZIAH

Amos 7:10–17

[10]Then Amaziah the priest of Bethel sent to Jeroboam king of Israel, saying, "Amos has conspired against you in the midst of the house of

Israel; the land is not able to bear all his words. ¹¹For thus Amos has said,

'Jeroboam shall die by the sword,
 and Israel must go into exile
 away from his land.'"

¹²And Amaziah said to Amos, "O seer, go, flee away to the land of Judah, and eat bread there, and prophesy there; ¹³but never again prophesy at Bethel, for it is the king's sanctuary, and it is a temple of the kingdom."

¹⁴Then Amos answered Amaziah, "I am no prophet, nor a prophet's son; but I am a herdsman, and a dresser of sycamore trees, ¹⁵and the Lord took me from following the flock, and the Lord said to me, 'Go, prophesy to my people Israel.'

¹⁶"Now therefore hear the word of the Lord.

You say, 'Do not prophesy against Israel,
 and do not preach against the house of Isaac.'

¹⁷Therefore thus says the Lord:

'Your wife shall be a harlot in the city,
 and your sons and your daughters shall fall by the sword,
 and your land shall be parcelled out by line;
you yourself shall die in an unclean land,
 and Israel shall surely go into exile away from its land.'"

The account of the prophet's visions is now interrupted by a scene depicting a confrontation between Amos and Amaziah, the High Priest of the royal Israelite shrine at Bethel. This occasion of confrontation may well have been the final episode in Amos' brief ministry in Israel; its location in the book, however, is determined by the substance of the third vision and the message emerging from it. In the oracle following the vision of the plumb line, Amos had spoken the words of God: "I will rise against the house of Jeroboam with the sword." Apparently the declaration of those words, making specific reference to Israel's royal family, precipitated the conflict scene described here.

The narrative is unique in the book of Amos, being the only passage in which we are provided with clear details of the historical setting and personal encounters in the prophet's ministry. Its purpose, however, is not strictly historical or biographical; indeed, from a biographical perspective it is a frustrating narrative, for we are left guessing as to what was the final outcome of this clash of two powerful personalities. From the perspective of the book as a whole, the purpose of the narrative is to make clear the setting and meaning of the oracle against the High Priest and his family with which it concludes (verse 17). It is legitimate, nevertheless, to learn from both the narrative and its concluding message.

(i) *The confrontation* (verses 10–15). Prior to the actual confrontation, Amaziah sent a message to King Jeroboam II. The High Priest had heard, or been told, about the prophet's proclamation of judgment against the royal household. And Amaziah, as chief priest at Bethel, was a servant of the king, for Bethel had been a royal sanctuary for a long time. (In the text, Amaziah is simply called "the priest of Bethel", but as the establishment would have had many priests, the expression implies "*the* priest", or the High Priest.)

The message to the king implies that Amos is guilty of conspiracy, or even treason. His prophetic ministry is interpreted as an act of conspiracy against the king by a foreign prophet, whose actions are said to be stirring up the people to a dangerous state. The message was partly true and partly false. It was true that Amos had spoken against the royal household (7:9); it was not true that he had specifically said that Jeroboam would die by the sword, as Amaziah claimed (7:11). It was no doubt true that the people were stirred up by the prophet's preaching; there was nothing to suggest, however, that they were stirred towards conspiracy, but only by anxiety with respect to the possibility of judgment.

Amaziah is thus a representative of the establishment who wants to preserve the status quo. He had a good position in Bethel, considerable influence and power and wealth. He enjoyed the privilege of being the king's representative in the town of Bethel. But Amos was stirring things up and spoiling the usual smooth flow of affairs. He was condemning in public the cult and the great festivals. He was upsetting the populace whose offerings helped to maintain Amaziah in the life of luxury to which he had become attached. This foreign prophet was a fly in the clear ointment of the High Priest's life and must be removed. And what better way to remove him than to activate the king's authority from Samaria? If the facts needed to be twisted a little to that end, so be it. And if in reality Amos spoke the true word of God, well, Amaziah would rather not hear that word when it threatened his sinecure.

There then follows the actual confrontation between the two men (verses 12–15), and one must suppose that by this time Amaziah had secured some warrant from the king. Amaziah instructs the prophet to return to Judah, implying that he should flee before being arrested for conspiracy. And the priest implies, no doubt deliberately, that the purpose of Amos' prophesying was simply to make money. There were indeed professional prophets who made a living by their services; when Amaziah says to Amos "eat bread there" (in Judah), he is employing an expression which means: "make your living there, not here". Thus Amaziah not only prohibits Amos from ministering in Bethel, but he impugns his motives; he implies that Amos' only goal was personal gain.

Amos was not a diffident man and responded first to the High Priest's instruction with respect to his motives. "I am no prophet . . ."; he means that he is not a professional prophet, paid for his services, nor was his father before him. In normal life, he was responsible for cattle, fruit-farming, and sheep (see further in the Introduction). The response implies that Amos had a perfectly good living without needing to engage in prophetic moonlighting. He acted as a prophet in Bethel for one reason, and only one reason: the Lord had said to him, "Go, prophesy to my people, Israel" (verse 15). And so Amos had obeyed.

(ii) *The message to the High Priest* (verses 16–17). Having affirmed his credentials, Amos now continues to declare a divine oracle addressed specifically to Amaziah and his family. Amos had been told, "Do not prophesy". But God had spoken, and so no human injunction to silence could cause him to refrain from speaking.

The message to Amaziah is not a pretty one. The High Priest's wife would become a prostitute in the city; his children would be slain in battle. His land holdings would be divided up and given to others, and he himself would die in a foreign land. The context in which all these judgments must be interpreted is that of exile, following military defeat, as is made clear in the last line of verse 17. After the city's defeat, Amaziah would be sent into exile, there to die eventually. His wife, left in Bethel without any means of support after years of luxurious living, would turn to prostitution as an ignominious means of survival. And their children would be dead.

The conclusion of the passage brings home a frightening truth with respect to Amaziah's position. Behind the great confrontation scene there appears to have been one basic desire on the priest's part. He did not want God's truth to be proclaimed. And the reason he tried to prohibit its proclamation is that it might have undermined the comfortable niche he had established for himself in the "Church". From the perspective of distance in time, his actions seem crazy: why should Amaziah prohibit the proclamation of the Lord's word, when his own name and office identified him as a servant of the same Lord? (*Amaziah* means "the Lord is strong".) But what seems crazy in others' lives can all too easily become a part of our lives. Having established for ourselves a comfortable niche in the Church, we resist everything that would threaten it.

THE VISION OF THE END

Amos 8:1–3

[1]Thus the Lord God showed me: behold, a basket of summer fruit. [2]And he said, "Amos, what do you see?" And I said, "A basket of summer fruit." Then the Lord said to me,
  "The end has come upon my people Israel;
    I will never again pass by them.
[3]The songs of the temple shall become wailings in that day,"
                                        says the Lord God;

"the dead bodies shall be many;
   in every place they shall be cast out in silence."

After the interlude concerning Amos and Amaziah, the account of the series of visions continues. The fourth vision, like the third, begins with a description of something that Amos sees; then there follows a dialogue between Amos and God which issues into a statement of divine judgment.

Amos sees a basket containing "summer fruit"; the expression refers to those fruits that come to fruition at the end of the growing season, in late August and September. Though several types of fruit could be embraced by the expression, the primary designation is probably a fruit-for-eating, such as a fig. If the vision were prompted in any manner by physical circumstances, then it is probable that this visionary experience was in late summer or early autumn, some half-year later than the first vision of springtime (7:1–3).

Amos is asked what he sees, and he responds: "A basket of *qayits* ['summer fruit']." To which the Lord responds: "The *qets* ['end'] has come". Thus the substance of the vision introduces a word play *(qayits/qets)*, which in turn introduces an oracle concerning Israel's end. The two words, *qayits* and *qets*, are not etymologically related, so it is their sound that is the basis of association. But the symbolism nevertheless goes beyond sound to meaning: just as the fruits in question come at the end of summer, so also Israel's summer is almost over and the harvest of judgment is ripe for the picking.

The meaning of the vision and the attached oracle are among the most solemn ever pronounced by Amos. The end had now come. The happy songs traditionally associated with harvest home at summer's end would be exchanged for wailings when the prophesied end became a reality. Dead bodies would be strewn about the land like the stalks and stubble left over after a harvest has been cut. The fresh field of promise, which was the beginning of Israel's life, would at last become a field of corpses, hung over by the stench of death.

The fourth vision is terrifying, both in its significance for Israel and its delivery on the part of Amos.

(i) For Israel, the message was clear: it was now too late to change the future, which had been determined and fixed by a long history of sin. The prophetic message served no longer as a warning, allowing the possibility of repentance; it was simply a statement, intimating the end. Like the sentence of death proclaimed in court of law by a solemn judge, the words following the vision make us pause for a moment and think. It is indeed possible to go too far. One can in fact practise evil so persistently that a death sentence is inevitably proclaimed. There does actually come a point at which all excuses are useless: the death sentence is proclaimed and nothing can change it. The message of Amos offered no consolation whatever to Israel; it may still serve as a warning, however, to those of subsequent generations. Evil is not a light matter, something to be played with casually; its end is death.

(ii) The vision and its message must have been no less terrifying to Amos. It was not an easy statement he was told to declare. Nor was it even an easy thing to accept. Did not the fact that Amos had been called to a prophetic ministry imply a divine mission of mercy? Did God need a town-crier whose only task was to declare death? For a short time in his ministry he had been able to say: "Seek the Lord and live" (5:6). Now all he could say was, "It's too late; you must die."

Like the physician who must inform a patient that an illness is terminal, that there is nothing further medical science can do, and that there are only a few weeks still to live, so must Amos address Israel. And just as a physician cannot say such words easily, belonging to a profession dedicated to the healing of sickness and the alleviation of suffering, likewise Amos cannot speak the words lightly. The physician seeks to heal the body, the prophet seeks to heal the spirit, and neither can casually accept the onslaught of death; each suffers in what seems to be defeat. Yet neither physician nor prophet were promised that their task would be an easy one.

ISRAEL'S COMING RUIN

Amos 8:4-14

⁴Hear this, you who trample upon the needy,
    and bring the poor of the land to an end,
⁵saying, "When will the new moon be over,
    that we may sell grain?
And the sabbath,
    that we may offer wheat for sale,
that we may make the ephah small and the shekel great,
    and deal deceitfully with false balances,
⁶that we may buy the poor for silver
    and the needy for a pair of sandals,
    and sell the refuse of the wheat?"

⁷The Lord has sworn by the pride of Jacob:
    "Surely I will never forget any of their deeds.
⁸Shall not the land tremble on this account,
    and every one mourn who dwells in it,
and all of it rise like the Nile,
    and be tossed about and sink again, like the Nile of Egypt?"

⁹"And on that day," says the Lord God,
    "I will make the sun go down at noon,
    and darken the earth in broad daylight.
¹⁰I will turn your feasts into mourning,
    and all your songs into lamentation;
I will bring sackcloth upon all loins,
    and baldness on every head;
I will make it like the mourning for an only son,
    and the end of it like a bitter day.

¹¹"Behold, the days are coming," says the Lord God,
    "when I will send a famine on the land;
not a famine of bread, nor a thirst for water,
    but of hearing the words of the Lord.
¹²They shall wander from sea to sea,
    and from north to east;
they shall run to and fro, to seek the word of the Lord,
    but they shall not find it.

¹³"In that day the fair virgins and the young men

shall faint for thirst.
14Those who swear by Ashimah of Samaria,
  and say, 'As thy god lives, O Dan,'
  and, 'As the way of Beer-sheba lives,'
  they shall fall, and never rise again.''

In this passage, which is a collection of various oracles and summary statements from the prophet, the theme of the fourth vision
is developed and illustrated: the end was coming for Israel. In
different ways, the nature of that coming end is illuminated, its
judgmental character and the plight of the people in the last days.
There are four sections to the passage, each employing some
phenomenon from the natural world as a description of the end.

(i) *Earthquake* (verses 4–8). At the beginning of the book,
Amos' ministry is introduced as occurring "two years before the
earthquake" (1:1). Now, once again, an earthquake is referred to
(verse 8); it still lies in the future, but it is described not simply as a
phenomenon of nature, but as an act of divine judgment. Almost
certainly the event has not yet happened; its effect is described as
being like the rise and fall of the Nile in flood, which is inappropri-
ate as a descriptive simile, but effective enough in describing the
end result. The land would be devastated, tossed about and
sinking flatly at last in the aftermath of chaos.

The act of judgment is quite explicitly tied to one aspect
of Israel's moral failure. The searchlight of judgment falls on
Israel's merchant classes, those who grew rich by trade, oppressing the poor in their climb towards wealth. The prophet's description is colourful. These greedy merchants are anxious for the
festivals (the "new moon", verse 5) and the sabbaths to be over,
so that they can open the corn market again and resume business.
For them, the day of rest was a day wasted, a day in which the
poor could be exploited and profit accumulated. And the merchants did not observe the standards of the Better Business
Bureau: they sold light measure for top price. And when the
hungry were too poor to pay for food, the merchants traded corn
for human lives. The poor themselves could be sold to other rich
persons as slaves for a quick profit.

Of all the ills that may assault a human society, rapacity is perhaps one of the most common and the most dangerous. It is a grasping lust for money and power, a predatory instinct that makes the lives of others mere prey in the path of one's own advancement, and an acceptance of extortion as a normal part of business practice. Its goal is entirely the satisfaction of self, its victim all those weak enough to be used for personal ends. It is indeed a kind of religion, evoking in its adherents profound love of the self and happy acceptance of the ruin of others. But rapacious greed is a cult so fundamentally foreign to the whole truth of God that it must be condemned. And Amos perceives its foundations to be so firm that only an earthquake can shatter its proud structures.

(ii) *Eclipse* (verses 9–10). Now Amos refers to a second catastrophe, more ominous than actual, namely a total eclipse of the sun. Scientific calculations have indicated that at least two total eclipses must have occurred during the prophet's lifetime: one on February 9, 784 B.C., the other on June 15, 763 B.C. But the scientific knowledge which makes such calculations possible in our own age was not available to Amos and his contemporaries. And whereas today we may be alerted to a coming eclipse in the newspaper and may troop outside to watch it, warning children of the danger to their eyes, such was hardly the case in the ancient world. Even today, an eclipse is an awesome thing to observe; in centuries past, it was a source of profound fear and anxiety, intimating disorder in the cosmos.

The reason for the coming eclipse is intimated in verse 10. It would turn the cheerful festivals into times of misery; it would transform the happy days into days of lamentation and mourning. Amos is continuing his critique of Israel's cult (see also 4:4–6 and 5:21–24). But the relation between the judgment and the crime is an effective one. On the festival days, light was celebrated: the light of God's creation, the light of God's truth, indeed the light of life itself. But the collapse of the cult, its hypocrisy covering a nation's life of darkness, had made a mockery of the true meaning of the festivals. And so the day of light would become a day of darkness, the eclipsed sun symbolising that the light of God's countenance would be hidden from Israel. One cannot celebrate light and live in darkness. And if we really desire the light of God's countenance to shine upon us, then we must walk in the light.

(iii) *Famine* (verses 11–12). In this message, that which is symbolized overpowers the symbol. From the context, one may suppose that Amos anticipated the advent of a real famine. But his message focuses on something deeper, something profoundly more worrisome, a famine of the "words of God". A time would come when the people of Israel would wander far and wide across the land, from extremity to extremity, seeking the Lord's word, but they would be unable to find it. One of the ancient fundamentals of Israel's faith was that "man does not live by bread alone, but that man lives by everything that proceeds out of the mouth of the Lord" (Deut. 8:3). Ultimately it was God's word that made life possible; by that word the creation of the world was established, by that word redemption was secured from Egyptian slavery, and by that word human beings found the meaning of their lives in relationship with God. The coming famine of the word could culminate in the starvation of the spirit, not the body, but when the spirit dies within a person the carcass is of little value.

Jesus, in resisting the temptation in the wilderness, was aware that "man shall not live by bread alone, but by every word that proceeds from the mouth of God" (Matt. 4:4). But he went further in illuminating the divine word upon which a person must feed. "My food is to do the will of him who sent me, and to accomplish his work" (John 4:34). To feed upon the divine word is to obey the divine will. But in ancient Israel the long history of disobedience was also the failure to feed upon the divine word. From such, eventually, the divine word would be withdrawn; only in the hunger pangs of death, when it was already too late, would people search once again for a bread that had been withdrawn.

(iv) *Drought* (verses 13–14). Those who worshipped at the various religious shrines associated with the nation's perverse faith would "faint for thirst." The implication is that they would eventually die of thirst in the coming drought.

There are considerable difficulties in the interpretation of verse 14. "Ashimah of Samaria": the expression may refer either to a foreign god, *Ashimah*, or it may be translated "the *guilt* of Samaria" (AV: "sin of Samaria"), an allusion perhaps to an idolatrous golden calf set up in Samaria, the nation's capital. The reference to Dan, a shrine in the north of Israel, may allude to a bull-image set up there (1 Kings 12:29). And Beersheba, located in the south of Judah, was an ancient shrine still visited by pilgrims from the northern state (see 5:5). Whether the prophet alludes to pagan worship as such, or whether he specifies the false and idolatrous worship of the Lord, remains uncertain; what is certain is that Israel's worship has become thoroughly corrupt and therefore totally unacceptable.

The judgment is that all the young shall die (verse 13), thereby emphasizing the message of the nation's end (8:1–3). Young men and women are more resistant than the old, but even they would collapse in the coming drought. And when a nation's youth are gone, there is no hope for the future. They carried the hope for a coming generation, so that their deaths would reinforce all the more the death of future hope. Thus the prophet, in these various messages, removes all shadow of doubt from those whom he addresses concerning the finality of Israel's coming judgment.

THE VISION OF THE LORD OF JUDGMENT

Amos 9:1–10

> [1]I saw the Lord standing beside the altar, and he said:
> "Smite the capitals until the thresholds shake,
>   and shatter them on the heads of all the people;
> and what are left of them I will slay with the sword;
>   not one of them shall flee away,
>   not one of them shall escape.
>
> [2]"Though they dig into Sheol,
>   from there shall my hand take them;
> though they climb up to heaven,

from there I will bring them down.
³Though they hide themselves on the top of Carmel,
    from there I will search out and take them;
and though they hide from my sight at the bottom of the sea,
    there I will command the serpent, and it shall bite them.
⁴And though they go into captivity before their enemies,
    there I will command the sword, and it shall slay them;
and I will set my eyes upon them
    for evil and not for good."

⁵The Lord, God of hosts,
he who touches the earth and it melts,
    and all who dwell in it mourn,
and all of it rises like the Nile,
    and sinks again, like the Nile of Egypt;
⁶who builds his upper chambers in the heavens,
    and founds his vault upon the earth;
who calls for the waters of the sea,
    and pours them out upon the surface of the earth—
the Lord is his name.

⁷"Are you not like the Ethiopians to me,
    O people of Israel?" says the Lord.
"Did I not bring up Israel from the land of Egypt,
    and the Philistines from Caphtor and the Syrians from Kir?
⁸Behold, the eyes of the Lord God are upon the sinful kingdom,
    and I will destroy it from the surface of the ground;
    except that I will not utterly destroy the house of Jacob,"
                      says the Lord.

⁹"For lo, I will command,
    and shake the house of Israel among all the nations
as one shakes with a sieve,
    but no pebble shall fall upon the earth.
¹⁰All the sinners of my people shall die by the sword,
    who say, 'Evil shall not overtake or meet us.'"

In the account of the fifth vision, it is clear that the progression is from bad to worse. In the first two visions, judgment had been threatened and then averted. In the third vision, disaster seemed inevitable; in the fourth, it was Israel's final end which was given prominence But still the prophet has not finished; the fifth vision affirms yet again the finality of the nation's coming collapse. The last three visions are like the progression of a long funeral day: first, there is a service for the deceased in the home, then a further funeral service in the church, and finally a service beside the open grave. In this final vision narrative we see Amos standing, as it were, beside the nation's open grave; the body of the deceased is about to descend into the dirt.

The setting of the vision is a sanctuary, presumably the Israelite sanctuary at Bethel which has already figured so prominently in the prophet's ministry. Amos sees the Lord standing beside the altar and he hears him speak. The altar was the place which symbolized the making of peace between God and Israel, but the words which are spoken are not words of peace. The Lord declares destruction: it would begin with the sanctuary itself and those within, spreading out from there to encompass the entire population. None would be able to escape the trembling earthquake of destruction. Neither the world beneath nor the heavens above, neither mountain nor ocean, would offer an avenue of escape, for God had set his eyes upon Israel "for evil and not for good" (verse 4).

There follows a hymnic passage, extolling the might of God over all the forces of nature (verses 5–6). At first it might appear out of context in the aftermath of the vision, but the intent of the verses soon becomes clear. The God of judgment, revealed in the vision, is Lord of heaven and earth; he has the control of the world of nature which is necessary if he is to make good his threat.

And then, as if someone had raised an objection, Amos reinforces the point that in a time of judgment Israel's election offers no special status. The chosen people, redeemed from Egypt, were simply one more nation among the nations of the world. They were essentially no different from the "Ethiopians' (more precisely the Nubians, who lived along the southern reaches of the Nile), or from the Philistines who had come from Caphtor (see 1:6–7), or from the Syrians from Kir (see 1:5). All the nations had a place in God's international scheme of things, but that meant also that all nations had a responsibility for righteousness and justice. And Amos declares that the "eyes of the Lord

God are upon the sinful kingdom" (verse 8); evil and injustice not
only invite judgment, but also eliminate any privilege associated
with election. And so the judgment of God must fall and the
people must perish.

The prophet's final vision and the elaboration added to it
reinforce two of the basic themes of his ministry.

(i) *Judgment begins in the sanctuary.* It radiates out from there
to encompass every other aspect of the nation's life. The reason is
not that there was more evil practised at the sanctuary than, for
example, in the stores of the rapacious merchants. Rather, the
sanctuary was always the centre of the nation's life. From there,
there should have radiated forth the knowledge of God and the
principles of truth and righteousness. But if the sanctuary could
not be the centre of Israel's life, then it could still be the centre of
the nation's death.

Righteousness and justice must be preserved at the centre,
whether of the Church, or of individual lives. When they are
absent there, they will disappear elsewhere. And if the life-giving
spirit of God does not flow from the centre to permeate the
whole, then the judgment of God may fill the vacuum.

(ii) *There are no privileges when righteousness and justice have
been abandoned.* To the very end, it seems, there were those who
protested all would be well, pointing to Israel's status as a privileged and elect nation. But when the responsibilities of privilege
are jettisoned, the position of privilege also goes. Privilege is
never just a special status. It is true that it is undeserved, given as
an act of grace, and cannot be earned. Yet for all the fact that one
cannot earn a place of privilege in God's sight, but only accept it,
one also must accept the responsibilities that come with it. There
is a basic insight here into the nature of the gospel. One can never
earn the privilege of God's grace, but nor can one abandon its
responsibilities without denying the privilege itself. Like "Love
and Marriage", as the old popular song used to go, "you can't
have one without the other."

Too much stress should not be laid on the final verses of this
section, which seem to hold out a little hope for the future. The
last line of verse 8 suggests that God will not *utterly* destroy Israel,

and verses 9–10 use the metaphor of a sieve which will not let good pebbles fall through, only the dirt. Because these "after-thoughts" slightly mitigate the gloom that pervades Amos' preaching, many scholars suppose that they were added later by a less radical hand. But even if they are Amos' own, *afterthought* is the operative word. All they in fact do is to leave a toe-hold for God's mercy one day (but certainly not now) to use. And perhaps, even for an Amos, that is as it should be.

POSTSCRIPT: HOPE FOR THE FUTURE

Amos 9:11–15

> 11"In that day I will raise up
>   the booth of David that is fallen
> and repair its breaches,
>   and raise up its ruins,
>   and rebuild it as in the days of old;
> 12that they may possess the remnant of Edom
>   and all the nations who are called by my name,"
>   says the Lord who does this.

> 13"Behold, the days are coming," says the Lord,
>   "when the ploughman shall overtake the reaper
>   and the treader of grapes him who sows the seed;
> the mountains shall drip sweet wine,
>   and all the hills shall flow with it.
> 14I will restore the fortunes of my people Israel,
>   and they shall rebuild the ruined cities and inhabit them;
> they shall plant vineyards and drink their wine,
>   and they shall make gardens and eat their fruit.
> 15I will plant them upon their land,
>   and they shall never again be plucked up
>   out of the land which I have given them,"
>   says the Lord your God.

The book which has been dominated throughout its nine chapters by the dark clouds of judgment ends abruptly with this more cheerful message of hope. A day is still to come, it is affirmed in these verses, in which the people will be restored to their land, there to live in God's bounty and prosperity.

The change in tone (even taking into account the chinks of light in verses 8–10) is so remarkable that, not unnaturally, a debate has arisen amongst the scholars as to whether the concluding verses are authentic to Amos, or whether they are an addition of a later age. Those who argue that this section is a later addition stress the change in tone and in theological substance, note the apparently Judean (rather than Israelite) perspective in the reference to the "booth of David" (verse 11), the later historical perspective implied of Edom (verse 12), and various other fine points of literary criticism. On the other hand, those who hold that this is an authentic part of Amos' work argue that the change in tone, the following of judgment with a message of ultimate hope, is not peculiar to Amos. Similar contrasts in theological thought may be seen in the writings of the prophet's contemporaries: Hosea, Micah and Isaiah. (It should be added, of course, that a similar debate rages with respect to those books!) And indeed a similar contrast in religious thought can be seen in works from Israel's neighbours, such as the Egyptian "Prophecy of Neferrohu".

A debate of this kind is not easily resolved; it would be fair to say that the majority of modern scholars consider the section to be a postscript from a later period, perhaps the Judean exile of the sixth century B.C. The postscript would then add the final perspective from which later generations were expected to read the prophet's dark threats of judgment. But, in the absence of original manuscripts and other information, the argument will probably never be concluded to everyone's satisfaction.

Whichever perspective one chooses in interpreting the final verses of Amos, it is important to recognize that they remain a part of the canonical text of Holy Scripture. One is not being unfaithful to the Bible, as God's Word, by taking the view that these verses are from a later hand. Whether they come from Amos, or whether they represent an addition from an editor or disciple, they are a part of the Bible. And with respect to our reading of the Book of Amos, they are an extremely important part of the text as a whole. In the book we have been provided with limited insights concerning the prophet's ministry and message. But we need to know also why the prophet's message was preserved for later generations. It is crystal clear how important the message of Amos was to ancient Israel; does it have the same importance for subsequent generations? The final verses round out the message of the prophet. They do not contain a summary, for these verses, taken alone, would give a very lopsided view of the whole picture. But they contain nevertheless an important insight: even after the darkest message of judgment, and indeed even after its fulfilment, there remains a word of hope.

Beyond all the disaster of judgment, a day of rebuilding is anticipated; it is *rebuilding*, for the judgment must inevitably come to pass. The broken world of the chosen people would be restored, the crops and harvests of the land would be plentiful once again, and new cities would arise from the ruins of the past. And the restoration of the chosen people, when it occurred, would be permanent; the new growth of the nation would never again be destroyed. Thus does the book end, and this final bright perspective must be added to those darker ones that precede it.

We take leave of the Book of Amos with the sense of having encountered one of God's most remarkable servants. A citizen of Judah, his agricultural business interests took him north to the nation of Israel. But Amos was a man of faith, not merely a businessman. The faith was not left in Tekoa when he took off on business; wherever he went, he saw the world and human society from the perspective of his faith in God. And being a sensitive man, he heard the divine vocation. For a short period of his life, this remarkable layman served as a prophet, declaring a particularly unpleasant and unpopular message in a land where he was a foreigner. Amos is extraordinary for his obedience and his courage; no less significant are the clarity and immediacy with which he proclaimed the prophetic word.

In his own time, the relevance of his message would have been clear to all who heard it, though it would not have been easy to accept and act upon. And, perhaps because it was relevant in its own time, the message seems to have lost little of its power and relevance in another world and another age. It is true that the message was given to Israelites, and we read it as gentiles. It is true that it was declared in Hebrew, while we read it in English. But for all the changes of circumstance, history, and culture, the fundamentals of the society Amos saw and of our own have remained, sadly, much the same. Now, as then, injustice remains to mar human society; righteousness is most evident by its absence. The established forms of religion prosper in their own way, but we cannot but wonder at what the sermon of Amos would be directed if he were the visiting preacher at one of our great church festivals. He would probably still have to preach the same old message of judgment: "I hate, I despise your feasts, and I take no delight in your solemn assemblies" (5:21). For he could see, in a way that we cannot easily see, through the veneer that religion may become; his eyes penetrated the shell of hypocrisy and saw within the presence of evil and injustice. And when we begin to grasp this vision of Amos, and apply it to ourselves and our contemporary institutions, we also realize that we must hear his message of judgment before we turn to the oracle of salvation with which the book ends. It is a solemn thought that Amos' first audience lived to experience the judgment, but died before any day of salvation dawned. The book has been preserved, in part, to warn its readers in later generations of the folly of pursuing a path that leads to disaster.

INTRODUCTION TO
THE BOOK OF OBADIAH

AUTHORSHIP, DATE AND CIRCUMSTANCES

The Book of Obadiah claims the honour of being the shortest book in the Old Testament; its brevity, however, is not matched by ease of interpretation.

The problems begin with the difficulty of identifying the book's author. He is called *Obadiah*, meaning "the Lord's servant", but nothing is known of his life. There are eleven other persons in the Old Testament bearing the name Obadiah, but not one of them can be linked with any certainty to the writer of this short prophetic book. He was a prophet; this much can be discerned from his regular ascription to God of the origin of his words (verses 1, 4, 8, 18). Some scholars have attempted to determine something of the writer's character from the substance of his message, but such a procedure is precarious at the best of times. So we must be content to recognize the author as a named, but essentially anonymous, prophet; his message was preserved, but the medium remains unknown.

Some assistance might be provided in identifying the author if it were possible to pin down the century in which he lived, but even this cannot be done with certainty. Whereas the books of many prophets, such as Hosea, begin with a precise statement of date, linking the prophetic ministry to the reigns of kings or to significant events, Obadiah's book, after the briefest of introductions, plunges directly into the subject matter. Proposals with respect to the book's date have ranged from as early as the ninth century B.C. to as late as the fifth century B.C. With such disparity, it is clear that the internal evidence of the book, upon which hypotheses of date must be constructed, is thoroughly ambivalent.

The central subject of the book is the small state of Edom, against which the prophet's message is directed. If the event in Edom's history which precipitated the prophecy could be determined, it might then be possible to propose a date for the book and learn a little more about the author. But though a certain amount is known of Edomite history, several parts of the history could be associated with this short prophetic book; hence, the uncertainty remains.

Edom was situated, in modern geographical terms, in the southern part of the territory now belonging to the kingdom of Jordan. Its northern territory flanked the eastern shores of the Dead Sea, and it extended southwards alongside and beyond the great rift valley, the Arabah. Though bordered by the desert on the east and south, Edom was a land that was just habitable as a consequence of the rainfall on its mountains, slopes, and the plateau bordering the western escarpment. This moderate rainfall made possible some farming.

The territory of Edom, though originally the domain of nomadic peoples, had been settled about 1300 B.C., shortly before the Hebrew settlement in Palestine. In addition to agriculture, the small kingdom flourished by virtue of its control of various ancient trading routes. To the north, the highway led up the Arabah, and eventually through the Jordan valley and beyond to Damascus. The same highway extended to the south, leading to Arabia and the ocean routes with ports on the Gulf of Aqaba. Westwards, across the Arabah, a road led to the Mediterranean with its ports, and thence to Egypt. Thus, through trade and agriculture, Edom acquired for several centuries a modest degree of wealth and influence in the ancient world.

Its towns, too, were defensible in times of military crisis, a consequence of their location in mountain strongholds. Most modern travellers in the kingdom of Jordan are familiar with the remains of the ancient city of Petra, a "rose-red city, half as old as time," as the Rev. John William Burgon called it. Though the Petra that remains was constructed for the most part at the end of, and after, the Old Testament period, either it or a settlement near it may have been the capital of ancient Edom. The enormous flat-topped chunk of rock that dominates the Petra basin, Umm el Biyara in Arabic (rising about 1,000 feet above the remains below), was a site of human habitation at least as early as the seventh century B.C., as witnessed by the excavation of various objects there in recent years, including a clay seal bearing a seventh century inscription.

From the time of Israel's earliest history, there were tense relationships between the Hebrews and the Edomites. In King David's time, Edom had become an Israelite colony; though it eventually broke away from colonial status, the kingdom never came to continuous and peaceful terms with Israel (and later Judah). In the fifth century B.C., the Edomites were eventually evicted from their land by another enemy, the Nabateans; many Edomites moved westward across the Arabah and settled in the southern part of Palestine, in territory that once belonged to Judah before that state's decline at the beginning of the sixth century B.C.

The book as a whole, though coming from a Hebrew prophet, is addressed to the nation of Edom; only brief references are made to Jerusalem and Israel. But the origin of the book, though it remains obscure, is related to some critical point in the history of Hebrew-Edomite relationships. Recognizing the uncertainty that must be attached to any historical hypothesis, it is possible nevertheless to propose that Obadiah's book comes from the decades following the fall of Jerusalem and Judah (587/86 B.C.). After that critical event, it seems that Edom took advantage of Judah's calamity, seizing land for itself and being merciless to the survivors of the Babylonian war and defeat of Judah. It was, perhaps, these actions of Edom that elicited Obadiah's mournful message of judgment on Edom.

THE MESSAGE OF OBADIAH

The particular substance of this little book is described as a *vision* (verse 1), yet it is not a vision in any pictorial sense, but rather an account in words of events that would come to pass. Edom's coming destruction would take place in battle at the hands of various foreign nations. Its military strongholds, built in mountainous locations and offering good protection, would be of no avail when their enemies came to destroy. The arrogance of the Edomites, born out of a false sense of security, would be utterly shattered on the day of their defeat. With such gloomy predictions the prophecy of Obadiah begins. Yet it becomes clear as the prophet contines to speak that Edom's coming judgment was to be a direct consequence of its sin. The catalogue of evil (verses 10–14) amounts to a condemnation for a form of fratricide, for though the Edomites were distantly related to the Hebrews, they had participated actively in the downfall of Jerusalem. Along with other nations, Edom would fall victim to the coming judgment of God, but a different future lay ahead for Israel. The exiles would return eventually to their own land and the Lord would be their King once more.

Throughout the book, expression is given to the prophet's understanding of God's judgment in human history. Edom had committed inhuman crimes and for such there would inevitably be punishment. Yet the writer states his views, not so much as a gloating outsider, but rather as one who has already experienced God's judgment in his own nation and in the destruction of its capital city, Jerusalem. But through the dark shades of future historical judgment, Obadiah perceives hope for the restoration of the chosen people; more than that, he expresses hope for the kingdom of God.

It would be foolish to pretend that Obadiah is a pleasant book to read. Not only is it overcast by the dark shroud of judgment and disaster, but at first reading it appears also to be stained by a spirit of vindictiveness. Does it not seem a little presumptuous for a Hebrew prophet to declare with such terrifying detail the coming disaster in Edom? And even when it is recalled that Edom had not behaved well towards Judah in its time of travail, there is a sense in which that behaviour was little more than retaliation. Edom was a former colony and had stored up a long history of resentment at former actions undertaken against it by the Hebrews. Certainly Judah had no right to point the accusing finger of judgment at Edom.

Yet, as is true of all prophecy, the essence of the book is that it contains the Lord's word (verse 1). And God was not partial; he had already judged his own people for their evil, and no less would he judge other nations. The essence of the theology throughout is that God is the Lord of human history; the evil acts of any nation, regardless of affiliation or national faith, invite divine judgment. And that theme, though delivered in Obadiah's time, contains a timeless truth. But there is also hope in the book. It is expressed initially in terms of Jerusalem and the promised land, but eventually it touches on a broader vision: "the kingdom shall be the Lord's" (verse 21). And beyond the calamities of current history, we must share this glimpse of the prophet's vision if we are to grasp the perpetual relevance of the book. We pray regularly, in the Lord's prayer, "thy kingdom come". In so doing, we give expression to the same hope as Obadiah that, beyond the crises of history, God's kingdom of peace may eventually be established in the world.

THE DECLARATION OF EDOM'S DOOM

Obadiah 1–9

¹The vision of Obadiah.

Thus says the Lord God concerning Edom:
We have heard tidings from the Lord,
    and a messenger has been sent among the nations:
  "Rise up! let us rise against her for battle!"
²Behold, I will make you small among the nations,
    you shall be utterly despised.
³The pride of your heart has deceived you,
    you who live in the clefts of the rock,
    whose dwelling is high,
who say in your heart,
    "Who will bring me down to the ground?"
⁴Though you soar aloft like the eagle,
    though your nest is set among the stars,
    thence I will bring you down,

                                   says the Lord.

⁵If thieves came to you,
 if plunderers by night—
 how you have been destroyed!—
 would they not steal only enough for themselves?
 If grape gatherers came to you,
  would they not leave gleanings?
⁶How Esau has been pillaged,
 his treasures sought out!
⁷All your allies have deceived you,
 they have driven you to the border;
 your confederates have prevailed against you;
  your trusted friends have set a trap under you—
  there is no understanding of it.
⁸Will I not on that day, says the Lord,
 destroy the wise men out of Edom,
 and understanding out of Mount Esau?
⁹And your mighty men shall be dismayed, O Teman,
 so that every man from Mount Esau will be cut off by slaughter.

Verse 1 forms an introduction to the book as a whole; verse 2 introduces the first prophetic oracle, namely the words of God which the prophet was to declare.

The book is entitled "the vision of Obadiah". Though the word *vision* may imply that God's word came to the prophet in a dream, or some other visual form, it developed the general meaning *revelation*; the substance of the following verses suggests that the divine message came to Obadiah in the form of words, which the prophet in turn was to declare in public. And the words, though they concern Edom with respect to substance, were to be addressed to the prophet's fellow citizens, the people who lived in Jerusalem and Judah. Indeed, the last words of the book are addressed specifically to those in the vicinity of Jerusalem; the message to Jerusalem emerged from the declaration concerning Edom's doom.

After the title line, the prophet elaborates in a little more detail the circumstances of the declaration of God's word, prior to delivering the prophecy as such. Two items prompted the prophetic ministry. (a) The Lord had spoken: "We have heard tidings from the Lord". And the prophet's role was to communicate these tidings to the people, in the traditional prophetic fashion. So far, the words indicate the normal fashion in which a prophetic activity would begin. (b) Concurrently, something was taking place in international affairs which prompted the ministry and indicated its timeliness. News had reached the people that war was being prepared by various nations against Edom. The words in quotation marks at the end of verse 1 are typical of the form of a summons to warfare in the ancient world. In context, however, they are equivalent to a modern newspaper headline: "WAR DECLARED AGAINST EDOM!" This item of international news was a part of the situation which precipitated Obadiah's ministry.

The substance of the oracle concerned the state of Edom, southeast of the Dead Sea (see further the Introduction to Obadiah). Former prophets, and others who may have been Obadiah's contemporaries, had prophesied concerning Edom. Amos had spoken of the coming punishment of Edom (Amos 1:11–12), as had that great prophet of the Exile, Ezekiel (25:12–14). Jeremiah had declared a long oracle of judgment against Edom (49:7–27) and, if it is correct to date Obadiah slightly later than the time of Jeremiah, it becomes evident that Obadiah drew in part upon the words of his predecessor in Judah (in particular, compare Obad. 1–5 with Jer. 49:9, 14–16). It is possible that the coincidence of external events created an awareness in Obadiah that the prophecies of his predecessors were nearing fulfilment; he may begin with these quotations in order to indicate that the words spoken by Jeremiah and others were about to be executed on the stage of human history.

The prophetic oracle begins with a declaration of the divine intent. Edom, a nation that had aspired to grandeur, deluded by its capacity to protect itself against external threat, would be reduced to nothing. The Edomites, with good reason, believed their land to be safe from the threat of foreign enemies. Their towns and strongholds were built in rocky locations offering extraordinary military protection. Sir George Adam Smith, in *The Historical Geography of the Holy Land*, wrote of Edom: "its west flank is a series of ridges, shelves, and strips of valley, mazes of peaks, cliffs, and chasms that form some of the wildest rock scenery in the world. In the sandstone above the Arabah are the Shiks, clefts or corridors between perpendicular rocks." The reference to "the rock" in verse 3 may in fact be translated *Sela* (literally "Rock"), an Edomite fortress located near the spot that later become Petra, or else a location further north in Edom, about two miles northwest of Bozrah. Whether a specific place or merely an allusion to the rocky terrain of all Edom's strongholds, the poetic words indicate the pride of a people whose national defence system seemed to them to be impregnable.

The certainty of Edom's downfall is then stressed by reference to the totality of its coming destruction. If thieves broke into a house at night they would steal valuable items, but practical considerations would dictate that they leave some things behind! Yet Edom would not be so fortunate; the entire land would be pillaged. And in the grape harvest, the pickers would traditionally leave behind them slim pickings for the poor, yet Edom would not be so lucky! (The metaphor may allude to the vineyards of Edom, for vines flourished on the lower levels of the limestone hillsides; many centuries later, the Roman naturalist Pliny, in his *Natural History*, referred to "Petritan wine", produced probably in the vicinity of Petra.) Likewise, Edom's wise men would be destroyed at the time of God's judgment (verse 8); Eliphaz, one of Job's supposedly wise counsellors, was described as a resident of the Edomite city of Teman, indicating perhaps that Teman, in Edom, was a "university town", known abroad for its learning. But such learning would be to no avail at the time of God's judgment. (Teman, which according to tradition was named after a grandson of Esau, Gen. 36:11, has been identified with the ruins excavated in Edomite territory at Tawilan, where the remains appear to be of a city that flourished between the eighth and sixth centuries B.C.) Just as the advice of Edom's scholars would be of no avail in the face of judgment, so too the nation's warriors would lose heart and be defeated. (*Mount Esau* is poetically synonymous with Edom; according to tradition, the land was populated by the descendants of Esau.)

From these opening verses the fundamental theological perspectives of Obadiah's short prophecy emerge.

(i) *God's sovereignty over the nations.* The divine "I" of verse 2 makes it clear that Edom's downfall would be a direct consequence of God's action in human history. The goal would be achieved through the instrumentality of human beings, namely the military movements of Edom's enemies, but the divine hand would be behind the events of history.

Thus it is clear from the very beginning that the prophet views the history of nations not simply in terms of human freedom, but rather within the perspective of God's active presence in the world. He does not view history as fore-ordained, as if it would unfold like an already printed map; rather, human history unfolds through human action, but those actions as such are mysteriously penetrated by the action of God towards the goals of judgment and justice. It is not easy to join with the prophet in this view of human history. The secular historian's viewpoint may seem more attractive: history may be understood in terms of cause and effect, in terms of human action and reaction, without the possibility of any external powers being taken into account in understanding historical process. A totally different view of history, comforting to the few who hold it, is that all history is determined and must inexorably run its course, unaffected by human action. But Obadiah goes to neither extreme. To an extent, history must be understood in terms of the actions of the humans who forge it; to an extent, it can only be understood ultimately within the larger perspective of God's sovereign justice. And this balanced perspective at once issues in human responsibility for the course of history, balanced by a faith that its outcome is yet within the divine purview.

(ii) *The power of pride.* Though Edom's sins are yet to be listed in detail, the nation's pride is already set forth in these opening verses. Although the ideas of "pride" and "height" are often used in conjunction, they are joined with striking effect in these verses. Edom's mountainous land rose to a height of more than 5,000 feet above sea level, and its garrisons and forts were secured in rocky heights. But the sense of security lent to Edom by its physical height had contributed concurrently to the loftiness of pride: "Who will bring me down to the ground?" (verse

3). God will, the prophet answers, for Edom's pride was rooted in evil.

THE DAY OF EDOM AND THE LORD'S DAY

Obadiah 10–16

10For the violence done to your brother Jacob,
    shame shall cover you,
    and you shall be cut off for ever.
11On the day that you stood aloof,
    on the day that strangers carried off his wealth,
  and foreigners entered his gates
    and cast lots for Jerusalem,
    you were like one of them.
12But you should not have gloated over the day of your brother
    in the day of his misfortune;
  you should not have rejoiced over the people of Judah
    in the day of their ruin;
  you should not have boasted
    in the day of distress.
13You should not have entered the gate of my people
    in the day of his calamity;
  you should not have gloated over his disaster
    in the day of his calamity;
  you should not have looted his goods
    in the day of his calamity.
14You should not have stood at the parting of the ways
    to cut off his fugitives;
  you should not have delivered up his survivors
    in the day of distress.

15For the day of the Lord is near upon all the nations.
  As you have done, it shall be done to you,
    your deeds shall return on your own head.
16For as you have drunk upon my holy mountain,
    all the nations round about shall drink;
  they shall drink, and stagger,
    and shall be as though they had not been.

As Obadiah continues to address his words to Edom, the true nature of that nation's evil emerges. The Edomites, according to the ancient traditions of the Hebrews, were relatives; they were the descendants of Esau, the brother of Jacob. But their actions had not been the actions of a brother. They had participated in violence against the Hebrews; they had watched calmly while foreigners devastated the city of Jerusalem. By both violent action and heartless inaction, they had not only sinned, but been the instruments of injustice in the relationships between nations. The prophet, recalling vividly in his mind the horrors of the time of Jerusalem's sack (verses 12–14), issues a series of eight condemnations, specifying the various evils which Edom should not have perpetrated. But Edom's evil would have its own natural consequences. What they had done would be done to them; their acts of injustice would rebound upon them, but with full justice. The fratricidal acts of Edom would continue to haunt the nation, bringing about eventually its own demise.

In this section of the prophet's oracle, the central theme of the message is the word *day*; the theme is developed in two different directions, which are then strikingly contrasted.

(i) In verses 11–14, the word *day* is employed ten times. It is an historical reference, referring not to a 24-hour period, but rather to the time (approximately a month) during which the city of Jerusalem was sacked and partially destroyed by the Babylonian armies. What was for Judah a "day of distress" had become for Edom a day of delight. They gloated and boasted, rejoiced and participated, looted and assisted in Jerusalem's fall. Every inclination towards justice, every lingering memory of fraternal affection, indeed all basic humanity, had been set aside in the pursuit of personal advantage. Jerusalem's distress was Edom's pleasure. But now, Obadiah is stating, after the orgy of violence the accounts must be paid.

(ii) And so the prophet refers to another day, the "day of the Lord" (verse 15). The prophet Joel and others have developed this theme in greater detail; the Day of the Lord, while it has implications for salvation, is nevertheless a day of judgment for the world's evil nations. But Obadiah makes it very clear that the divine judgment on that day will not be arbitrary: "As you have done, it shall be done to you". In metaphorical language, the drunken orgy of evil on the holy mountain would culminate eventually in the alcoholic collapse of the drunkard.

The theological perspectives of Obadiah, in this portion of his message, highlight both the divine and the human dimensions of judgment.

(a) Running through the whole message is the prophet's conviction that God remains active in the affairs of human nations. He had not only observed Edom's actions towards Judah, but believed also that God had observed; and knowing something of divine justice, from his own and his nation's experience, he believed that the God who knew of Edom's folly must also act in judgment. Thus he proclaims: "the day of the Lord is near" (verse 15).

(b) But the conviction concerning God's justice and judgment with respect to the nations is balanced by an assurance that acts of evil bear within them the seeds of their own destruction. What Edom had done would affect what would be done to Edom; justice would be seen to be done in the corollary between the punishment and the preceding crime.

This twofold perspective of judgment is essential if we are to grasp not only the message of the prophets, but also the nature of judgment itself. From a human perspective, we cannot affirm the latter point by itself. Evil does not always seem to return to judge the perpetrator, as if it were some fundamental law of nature. It is only when we have faith in the sovereign justice of God that we may perceive the relationship between evil and the settling of accounts in judgment. In human terms, judging in the short period by the data of history itself, we cannot always know that justice is done. Obadiah proclaims the coming judgment in faith, though we do not know that he lived to see it. But we also perceive from Obadiah's message that judgment, when it comes, is not simply a manifestation of God's wrath; it is, in a sense, manufactured by its recipients, the consequence of the acts reverberating upon the actors.

Though Obadiah addresses a nation, his message is equally pertinent to individuals. He portrays clearly the opportunism of Edom, the mean streak that evokes glee in another's weakness, and the avarice that prompts the exploitation of another's grief for personal gain. It is easier to see such faults in the portrait of another than to perceive them in oneself. Yet Obadiah, like every other prophet, speaks not only to his own world, but holds up also a mirror for other generations. We do well to reflect upon the evils of Edom, for we may discern therein the outline of our own reflection. And if we see ourselves in the prophet's glass, we should also pay heed to his words: "As you have done, it shall be done to you." It is only repentance, and subsequent forgiveness, that breaks the vicious cycle of evil.

THE KINGDOM OF THE LORD

Obadiah 17–21

17But in Mount Zion there shall be those that escape,
    and it shall be holy;
  and the house of Jacob shall possess their own possessions.
18The house of Jacob shall be a fire,
    and the house of Joseph a flame,
    and the house of Esau stubble;
  they shall burn them and consume them,
    and there shall be no survivor to the house of Esau;
      for the Lord has spoken.
19Those of the Negeb shall possess Mount Esau,
    and those of the Shephelah the land of the Philistines;
  they shall possess the land of Ephraim and the land of Samaria
    and Benjamin shall possess Gilead.
20The exiles in Halah who are of the people of Israel
    shall possess Phoenicia as far as Zarephath;
  and the exiles of Jerusalem who are in Sepharad
    shall possess the cities of the Negeb.
21Saviours shall go up to Mount Zion to rule Mount Esau;
    and the kingdom shall be the Lord's.

At the end of Obadiah's message, the focus falls for the first time on the future fate of Obadiah's fellow citizens and their land. Now the prophet speaks of Zion and the chosen people, though their future is one that is ultimately related to Edom's demise. For the same "Day of the Lord" that would mark Edom's doom would also be a day of salvation for Judah. Mount Zion would be a holy mountain once again, the worship of its Temple restored; and the citizens of the land would repossess those territories of which they had been dispossessed by Edomites and other foreigners. What links these verses to the preceding passage is the instrumentality of Judah in Edom's judgment. To the citizens of Edom, the prophet had said, "As you have done, it shall be done to you" (verse 15); now we perceive that those to whom the Edomites had been so ruthless would also serve as the instruments of Edom's judgment. As a fire burns up the dry stubble after the harvest, so too Judah's restoration to strength would mark the burning and destruction of Edom. Thus, Obadiah reveals that Edom's coming judgment day would be a day of deliverance for Judah. And likewise, Judah's recent judgment and fall at the advent of Babylonian armies would be reversed in the coming collapse of Edom.

The anticipation of Edom's fall through the instrumentality of a revived Judah evokes from the prophet a still broader vision of the future. He looks forward to a time when all the lost lands of a once splendid kingdom would be regained. The catalogue of lands to be repossessed (verses 19–20) begins with Edom, but then broadens to encompass all the territories that had once constituted the nation of Israel in King David's time. And the verses do not merely catalogue the retaking of lost land; the prophet, by indicating that these future changes would take place in part through the actions of those returning from exile, conveys to his own people a powerful promise for the future.

The geographical vision of verses 19–20 is extensive. The *Negeb* was the broad tract of territory that lay in the southernmost part of Judah (namely the southern region of the modern state of Israel). This region was penetrated and partially populated by Edomites following the fall of Jerusalem (587 B.C.), but now the prophet anticipates a time of reversal when the people of the Negeb would expand eastwards into the mountainous region held by the Edomites. The *Shephelah*, lying between the Mediterranean Sea and the foothills of the Judean highlands, would be expanded towards the south, as its inhabitants repossessed the lands in the vicinity of Gaza that the Philistines and their descendants had possessed. To the north, in the territory that once was central to the state of Israel, the hill country of Ephraim, with its key city of Samaria, would be retaken. And the Benjaminites, living in a narrow strip of territory just north of Jerusalem, would expand eastwards across the Jordan into *Gilead*, the northern portion of the modern kingdom of Jordan. The location of *Halah* is not known with certainty (verse 20: indeed the Hebrew text is difficult and the translation uncertain); it was probably a region in northwestern Mesopotamia and is referred to here as one of the places from which exiles would return to the promised land, settling on the Mediterranean coast in territory that had been taken over by the Phoenicians. (*Zarephath*, or Sarepta, was located on the coast a few miles south of Sidon. Recent excavations at Sarepta, by American archaeologists, have revealed the remains of the city, dating back to Old Testament times.) The location of *Sepharad* is not known with certainty. In later Jewish history, the word was used to designate Spain, but in the present context it may refer to a region at, or close to, Sardis (in western Turkey, in modern geographical terms), where ancient inscriptions have provided evidence of an early Jewish settlement. From such remote places, those in exile would return to reclaim their promised land.

The short book of Obadiah ends with the affirmation of faith that "the kingdom shall be the Lord's" (verse 21). The message of the book as a whole can be summarized in the following points.

(i) *To Edom, there is a message of judgment.* Evil, in the world of nations, does not go unpunished, but returns to judge the evildoer. The prophet thus emphasizes not only the consequences of evil, but also the principles of justice. Despite what may seem to be the evidence of human history, namely that evil abounds and justice never comes, Obadiah affirms the principles of justice in God's dealings with the world's nations.

(ii) *To Judah, there is a message of hope.* Though the prophet and his compatriots lived still with the vivid memory of terrible judgment, the loss of their land, and the destruction of the holy city, beyond the rubble of present experience lay hope for a new land. And though the substance of hope still lay beyond the horizons of Judah's experience, it was a source of strength that would enable the people to continue to live and to create a new future.

(iii) *God is sovereign in human history.* The prophet's faith in God is such that he cannot perceive the events of history to be merely accidental or coincidental; in some fashion, albeit mysterious, history is moving towards the fulfilment of God's purpose. And yet Obadiah does not view the actions of persons and nations to be merely those of puppets, dangled from some divine string. Persons and nations are responsible for their actions; both judgment and salvation are a consequence of those actions. God's sovereignty in human history, as the prophet perceives it, does not supersede human action and responsibility, but works in and through the movements of history towards the divine goal.

(iv) *The goal of human history is the kingdom of God.* In the immediate context, it is the restoration of the kingdom of God in the promised land of which the prophet speaks. But in the larger biblical perspective, we may perceive a greater message. Obadiah's message closed with an anticipation of the coming kingdom (verse 21); the ministry of Jesus began with proclamation of a coming kingdom (Mark 1:14–15). The kingdom of God was to be established, from the New Testament perspective, in the death and resurrection of Jesus Christ. And yet, within that new kingdom of God, which is the Church of Christ, we continue to take Obadiah's hope upon our lips and make it our prayer every time we use the words of the Lord's Prayer: "thy kingdom come!"

INTRODUCTION TO THE BOOK OF JONAH

The short Book of Jonah is something of an oddity in the larger context of the Book of the Twelve Prophets. The other eleven books, though occasionally containing elements of biography and history, are essentially prophetic books; that is, they contain the prophetic statements and sermons of the prophets after whom the books have been named. But such is not the case with Jonah; the book contains a story, and the prophetic word of God occupies only a tiny portion of the book as a whole.

From a technical perspective, the book is anonymous; we are not told who wrote it, and hence we can have little certainty as to the date at which it was written. The principal character of the book is clear: it is Jonah, son of Amittai, who is referred to briefly in the historical narratives of ancient Israel (2 Kings 14:25) as a northern prophet from Gath-hepher, in the vicinity of Galilee. Jonah's prophetic ministry, of which very little is known from the single reference in 2 Kings, took place in the first half of the eighth century B.C., during the reign of King Jeroboam II. But whereas the period of the prophet's life is known, the date at which the book named after him was written remains unknown. In all probability it was written at a much later date, between the sixth and fourth centuries B.C.

THE STORY OF THE BOOK

Not only is the book unusual in the context of the Twelve Prophets; the story is also unusual, indeed comical in places. It begins conventionally enough with the prophetic call coming to the Lord's servant: "Arise, go to Nineveh" (1:2). But, from this point on, everything is the opposite of what one might expect in a prophetic narrative.

Jonah is told to go to Nineveh (northeast of Israel), a long trip over land. So immediately he sets off in a westerly direction for Joppa and buys a ticket for the slow boat to Tarshish (perhaps Tartessus, in Spain). But flight from the divine call was impossible; the ship for Tarshish was caught in a ferocious storm. But Jonah, who was too frightened to go to Nineveh and preach, slept peacefully through the storm while the old salts and seasoned sailors were on the verge of nervous breakdown. Jonah, on being identified as the probable cause of the storm, invites the crew to toss him overboard, again betraying no fear! The sailors reluctantly agree, and the storm abates. Jonah meanwhile is swallowed by a great fish, in whose belly he spends three gloomy days and nights. Jonah's repentance and prayer are followed by the deliverance; the great fish spews out its unwelcome burden on the beach, and then Jonah sets off for Nineveh. There, Jonah preaches the prophetic word, warning the citizens of that great city of their impending doom, unless they repent of their evil ways. To the prophet's horror, his evangelistic message is heeded by Nineveh's citizens; they turn away from their violence and evil and are spared from divine judgment. This is simply too much for the petulant and peevish prophet, whose anger is irrationally aroused by God's act of mercy. But, in the final verses of the book, the prophet (who has now decided that it would be better to be dead than live through such ignominy!) is taught a lesson concerning the nature of God's mercy.

THE PROBLEM OF INTERPRETATION

The short synopsis of the story already indicates the problem of interpreting this curious book. What kind of literature is it? How is it to be interpreted? Is it history? Or parable? Or some other kind of text?

In the ancient history of both Judaism and Christianity, there existed various theories as to the proper interpretation of the book. One of the oldest theories is that the book should be interpreted as an historical, prophetic narrative; it described, in this interpretation, an incident in the ministry of the prophet

Jonah. It should be admitted that such an interpretation is possible. Its starting point is the reasonable observation, based on the reference in 2 Kings, that Jonah was indeed an historical prophet (albeit a very obscure one). And, from a certain perspective, it has seemed to some interpreters that the New Testament references to Jonah imply an historical interpretation (Matt. 12:40 and 16:4; Luke 11:29).

But though it is possible, the historical interpretation is not probable. Every aspect of the story is so different from the conventional prophetic narratives that one suspects a different approach to the text is more appropriate. The role of the great fish and the plight of the belly-aching Jonah raise not so much the issue of miracle as they do of coarse humour. (We can almost sense the hilarity in the audience as the hairy prophet is swallowed—and is later coughed up, reeking of fish.) And while it was the custom of some interpreters a century ago to scour the annals of unusual maritime experience, such an effort in a sense misses the point. (It used to be fashionable to refer to the experience of a certain James Bartley, who in 1891 claimed to have fallen overboard from the whaling ship "Star of the East". He was then swallowed by a sperm whale, according to his account, and survived in that beast's belly for a day and a night, before escaping to tell his tale ashore. But that supposed incident, while a fascinating part of maritime lore, was probably not authentic. Indeed, the widow of the ship's master affirmed afterwards that no sailor went overboard during the term of her husband's captaincy of the vessel!) That the unusual or miraculous may indeed happen is not at issue; what is at issue is the nature of the book, its literary type, and hence the appropriate method of interpretation.

A second ancient interpretation of the book took as its starting point the view that the Book of Jonah must be interpreted as a kind of parable. The writer took a real, but virtually unknown, character called Jonah and constructed a parable around that figure to convey a theological message. The story of Jonah is thus, in general terms, parallel to such New Testament parables as the "Good Samaritan". And just as the parable of the "Good Samaritan" ends with a question (Luke 10:36), inviting the hearer to reflect upon its meaning, so too does the Book of Jonah end with a question (4:11), inviting the reader to reflect upon its meaning.

In the interpretation that follows the details of the story, and the meaning of the parts, are examined in more detail. But, though recognizing the hypothetical nature of any interpretation, the overall context in which the interpretation is presented is the view that the book should be read as an extended parable.

THE TEACHING OF THE BOOK

The book has both a central theme and a number of minor lessons that emerge along the way. Minor points, by way of example, are illustrated in the matter of obedience and disobedience: the prophet's disobedience to the divine call culminated only in disaster. But the central teaching of the book concerns the nature of God and above all the nature of God's mercy toward all mankind.

The prophets of Israel were for the most part nationalistic; God was the Lord of Israel and, through his prophets, addressed the chosen people. But in addition, as Jonah's book makes clear, God was also profoundly concerned with the behaviour and lot of all mankind. The violence and evil of the gentile citizens of Nineveh were of no less concern to God than was the evil of his own people. Yet the mercy of God always seeks to turn aside evil and offer mercy to those who repent. The parable of a prophet sent to Nineveh demonstrates the concern of God for gentiles and the possibility of gentiles repenting and finding God's mercy. Thus, for the gentile reader of the Old Testament, the book of Jonah not only reveals the grand nature of a compassionate God, but also opens the door of the more particularistic streams in ancient Judaism to a vision of the universal God.

THE CALL OF JONAH

Jonah 1:1-3

[1]Now the word of the Lord came to Jonah the son of Amittai, saying, [2]"Arise, go to Nineveh, that great city, and cry against it; for their

wickedness has come up before me." ³But Jonah rose to flee to Tarshish from the presence of the Lord. He went down to Joppa and found a ship going to Tarshish; so he paid the fare, and went on board, to go with them to Tarshish, away from the presence of the Lord.

The Book of Jonah begins in a conventional fashion for a prophetic work; no doubt the first readers, or those who first heard the story, would have been lulled by a sense of familiarity with the words of verse 1. "The word of the Lord came to Jonah", as it had done to so many other prophets; the Lord spoke the word, and it was the prophet's duty to respond. But verse 1 is one of the very few conventional verses in the entire book; in verse 2, the substance of the divine call immediately strikes a jarring note. "Go to Nineveh", the great pagan city of Assyria, renowned throughout the ancient world as a symbol of power and might. And the jarring note continues in verse 3: having been ordered to Nineveh, Jonah promptly took off for Tarshish. Thus does the writer of this ancient book make effective use of language and style; the familiarity of the opening sentence is rudely contrasted by the peculiarity of what follows. From the very beginning, the reader is alerted to the fact that this is not to be a normal book.

The opening verses of the Book of Jonah not only grasp the reader's attention, but also establish the fundamental themes to be developed in the story that follows.

(i) *It is God who speaks first; his words express his universal concern* (verse 2). The wickedness of Nineveh has weighed on his mind and requires attention; he determines to send Jonah to the city as his messenger.

Nineveh was an enormous city in Assyria, which served from time to time as the capital city of the great Assyrian Empire. The ruins of Nineveh are situated beside the River Tigris, just across the river from the modern city of Mosul in Northern Iraq. Excavations have been conducted there since the nineteenth century and have laid bare the splendour of the city that once was, with its fine palaces, superb works of art, and great libraries. The undoubted grandeur that once typified the physical ambience of Nineveh was no guide, however, to its moral character. The writer describes its character simply as "wickedness", not elaborating on the forms that urban evil assumed. But evil of all kinds was a matter of concern to God.

Within the universal perspectives of Christian faith, we may not at first be struck by the extraordinary nature of these divine words. In Old Testament times, God was conceived as being concerned primarily with Israel, the nation of the chosen people. But here it is clear that the divine concern knew no limits. The evil of Nineveh, and hence its possibilities of survival, were no less matters of weight in the mind of God than were the fortunes of Jerusalem. And so, in subtle ways, the writer of this book is going to broaden the horizons of his audience: Nineveh, a gentile metropolis of megalomaniacs and wickedness, mattered to God. And if we are to grasp the horizons of this ancient book, we too will have to stretch our minds. For all the petty prejudices that may confine us, God's concern knows no bounds. Moscow matters as much as Milwaukee, Entebbe as much as Edinburgh.

(ii) *The universal concern of God results in action.* Having seen Nineveh's evil, he determines to despatch a messenger there. Though the explicit purpose of the messenger is not made clear in these verses, the book as a whole reveals that the messenger was to issue a warning intimating to the citizens of Nineveh the evil of their ways and calling for repentance before God. Thus, there are revealed the broader dimensions of God's care: it is not only the evil of Nineveh that concerns him, but also the necessity that its citizens turn from evil and discover the good. Jonah is sent on a mission, not to proselytize or make converts to his own faith, but simply to warn foreigners of the terrible consequences of their actions and to plead with them to turn from them.

(iii) The most striking substance of the opening verses of the book is *the anatomy of disobedience that is given here.* On being ordered to Nineveh, Jonah promptly set out in the opposite direction for Tarshish. The exact location of Tarshish is uncertain, and in the ancient world there were probably many places called *Tarshish* (the name designating towns that were built on the activity of mining and smelting). One such Tarshish was in the western Mediterranean, either in the territory that is now Spain, or on the island of Sardinia (where archaeologists have discovered Phoenician inscriptions from the ninth century B.C. bearing the word *Tarshish*), and it is probably this location that is intended in the story.

It is not clear yet, at this point in the story, why Jonah was so immediately and directly disobedient. He was told to go one way, but went the other. It was probably not fear that prompted the disobedience; indeed, in the boat scene that follows, Jonah emerges as something of an intrepid character. And it would be too simple to describe him as being simply perverse. At best, perhaps all that can be said is that Jonah did not share in the least God's concern and compassion for Nineveh. It was of no consequence to him that a distant and foreign city was evil. The fate of its citizens, as a consequence of their evil, had never crossed his mind. Jonah had enough to do in life as a citizen of his own nation, without being concerned with other nations. Yet he did not remain at home when the call came. Perhaps the reality of the divine call was so clear, and so unpleasant, that he decided that the most appropriate course of action was to put as much distance between himself and Nineveh as possible. An ocean cruise would be pleasant; a few days on the beach at Tarshish would be a splendid tonic. And so he disobeyed.

The writer of the book has chosen his language carefully to convey the implications of disobedience. Jonah was called to go to a place in the east, so he set off for the west. He was told to go to Nineveh, but "went down" to Joppa, and there "went down" (as the Hebrew text states literally) into a ship. And twice the writer stresses that Jonah's westward journey was away "from the presence of the Lord." The act of disobedience always has attendant circumstances, for the point of decision makes it impossible for things to remain as they were. The one who disobeys cannot remain in God's presence and fellowship, for the act of disobedience is always a journey away from God. And the one who will not go up, in response to God's challenge, inevitably finds that the path in life following disobedience is a downward path.

(iv) A final perspective to consider with respect to the opening verses of the book is *their effect upon the audience.* The opening words are familiar: God called a person to be a prophet. If it is correct that the book survived in the south, in Judah or Jerusalem, the identity of the person may have evoked in the audience lack of sympathy: Jonah was from the north country, and everybody knew that northerners were a disobedient lot (that, at least, would have been a popular view in the south). And then the prophet's destination would have caused surprise: Nineveh lay nowhere within the confines of the promised land. And finally, the call to obey was followed by disobedience; other prophetic books describe the struggle that precedes obedience, but none begin with downright disobedience. But the shock of the audience would be followed by complacency: what more could you expect from a northerner, practically a foreigner, being despatched on a mission to the gentiles!

The initial reactions are spontaneous, but as with all good parables, as the story continues, we will see not simply the comic and grotesque character of Jonah, but also a mirror in which our own image may gradually be discerned.

A STORM AT SEA

Jonah 1:4–10

⁴But the Lord hurled a great wind upon the sea, and there was a mighty tempest on the sea, so that the ship threatened to break up. ⁵Then the mariners were afraid, and each cried to his god; and they threw the wares that were in the ship into the sea, to lighten it for them. But Jonah had gone down into the inner part of the ship and had lain down, and was fast asleep. ⁶So the captain came and said to him, "What do you mean, you sleeper? Arise, call upon your god! Perhaps the god will give a thought to us, that we do not perish."

⁷And they said to one another, "Come, let us cast lots, that we may

know on whose account this evil has come upon us." So they cast lots, and the lot fell upon Jonah. ⁸Then they said to him, "Tell us, on whose account this evil has come upon us? What is your occupation? And whence do you come? What is your country? And of what people are you?" ⁹And he said to them, "I am a Hebrew; and I fear the Lord, the God of heaven, who made the sea and the dry land." ¹⁰Then the men were exceedingly afraid, and said to him, "What is this that you have done!" For the men knew that he was fleeing from the presence of the Lord, because he had told them.

Jonah's flight from God is one of perpetual descent. Having gone down to the port of Joppa, and there having gone down into a ship, he now goes down beneath the deck (verse 5), hoping to rest after his trying experience! But though the fleeing prophet thinks he has found some respite at last, there is no peace for the ship in which he has set sail. A great storm blows up, tossing the waves with such violence that the small ship threatens to break up. The sailors, not without experience in the tempests of the eastern Mediterranean, begin to take emergency measures. They cast overboard the cargo, raising the ship in the water and hoping thereby to reduce the risk of wreck. But the storm does not abate nor the danger of disaster subside; in desperation, the sailors call upon their various gods for help, driven to an unfamiliar piety by the jeopardy of their situation. Despite their pleas, the tempest continues to take its toll; it seems that death by drowning must be their fate.

And then Jonah is found, snoozing on the lower decks; doubtless the captain found him there, as he supervised the removal of the final bottles and bales of cargo to be cast overboard. The captain is furious to find him sleeping in such a time of crisis; the very least Jonah could do was to join the others in prayer for deliverance. "What do you mean, you sleeper!" he cries, and in calling Jonah a *sleeper*, he has unwittingly captured the unhappy man's entire character and life.

Jonah joins the sailors on the deck, where an urgent and morbid conference is taking place. All possible physical measures to avert a wreck have been taken, yet still the ship shows every sign of sinking. Recognizing in the ferocity of the storm the sign of some divine intervention in nature, the sailors cast lots in an attempt to determine the person who might be the cause of mortal peril. The lot falls inevitably upon Jonah, and his companions in danger pour forth their questions, seeking to determine what he has done to cause their current crisis. And so Jonah speaks, describing his disobedience, and even as he speaks he is becoming, without any clear intention, a prophet of the God of the Hebrews.

As the story-teller unfolds his tale, he creates not only interest and tension, but gradually begins to elaborate upon the moral and religious themes of his parable.

(i) *The gentile sailors on the ship typify the human condition as a whole.* Threatened by shipwreck and drowning, they are drawn together in their common toil, casting into the ocean the heavy cargo that might submerge their fragile float upon the ocean's waters. But as work fails to reduce their danger, they turn to their gods; their common toil is replaced by diversity of faith, as each calls upon this or that supposed deity for assistance and rescue.

It is the common danger that has brought the crew to this decisive point in their lives. Skilled in seamanship and experienced in the hazards of life on the ocean, they are nevertheless helpless in the grip of the tempest that would destroy them. In the face of death, they are ready for a new understanding of life.

(ii) *There is one man on board who could provide an understanding of life, even in the shadow of death.* His name is Jonah, but he is a sleeper. While the gentiles are awake, working feverishly in the search for salvation, Jonah is asleep in the hold. Having once disobeyed God's call to minister to gentiles in Nineveh, he now sleeps calmly through the more immediate danger threatening his shipboard companions. Jonah, the sleeper, has become a despicable figure; he rests in peace while those without faith can find no peace. In the quietness of slumber, he has banished care from his mind, while those in need of care are torn by anxiety. And worst of all, the storm that imperils the ship and all its crew is a direct consequence of Jonah's disobedience; having refused to care for the citizens of Nineveh, he has discovered that his careless indifference has spread like a plague to threaten the lives of others. The flight from responsibility has brought with it a new and immediate responsibility for the lives of an entire ship's crew.

(iii) *The one who refused to be a prophet to the gentiles of Nineveh is compelled at last to become a prophet to gentile sailors.* In response to their urgent questions, he admits: "I fear the Lord, the God of heaven, who made the sea and the dry land" (verse 9). And in reply to their further probing, Jonah acknowledges that his presence on board is a consequence of his attempted flight from God. Thus the gospel that should have been proclaimed in obedience to those in Nineveh is wrung out from the prophet's lips in a storm at sea. And the awesome circumstances make the unwilling prophet's words terribly believable. The sailors, having seen already the futility of their own prayers in time of peril, now are given a glimpse of a God whose might controls even the forces of the ocean.

Jonah's final precipitation into prophethood is not without its colouring of personal grief and sorrow. If only he had been obedient, the lives of these sailors would not be at risk. If only he had been obedient, he could have been a prophet with some honour in the fulfilment of his vocation. But life is full of "if onlys", and his chosen course had reduced him to this sorry estate, a grudging prophet in the eye of a storm. At last, he had found the truth, though as Sir George Adam Smith wrote of Jonah, "the truth, which might have been the bride of his youth and his comrade through a long life, is recognized by him only in the features of Death." For the consequence of his prophetic word was that he was to be cast overboard, an offering to the restless waves of the storm-tossed sea.

MAN OVERBOARD!

Jonah 1:11–17

¹¹Then they said to him, "What shall we do to you, that the sea may quiet down for us?" For the sea grew more and more tempestuous.

¹²He said to them, "Take me up and throw me into the sea; then the sea will quiet down for you; for I know it is because of me that this great tempest has come upon you." ¹³Nevertheless the men rowed hard to bring the ship back to land, but they could not, for the sea grew more and more tempestuous against them. ¹⁴Therefore they cried to the Lord, "We beseech thee, O Lord, let us not perish for this man's life, and lay not on us innocent blood; for thou, O Lord, hast done as it pleased thee." ¹⁵So they took up Jonah and threw him into the sea; and the sea ceased from its raging. ¹⁶Then the men feared the Lord exceedingly, and they offered a sacrifice to the Lord and made vows.

¹⁷And the Lord appointed a great fish to swallow up Jonah; and Jonah was in the belly of the fish three days and three nights.

The ship's crew was not a lynching party. Having determined the cause of their catastrophe, they did not immediately seize the prophet and cast him over the side to the mercy of the waves. Though the ocean was becoming still more tumultuous, they questioned him, asking what should be done. For Jonah, the answer was clear: he knew now, with the terrible clarity that the encounter with death can bring, that it was his own action that had called forth the tempest. And at last compassion is wrung out of the indifferent Jonah; it was he who had brought the ship's crew into such peril and he alone could avert it. So Jonah, in a rare moment of courage and compassion, instructs the sailors to throw him into the sea.

Still the mariners resist resort to such drastic measures. They pull mightily on their oars, struggling to bring the ship back to land and safety, but the increasing violence of the tempest makes their task impossible. Then, every other avenue having failed, they cast Jonah into the sea; immediately the storm ceased and the waves subsided. The sailors continued their voyage on a calm ocean; as for the prophet, a great fish was to become his home for three days and three nights.

The theme of this portion of the narrative is that of conversion: it embraces both Jonah and the crew.

(i) *Jonah's conversion is from the path of disobedience to the path of obedience*, from the shirking of responsibility to the acceptance of it. It is too late now, he realizes, to change his mind and go to Nineveh; the least he can do is to offer himself as a sacrifice, in an effort to avert the danger he has brought upon others. At last he accepts responsibility for his actions. In a strict sense, Jonah's offer is not a particularly noble act; were it not for him, there would be no crisis. He is simply accepting the consequences of a course of action he had chosen with full consciousness. And yet, for all that, there is an element of nobility and courage in Jonah's words to the sailors. A lesser person might still have sought to hide behind the cloak of dissemblance, accepting no responsibility for the crisis and trying to the very last to save his own skin. But Jonah has finally come face to face with himself; he does not like what he sees! He has failed not only in his responsibility to God, but has brought disaster to his fellow human beings. He sees himself, quite rightly, as a failure. His final act, the offer of his life, is only in part a sacrifice for his companions; in part it is the dreadful recognition that his life is no longer of value, that having missed its purpose, it is no longer worth living.

Jonah's plight is a vivid illustration of the cul de sac in the path of life down which we may choose to walk. Fleeing from the truth, we are forced to confront it in the face of death. Attempting to abandon responsibility for our fellow human beings, we find we are responsible nevertheless and may bring their lives to risk. Deciding upon disobedience to the divine call as a way of life, we discover that there is no fulness of life outside obedience. For Jonah, his conversion was at the door of death, as it must have seemed to him then. But even as he turned from his chosen path back to the once-neglected God, the realization came upon him of the tragedy of a wasted life.

(ii) *The conversion of the sailors is depicted as a turning from false and pagan faiths to a recognition of the Living God.* They are not portrayed, prior to their conversion, as sinners of the darkest dye; indeed, their dignity and general humanity emerge in positive light in contrast to the character of Jonah. But for all their honour, they do not know God and thus, prior to Jonah's confession, they have no route to rescue from the storm at sea. When they perceive in Jonah's testimony the power of God, they still do not act hastily; as long as possible, they resist the drastic course of action advised by the prophet. And even when eventually they cast Jonah off the ship, they pray to God for forgiveness (verse 14), following his instructions, yet fearful lest they should take the life of an innocent man. And after the storm has ceased, they offer sacrifices to God and commit themselves to him in a new awareness of his might.

In contrast to the petulant and perverse prophet, the sailors are portrayed as fundamentally decent human beings. They were a rough lot, no doubt, but they had their own brand of piety and their own standards of honour. They behaved well toward Jonah, even when they discovered he was responsible for their plight. But for all their decency and positive human qualities, they were on the verge of drowning in the depths; they needed to be rescued. And again we perceive the way in which the sailors portray the pathos of the human condition. We are misled, in the modern world, if we think that the only truly splendid "conversions" are of those whose former lives were dedicated to the relentless pursuit of evil. I once met a young man who sincerely regretted that his earlier life had not been more reprobate, for then, he said, his conversion to the Christian faith could have been truly spectacular. Those simple sailors, no doubt having their share of human decency, simply needed one to save them from their plight. They found that deliverance in God, and such is the path of all true conversion.

JONAH'S PRAYER

Jonah 2:1–10

1Then Jonah prayed to the Lord his God from the belly of the fish, 2saying,
"I called to the Lord, out of my distress,
    and he answered me;
out of the belly of Sheol I cried,
    and thou didst hear my voice.

[3]For thou didst cast me into the deep,
   into the heart of the seas,
   and the flood was round about me;
 all thy waves and thy billows
   passed over me.
[4]Then I said, 'I am cast out
   from thy presence;
 how shall I again look
   upon thy holy temple?'
[5]The waters closed in over me,
   the deep was round about me;
 weeds were wrapped about my head
[6]   at the roots of the mountains.
 I went down to the land
   whose bars closed upon me for ever;
 yet thou didst bring up my life from the Pit,
   O Lord my God.
[7]When my soul fainted within me,
   I remembered the Lord;
 and my prayer came to thee,
   into thy holy temple.
[8]Those who pay regard to vain idols
   forsake their true loyalty.
[9]But I with the voice of thanksgiving
   will sacrifice to thee;
 what I have vowed I will pay.
   Deliverance belongs to the Lord!"
[10]And the Lord spoke to the fish, and it vomited out Jonah upon the
dry land.

Jonah has passed from the frying pan into the fire. As he was cast
overboard by the reluctant sailors, his only prospect was that of
drowning. Now he finds himself in the belly of a great fish; he is a
long way from safety, but he is still alive and that is considerably
more than he had hoped for beforehand. Prior to being cast to the
waves, Jonah had gained some new perspectives on his miserable
life; now, still retaining those new perspectives, he turns to
prayer.

His prayer is similar to many of the psalms in the Psalter. From
a literary perspective it may be seen as an individual's psalm of
thanksgiving, in which gratitude is expressed for deliverance

from a terrible crisis. Yet the prayer is not quite typical of the parallel passages in the Book of Psalms. Many of its lines duplicate familiar lines in the Psalter (see, for example, Pss. 69:2; 30:3; 124:4; 42:5; 116:17–18; all of which contain words and phrases similar to Jonah's prayer); its author, in using the formulaic language typical of the Psalms, evokes a sense of familiarity in those who hear or read Jonah's prayer. Yet the sense of familiarity is only superficial, for Jonah's prayer is distinctive, its words indicating powerfully the watery abyss into which he sank. And it is not only a prayer of thanksgiving, but also a prayer for deliverance: Jonah has been rescued from drowning, but he is still in deep water! There is nevertheless a ring of expectation and hope in his words; having so narrowly escaped a watery grave, he now clings to a hope for complete rescue.

The prayer falls into three parts. (a) Jonah's initial cry of distress had been answered; he had survived, yet he still had little prospect of worshipping once again in God's Temple (verses 2–4). The language is full of allusions and subtle nuances. He cried out for deliverance "from the belly of *Sheol*" (namely death, or the watery grave), and God responded by transferring him to the belly of a great fish! The "heart of the seas" (verse 3) into which Jonah had been cast may be an allusion to *Yam*, a Canaanite god of chaos (Hebrew *yam* means "sea"). But for all his immediate deliverance, Jonah still remains cut off from God's presence, namely from the Temple which symbolized that presence in Israel (verse 4); thus, though he has been rescued, he looks forward in hope to a further act of deliverance. (b) The second part of the prayer repeats the substance of the first part in different words (verses 5–7). Jonah's fate had been all but sealed. The waters of the ocean had closed above his head, and the seaweed became tangled in his hair as he sank down to the "roots of the mountains" (verse 6, probably an allusion to the ocean floor). He was sinking towards that land beyond life, whose barred gates, once closed behind him, would never again open to allow exit; yet, at the last moment, God had pulled him back and given him another lease on life. There is a further wistful allusion to God's holy temple (verse 7), though Jonah remains far from its portals. (c) The prayer concludes with a reflection on the vanity of idolatry, a commitment to fulfil all vows to God, and a declaration of God's power to deliver (verse 8–9). As a consequence of Jonah's prayer and thanksgiving, the Lord prompts the great fish to spew out its unhappy load upon the beach.

Jonah's prayer develops further the message and the symbolism of the larger narrative to which it belongs.

(i) *The turning point in Jonah's life comes at the very depths of his pursuit of disobedience.* Since first he had said "No" to the divine call, he had gone *down* to Joppa, *down* into a ship, *down* into the hold, and at last *down* into the watery depths; the final descent into the ocean depths would have been his last, had there not been a change of heart before he was cast overboard by the sailors. But not until he was all the way down, finally stripped of his own buoyant sense of self-sufficiency, was deliverance possible.

The initial act of disobedience, which culminated in such disasters, required radical treatment if it were to be remedied. And sometimes, in our absence of obedience, we will be taken down to the very depths of the experience of disaster before a change is possible and we can set off once again in a new path through life.

(ii) *It is peril that prompts Jonah's prayer.* Just as the sailors before him, faced with the threat of drowning, prayed for deliverance, so too did Jonah, first as he sank through the waters, and second as he found himself alive, yet imprisoned in a piscine tomb. But the message is not simply that prayer must precede deliverance. The author is concerned to show that all desperate human pleas, whether uttered by Jew or gentile, fall upon the compassionate ears of God. All human beings may be reduced to critical circumstances; all, in fear and desperation, may cry out to God for salvation. And God is not partial in his listening; he is compassionate as much for gentile sailors threatened with drowning, as he is for a failed prophet plummeting downwards in the watery depths.

Thus, just as the author has impressed on us in chapter 1 that the God of Israel is concerned about pagan Nineveh, now we are shown again the breadth of his mercy. Here, as elsewhere, the ancient scriptures seek to remove the blinkers from our eyes, the constraints that would force God into the strait-jacket of our own prejudices and predilections. The ancient message was to inform the Jews that their God could not be confined to Israel; he was God also of the gentiles. And no less today do we require that broader vision of God, not easily grasped, that he is not confined to the Christian Church; his compassion extends to all mankind.

(iii) *Jonah's prayer is marked by elements of both pathos and humour.* He reaches at last the heights of spirituality in the depths of the ocean! But even as he finally achieves a degree of spiritual maturity, still he lags behind the gentiles, to whom earlier he had borne witness. His grudging testimony had led others to levels of faith which he had yet to achieve. It was not an easy lesson to learn; as the story continues, we will see that Jonah had not learned it well.

(iv) *After three days and nights in the fish's belly, Jonah was at last cast up on the beach.* This part of the story came later to be referred to as the sign of Jonah: as the prophet spent three days and nights in the belly of the fish, so too would the Son of Man spend three days and nights in the grave (Matt. 12:39–40). Jonah's experience, in other words, came to symbolize the death and resurrection of Jesus Christ from the grave. But the symbolism may extend further. The death and resurrection of Christ have meaning to the believer in the death we may die to sin and the new life we may receive in Christ. Jonah, as he sank in the depths, was undergoing a kind of baptism, dying to his old disobedient life; cast up on the beach, he was given a new life. But if we would appropriate that message from the story of Jonah, we must read further to see what he did with the new lease on life so graciously granted to him.

THE MISSION TO NINEVEH

Jonah 3:1–10

[1]Then the word of the Lord came to Jonah the second time, saying, [2]"Arise, go to Nineveh, that great city, and proclaim to it the message

that I tell you." ³So Jonah arose and went to Nineveh, according to the word of the Lord. Now Nineveh was an exceedingly great city, three days' journey in breadth. ⁴Jonah began to go into the city, going a day's journey. And he cried, "Yet forty days, and Nineveh shall be overthrown!" ⁵And the people of Nineveh believed God; they proclaimed a fast, and put on sackcloth, from the greatest of them to the least of them.

⁶Then tidings reached the king of Nineveh, and he arose from his throne, removed his robe, and covered himself with sackcloth, and sat in ashes. ⁷And he made proclamation and published through Nineveh, "By the decree of the king and his nobles: Let neither man nor beast, herd nor flock, taste anything; let them not feed, or drink water, ⁸but let man and beast be covered with sackcloth, and let them cry mightily to God; yea, let every one turn from his evil way and from the violence which is in his hands. ⁹Who knows, God may yet repent and turn from his fierce anger, so that we perish not?"

¹⁰When God saw what they did, how they turned from their evil way, God repented of the evil which he had said he would do to them; and he did not do it.

Jonah's life begins again. The Lord's word comes to him a second time, inviting him as before to undertake the mission of mercy to Nineveh. This time the prophet obeys, though there is little to indicate that he tackles his task with joy and gladness; nevertheless, he has learned at least to obey.

When Jonah at last reached the outskirts of Nineveh, after the long journey from the beach-head in his life upon which the great fish had vomited him, the task that faced him was a formidable one. Nineveh, we are told by the narrator, was a "great city, three days' journey in breadth" (verse 3). The reference is not to the central city core as such, though that was indeed a formidable walled metropolis, the circumference of its fortifications extending some eight miles, within which the great palaces and gardens were enclosed. Rather it was to "Greater Nineveh" that Jonah came, the suburban clusters and monotonous rows of drab houses in which dwelled the ordinary citizens of the city state. This larger area, as archaeological surveys have shown, spread out in a circle from the city proper, with a circumference of something like sixty miles (far greater than the modern city of Mosul, which adjoins the ancient site).

As Jonah began his trek through the bleak suburban sprawl, the appalling impossibility of his task dawned upon him. He was a foreigner in a strange land. He had been given a message to deliver to an alien people, whose countless dwellings he passed on every side as he trudged through the suburban streets. Perhaps he had been aware that his task could only bring despair when first he had disobeyed the divine command to go to Nineveh. And so, only a day's journey into Greater Nineveh, and still some distance from the splendid sights of the inner city, he begins his task. Feeling no doubt frightened, and not a little foolish, he proclaims to the masses around him his cheerless message: "Yet forty days, and Nineveh shall be overthrown!" (verse 4). It was not a message, one might have thought, designed to elicit a popular response.

But the shock and surprise, so characteristic of this book from its opening verses, continue in the description of the actions of the populace. As though primed by some divine hand, the suburbanites immediately respond to Jonah's preaching; they believe in God and turn aside from the evil which has become their daily diet in life. And so radical is their conversion that immediately those who have responded pass on the prophetic message to friends and neighbours. Like a brush fire whipped by the wind, the message travels quickly through the suburbs to the heart of the city; the king and his council hear it and they too respond. And what began as a populist movement is promulgated and strengthened by royal decree. The very heart of the city is transformed, though Jonah has only gone a third of the distance toward it in the fulfilment of his mission. The royal proclamation requires not only ritual response and fasting, of both humans and beasts; it calls also for a change of heart, for a turning from evil and the defeat of violence. The gentile city turns from the folly of its ways, not with any guarantee of grace, but only in the hope that God might turn aside his wrath and spare the city. And God does indeed "repent"; that is, he turns from his purpose of punishment and extends mercy to a repentant city.

With respect to Nineveh's role, the story has now reached its climax, though the prophet himself has not yet come to the fulfilment of his experience. Yet, in this narrative of mission accomplished, we may learn something both about the individual servant of God and about the human race as a whole.

(i) *Jonah, for all the unhappy nature of his task, was embarked upon a mission of enormous privilege.* Everything in his personal history suggested that he should not be given the privilege of participating in the work of God. Indeed, had he been drowned in the depths, he would have earned only his just deserts. But the word of God had come to him a second time; he had been given a second chance.

In terms of qualifications and rights, we are all like Jonah. Who can claim to be qualified for participation in the divine work? Who has not disobeyed in the past and forfeited any rights that might pertain to serving God? The service of God is thus, in a sense, always a second chance, always an undeserved privilege. And if vocation comes to us, we can never say that it is on the grounds of our gifts and qualities, or our capacities for the job at hand. The call of God is simultaneously a sign of mercy, in that he is willing to employ the unworthy, and also a sign of his greater purpose, his concern for those nameless masses whose drab and daily existence has not yet been illuminated by the divine light.

(ii) *But the narrator has also something to teach us about the human race as a whole in this portion of the story.* Its focal point is to be found in the sad suburbs of the city, not the splendid centre. And its interest lies first in great masses, not the king and his counsellors. The teller of the story has an extraordinary vision, one that is not easily communicated within the limits of human speech. It is not only that God is concerned with the gentiles as well as the Jews, though that is a part of it. It is that his mercy and care extend to all people, including those suburban and rural dwellers whose name will not find so much as a niche in the annals of human history. To such as these, Jonah preaches; these are they who first respond, whose response in turn triggers a change of heart even amongst royalty and that nation's noblemen. It is an extraordinary vision that we glimpse in these few brief verses. It is a vision of a multitude of human beings, diverse in their life-styles, disparate in the drabness of their daily existence, yet all

sharing a common need and a common capacity. The common
need is for God; the common capacity is their ability to repent.

THE WRATH OF JONAH

Jonah 4:1–5

> [1]But it displeased Jonah exceedingly, and he was angry. [2]And he
> prayed to the Lord and said, "I pray thee, Lord, is not this what I said
> when I was yet in my country? That is why I made haste to flee to
> Tarshish; for I knew that thou art a gracious God and merciful, slow to
> anger, and abounding in steadfast love, and repentest of evil. [3]There-
> fore now, O Lord, take my life from me, I beseech thee, for it is better
> for me to die than to live." [4]And the Lord said, "Do you do well to be
> angry?" [5]Then Jonah went out of the city and sat to the east of the city,
> and made a booth for himself there. He sat under it in the shade, till he
> should see what would become of the city.

From the very beginning, the story of Jonah has been characterized by shock and contrast; this new turn in the narrative is no
exception. Jonah was angry; we must suppose that his anger
was precipitated by the massive spiritual reform under way in
Nineveh and Jonah's surmise that the city would be spared the
experience of divine wrath. And so Jonah prays again (verses
2–3), though the tone of this prayer is entirely different from that
of his earlier prayer (2:1–10). Seeing what is happening to the
city, Jonah prays that God may take his life, for he has lost his
desire to live. God remonstrates with his peevish prophet, but to
no avail; taking up a station on the higher ground to the east of
the city, Jonah waits, still harbouring some hope that the city
might be destroyed.

The art of the narrator is at its most skilful in this portion of the
story. He easily draws his audience with him into a negative
reaction toward the petulant Jonah, yet the reaction to Jonah is
precisely the tool which, eventually, will force the story-teller's
message home to the hearts of his audience. What is the essence
of his message at this point?

(i) *Jonah's theology is in conflict with God*. While by now we are accustomed to Jonah's perverse reactions, it is not at first clear why the prophet was so angry. Was he angry because he had preached doom and destruction to Nineveh, and yet the passage of time seemed to indicate clearly that no doom would dawn on the city? Was his wrath evoked because the absence of divine judgment would cast doubt on his integrity as a prophet? Such is the interpretation that several scholars have proposed, but it is improbable.

Jonah was angry because his theology was in evident conflict with the nature and action of God. He had a strongly-based covenant theology, to which had been added the blinkers of too narrow an election theology. He knew that God loved Israel and extended his mercy to his chosen people; he felt, in the very marrow of his bones, that this special love of God to Israel should not be extended to gentiles, above all to evil gentiles such as the inhabitants of Nineveh. A part of Jonah's prayer was a quotation from ancient scripture: "I knew that thou art a gracious God and merciful..." (verse 2, compare Exod. 34:6–7); the context of those ancient words about God, as Jonah saw it, confined God's grace and mercy to Israel. But, he reasoned in his convoluted way, you couldn't trust God; he was supposed to love Israel alone, but it was beginning to look as if he loved Nineveh too. In short, Jonah was jealous.

The wrath of Jonah is thus an all-too-common human phenomenon. Having tasted the divine love, he could not bear to think of it being extended to others; blinded by his own jealousy, he wanted to restrict the compassion of God to himself and his own kind. And in his jealousy, evoked by a garbled view of love, he betrayed the fact that he had never really understood the love of God in the first place. Thus the narrator, by making the wrathful Jonah so comical a figure, seeks to remove the blindness from a multitude of other eyes, equally restrictive in their conception of divine love. And in the Church, no less than in ancient Israel, there is a perpetual tendency to try to confine God's love. Only those within the Church are the objects of divine compassion, so the argument runs. But the argument is fundamentally flawed. It seeks to chain God within the constrictions of narrow theology. Any strong theology must be so constructed that its perimeters can constantly be broken down, allowing new insight to flood in, enlarging the conception of a God who is ultimately beyond theology.

(ii) *Jonah's prayer reflects a reversion to his old estate.* This reversion reveals both the pathos and perversity of the obdurate prophet. For a short while, before being cast to the waves, it seemed that Jonah had seen the error of his ways and come to a new maturity in faith. And when the call had come to him a second time, he had obeyed, indicating again the appearance of a new commitment. But, tragically, this was still the same old Jonah. And, when things did not develop as he had hoped, he even remembered the objections of his former unregenerate days: "is not this what I said when I was yet in my country?" (verse 2). Jonah was a typical crisis convert: a deep and devout faith emerged suddenly in the eye of the storm, but when the tempest died down, his faith declined with it.

We can never rest casually on the conviction that, once we have been turned round in life, we shall always remain steadfast in our new direction. The traits of human nature are too deeply ingrained for that and require constant attention. But the narrator's art has again come to our aid. In the story, Jonah's fickle fluctuation between piety and perversity is openly displayed; if only we could see with clarity the same fluctuating tendencies in ourselves, we would learn from the story.

(iii) *Jonah is deluded with a false sense of nobility.* "O Lord, take my life from me," he prays (verse 3), echoing the noble prayer of Elijah (1 Kings 19:4). But there is no nobility in Jonah; his grand words delude only himself. He sees himself as a heroic figure in human history, let down once again by an unreliable deity. He has no self-knowledge, no perception of the pettiness of his position, and mocks only himself in his prayer for death. Such self-induced delusions are always dangerous. Deceiving ourselves into the belief that we are magnificent martyrs, we cannot partake of the perception of others that we are futile fools in our deluded estate. Only a hard-eyed realism as to who we are and what we are doing can deliver us from such false nobility as that of Jonah.

And yet, for all the folly of Jonah in his wrath, these verses end with a tone of charity. One could hardly blame God for anger at so vacillating a prophet. Yet the divine words are kind, charitable, tinged even with humour: "Do you do well to be angry?" (verse 4). The soft words, slightly caustic, should induce a little self-reflection in the wrongly wrathful Jonah.

THE DIVINE PITY

Jonah 4:6–11

> [6]And the Lord God appointed a plant, and made it come up over Jonah, that it might be a shade over his head, to save him from his discomfort. So Jonah was exceedingly glad because of the plant. [7]But when dawn came up the next day, God appointed a worm which attacked the plant, so that it withered. [8]When the sun rose, God appointed a sultry east wind, and the sun beat upon the head of Jonah so that he was faint; and he asked that he might die, and said, "It is better for me to die than to live." [9]But God said to Jonah, "Do you do well to be angry for the plant?" And he said, "I do well to be angry, angry enough to die." [10] And the Lord said, "You pity the plant, for which you did not labour, nor did you make it grow, which came into being in a night, and perished in a night. [11]And should not I pity Nineveh, that great city, in which there are more than a hundred and twenty thousand persons who do not know their right hand from their left, and also much cattle?"

Nineveh has been spared, but the prophet's therapy must still be completed. Jonah, sitting in his perch on the heights east of the city, was still hoping for a spectacular display of brimstone and judgment on the gentile city spread on the plain beneath him. By now he was virtually certain it would not happen, but he waited anyway. As protection from the sun, he constructed for himself a shelter of sorts, patched together from the sticks and grass that came to hand. It helped a little, but the sun's heat penetrated his fragile shade; the temperature and humidity aggravated the prophet's ill-humoured mood.

And so God, observing his prophet's plight, made a plant to grow rapidly alongside Jonah's flimsy shelter; the Hebrew word probably designates the quickly growing "castor-oil" plant, with its wide, shade-imparting leaves. Jonah, ever at the mercy of his fleeting and changing passions, finds his ill-humour turn to delight. What could be nicer on a hot summer day than the cool shade imparted by the leaves of a luxurious plant. Nature was a wonderful thing!

The trouble with nature was that it was totally unreliable. The weevils were at work. (The Hebrew word translated "worm" in RSV probably designates the "wood-worm", or vine-weevil, technically a type of beetle.) The plant that had provided such splendid shade was so weakened by the weevils that its foliage withered and its shelter was lost. And as if that were not bad enough, the scirocco began to blow; the hot air from the mountains of Iran combined with the unrelenting rays of the sun to reduce Jonah to a foul mood. Once again, he decided death would be better than continuing to live. But God spoke and inquired of Jonah whether his exasperation over a withered plant and wearisome weather were really sufficient to invite the supposed solace of death. "Yes," Jonah replied, without a moment's thought, and thus he invited the final divine speech in which the message of the book is made clear.

It is the immaturity of Jonah which stands out so starkly in this final scene of the story; that immaturity in turn is rooted in selfishness. First, Jonah wanted to die because he was jealous; the vast population of Nineveh would not die in judgment, a fate he believed they roundly deserved. Now he wants to die because he is suffering slight discomfort from the weather. Anything would be better than this horrendous heat! And the contradictory character of his position is evident for all to see. He is mad at God for the divine reluctance to obliterate an entire population. And he is mad at a plant for dying so inconsiderately and reducing his personal level of comfort. His emotions go up and down rapidly, like a lift controlled by a berserk computer. He was profoundly disappointed that God, creator of all mankind, did not wipe out thousands of his fellow human beings. And he was equally disappointed that God, creator of all plants and animals, would allow the weevils to waste a single plant. But there was a difference: the death of a plant was a considerable personal inconvenience to him, whereas the demise of the multitudes was of no immediate concern.

By now, the caricature of Israel in the person of Jonah has become so grotesque that the story might seem to have gone too far. But such is not the case. In the final question (verse 11), towards which the whole book moves, the narrator's purpose is driven home with considerable force. "Should I not pity Nineveh?" In the tradition of the audience to whom the story was first told, everything suggested the answer "No!" An evil gentile city should not experience the divine pity. But to say "No" after hearing the story of Jonah would be embarrassing, not to say petty. If God cares for castor-oil plants, not to mention cattle (verse 11), was it not possible that he also cared for people, even foreigners? It was a frightening thought, for if the Lord of Israel was also the God of Nineveh, wherein lay the special status of the chosen people?

And so we leave the book of Jonah with its final question ringing in our ears. Should God not pity? Can his love be restricted to this group of people and not extended to that? And the final question is phrased in the context of the multitudes; the city's masses, more than 100,000 in number, come to symbolize the world's perennial masses. Is there ever a time or a place where God should not, and cannot, pity? Leslie Allen wrote of the message of this book: "A Jonah lurks in every Christian heart, whispering his insidious message of smug prejudice, empty traditionalism, and exclusive solidarity." And we grasp the message of the book only when we eliminate the Jonah within us. As the great fish coughed up Jonah on the beach, so too must we eject from within us the Jonah of prejudice and shame.

FURTHER READING

Books marked * are more suitable for initial study.

L. C. Allen, *The Books of Joel, Obadiah, Jonah and Micah* (The New International Commentary on the Old Testament) (Eerdmans, 1976)

F. I. Andersen and D. N. Freedman, *Hosea* (The Anchor Bible) (Doubleday, 1980)

*D. Kidner, *Love to the Loveless. The Story and Message of Hosea* (Inter-Varsity Press, 1981)

*J. Marsh, *Amos and Micah* (Torch Biblical Commentaries) (SCM Press, 1959)

J. L. Mays, *Hosea* (Old Testament Library) (Westminster 1978)

J. L. Mays, *Amos* (Old Testament Library) (Westminster 1978)

*H. McKeating, *The Books of Amos, Hosea and Micah* (The Cambridge Bible Commentary on the New English Bible) (Cambridge University Press, 1971)

B. K. Smith, *Hosea, Joel, Amos, Obadiah, Jonah* (Layman's Bible Book Commentary) (Broadman Press, 1982)

G. A. Smith, *The Book of the Twelve Prophets*, 2 volumes (The Expositor's Bible) (Hodder & Stoughton, 1899)

*B. Vawter, *Amos, Hosea, Micah, with an Introduction to Classical Prophecy* (Old Testament Message, A Biblical-Theological Commentary) (Michael Glazier, 1981)

J. A. Ward, *Amos, Hosea* (Knox Preaching Guides) (John Knox Press, 1981)

*J. D. W. Watts, *The Books of Joel, Obadiah, Jonah, Nahum, Habakkuk and Zephaniah* (The Cambridge Bible Commentary on the New English Bible) (Cambridge University Press, 1975)

H. W. Wolff, *Hosea* (Hermeneia—A Critical and Historical Commentary on the Bible) (Fortress Press, 1974)

H. W. Wolff, *Joel and Amos* (Hermeneia—A Critical and Historical Commentary on the Bible) (Fortress Press, 1977)